A LAMP FOR INDIA
The Story of Madame Pandit

❀ *By Robert Hardy Andrews*

IF I HAD A MILLION
A CORNER OF CHICAGO
BURNING GOLD
LEGEND OF A LADY
GREAT DAY IN THE MORNING
LITTLE BIG MOUTH (MY FATHER SAID)

A LAMP FOR INDIA
The Story of
Madame Pandit

Robert Hardy Andrews

Prentice-Hall, Inc., Englewood Cliffs, N.J.

PRENTICE-HALL INTERNATIONAL, INC., LONDON
PRENTICE-HALL OF AUSTRALIA, PTY. LTD., SYDNEY
PRENTICE-HALL OF CANADA, LTD., TORONTO
PRENTICE-HALL OF INDIA PRIVATE LTD., NEW DELHI
PRENTICE-HALL OF JAPAN, INC., TOKYO

To two Great Ladies
born in August,
one of whom is
Irene, my wife

CONTENTS

To   Sm. Vijaya Lakshmi Pandit, M.P.
13 Akbar Road
New Delhi, India
Dear Mrs. Pandit:
You may well have forgotten, but I have not, that in 1954 while
we flew from Honolulu to Tokyo by way of Wake Island, you
read and patiently annotated a bulky manuscript I imposed on
you, and wrote on its cover "To Robert Andrews whose acquaintance I made in the air and whose writing makes me think
we shall be friends."
I hope most earnestly that we will still be friends, when you
read what I have written about you and those you have loved.
                     Always,
                          Robert Hardy Andrews

A LAMP FOR INDIA
The Story of Madame Pandit

Prologue

On January 30, 1948, in New Delhi, capital of the newborn Republic of India, a wizened, weary, dangerously mild, quite unexplainable maker of history whose millions of followers called him *Bapu*, Father, went to pray in public as he did every morning and evening, for peace among men of all colors, castes, and creeds.

He was weakened by imprisonment and self-imposed starvation, but his hands rested only lightly on the shoulders of his granddaughters who walked on either side. He had rejected bodyguards. Out of the waiting, silent crowd stepped a thickset stranger, saluting him with palms pressed together in the ancient gesture of *namasthe*, which signifies "You and I are one."

Mohandas Karamchand Gandhi returned the greeting. Then Nathuram Vinayak Godse, a fanatic of Gandhi's own birth-faith, pressed a revolver against the frail body and fired three shots: this because the Mahatma preached that Hindus and Muslims must learn to live together as brothers. As he

3

fell, Gandhi whispered *"Hai, Ram!"*, which is a way of saying "Thy will be done."

A few hours later, at her lonely listening-post in distant Moscow, Her Excellency Madame Vijaya Lakshmi Pandit, first Ambassador of Free India to the Union of Soviet Socialist Republics, heard New Delhi Radio broadcast the news of the mindless murder of the friend and guide whose path she had walked at cost few women could bear. Then she heard her brother, Prime Minister Jawaharlal Nehru, tell their country's people "The light has gone out of our lives, and there is darkness everywhere."

The Prime Minister wept. So did his sister. Then she remembered, as he would remember in days ahead, a poem they read together when they had yet to know or even know of Gandhi. It told of a time when the whole world thought the sun was dying, and there would be darkness on the earth forever. Then from a shadowed corner, an earthen lamp said "Light me, and I will do the best I can."

This is the story of a lamp that has shone against the night, not only in India, for half a century.

I ❀

"Light me and I will do the best I can."

I saw the lamp shine for the first time, 10,000 miles from India, on Wake Island, the loneliest dot of coral in the Pacific Ocean. Actually, Wake is not even an island, but only three jagged reefs twenty feet above water at the highest point. No castaway Crusoe ever survived on Wake. No one ever went there willingly until, in 1935, American adventurers pioneering the air route from Hawaii to Japan carved out an emergency landing-base.

Later, the United States Navy began setting up defense installations. These were only half-completed when on the morning of December 7, 1941, the Japanese attacked by air and sea. Three hundred and seventy-nine Marines and fifty-nine Navy pilots and mechanics held out for fifteen days, shooting down twelve planes, sinking five enemy ships including a submarine, inflicting more than five thousand casualties. Americans cheered a report, later decried as apocryphal, that Major J. P. S. Devereux signaled "Send us more Japs!" Naval Commander W. S. Cunningham's last message read "Enemy has

5

landed, issue in doubt." Then nothing more was heard from Wake, which the Japanese renamed Otorishima, until it was recaptured on September 4, 1945.

In October 1954, twisted bits of battle wreckage still stood here and there. Scattered around them were two thousand unmarked graves. Scotty Lewis, our gangling Texan pilot, said there had been two palm trees on Wake, until a couple of maintenance monkeys went Wake-happy and butted them down with bulldozers, just to break the monotony. This was easy to believe, where the wind always cries and the only other sound is the foolish chatter of gooney birds strutting along the airstrip, and all you can see is ocean as empty as the sky.

But Her Excellency Madame Vijaya Lakshmi Pandit, the only woman who has been president of the General Assembly of the United Nations, knew from old experience how to be free in a prison. She kicked off her sandals, loosened her mane of silvery hair, stepped into the surf, shivered, smiled, and talked without weighing words before she spoke them.

No correspondents jotted notes. No artful diplomats set cushioned traps. For a while she could be a person, not a personage. Clearly she savored this, while she paced barefooted on the narrow beach, eight steps one way, then eight the other, as only ten years before she had paced like a caged tigress in a cell from which she might never be released.

She came from the highest post of world responsibility held by any woman in history. Next she would speak for the world's most populous democracy, as Ambassador to the once-mighty Court whose Empire she helped to destroy. She saw no reason for mentioning this. She chose to discuss her new grandson.

She had boarded the crowded Clipper at Honolulu, laden with toys much too elaborate for a baby. Surrounded by them in the plane's least comfortable rear row, she made herself smaller when she saw her seatmate approaching. He was American, huge, and very drunk. As he passed, he stumbled over my foot and fell on me. We traded apologies, and by immediate mutual agreement adjourned to the tiny bar in the Clipper's belly.

Sir Walter Raleigh spread his velvet cloak as carpet for a Queen. My chivalry, if it was that, called for matching double Scotches with my new-found friend, until he collapsed on a bench. I loosened his necktie, and left him snoring there.

If Vijaya Lakshmi Pandit guessed what had transpired, she gave no sign. But she had room to rest until at daybreak the Clipper lumbered down through thickening clouds and delivered us on Wake, where Scotty Lewis said we might be delayed indefinitely. She complained only mildly. "I had it all arranged," she said. "I was to babysit in Tokyo tonight, while my daughter and her husband go to a party. I had so looked forward to that."

2.

Vijaya means *Victory*, and Lakshmi is the Hindu goddess of fortune. She was not named Victory-Fortune until her wedding day; and in the bitter after-years a lesser woman might have seen a mocking lie in her marriage-names. But as the world knows of her, few if any claimants can match her right to be called Woman of the Century.

No other woman has risen higher in her times: first to serve as the first woman Cabinet Minister in India, then first Ambassador of Free India to the Soviet, head of India's first United Nations delegation, Ambassador to the United States, and finally, United Nations president. All this although when she married, at not quite twenty-one, life expectancy for women in India averaged thirty years.

At forty-three, she was widowed. Tradition three thousand years old condemned her to death in life, in cloistered dependent seclusion. Her refusal to be ruled by any code but her own, the first of many such in her career, opened locked doors for uncounted members of her sex. She was fifty-four when we met on Wake. Still she looked ahead, not back.

She said nothing about police bursting in to search her home at midnight, about arrests and imprisonments and prison privations, forced separations from those she loved, family tragedies, heartbreak: the price she paid for a dream that came close to ending in nightmare. On Wake, where for a few hours time stood still, she chuckled about New York taxidrivers.

"When we still met at Lake Success, before the Big Glass House was built in Manhattan, invariably if it rained my car failed to show up. I'd stand in the rain feeling small and lost, my *sari* drenched, my self-importance washed away. Without fail, the worst-looking taxi imaginable would come snarling out of the night. The pirate at the wheel would growl 'Get in, Mrs. Pandit!' In I'd get. Away we'd go. I knew I was perfectly safe. All I had to do was listen."

From Flushing Meadow to the Waldorf-Astoria, each cabbie in his turn harangued her over his shoulder, cataloguing her mistakes that day at the U. N. "I couldn't have interrupted if I'd wanted to, which I didn't. I had a friend. He was disappointed in me, but forgave me. After all, I was a woman, and from India."

Arrived at the Waldorf, procedure was always the same. "I'd ask 'How much do I owe you?' He'd say 'Why, not a dime, Mrs. Pandit. We had a very interesting conversation. Take it easy, now!' Off he'd drive. I'd never see him again. But next time there'd be another, just as gruff and opinionated and kind. I learned to like Americans from them."

Ten years before that day on Wake, she was lost in her own homeland, penniless, alone but for her youngest daughter, Rita, then fifteen. She saw no future, and was almost drained of hope and faith. Her two older daughters, Lekha and Tara, were half a world away, at Wellesley in the United States. There was no way she could join them. She might be jailed again before they could come home to India.

Her brother, one day to be India's first Prime Minister, was in prison, in solitary confinement. His wife and their father and mother were dead, the victims of suffering endured in the crusade for freedom that now seemed to have led nowhere. "I shut myself in a room the size of the cell to which I might be returned at any hour. Friends invited me to come and stay with them. I said 'I won't come. You'd be sorry if I did.' They persisted. Finally I said 'All right, I'll come to dinner. But you'll wish I hadn't. I'll be a terrible guest.' "

Lightning flashed across a black wall of storm-clouds rolling down from Tokyo. She paid no heed. "There were uniforms all around me. I had had my fill of uniforms." Her hands made pictures. "The American general on my left asked why I was so sad and silent. I rejected sympathy. He declined to be dismissed. 'If you're so unhappy in India, why don't you leave?' I burst out: 'Because I can't. I have no money, and no papers, and nothing to go to anyhow.' Then I fled, without excusing myself."

Next morning, there was a uniform at her door. "I told myself 'Well, you deserve it.' I didn't deserve what I received." An admiring young American major presented official papers signed by her dinner-partner, General George E. Stratemeyer, that authorized her immediate departure for the United States. If she felt strong enough for less than first-class travel, she could fly to New York as extra passenger in an Air Force transport plane. "I said that after the jails I had been in and out of, a transport plane would be a palace."

She went to say goodbye to Gandhi, who was like her second father. He was at liberty only because the British feared he would die in their custody, if they kept him locked up any longer. He asked if she had made her peace with her husband's people. She said "I have never quarreled with Ranjit's family." This was true; but Gandhi knew the situation. Under Hindu law, since she had no son, her husband's considerable estate had passed, in the male line, to his brother. Neither she nor her daughters could claim any share in it. She would be provided for, so would they, only if, as orthodoxy required, she immured herself in a shadowed corner in the Pandit home. This she would not do.

Gandhi said "Courtesy and decency demand that you go to see Ranjit's relatives." She said "Not even to please you, Gandhiji." He told her "I see enough bitterness in your heart to cause you injury. You are going to a far country because you are unhappy and want to run away." He asked searchingly "Can you run away from yourself?"

She left him without answering, but next morning rose early and joined the prayer-meeting with which he began each day. *Lead Kindly Light* was sung, as it would be at his funeral pyre four years from that time. Afterward, she told him "As always, Gandhiji, you are right." She went to her brother-in-law, explained her plans, and asked for and was granted his blessing. Then she said on Wake Island, "I was more at peace with myself than I had been for longer than I cared to remember."

A stranger in a very strange land, she had some *saris* in a small suitcase, no other possessions and no plans beyond the moment, when she saw New York for the first time in 1944. It had never occurred to her, that she might be a heroine to Americans. She was asked to lecture, for fees that astounded her. For the first time in her life, she had money of her own.

When she wrote a large check to the Waldorf-Astoria, to pay for her oldest daughter's twenty-first birthday party, she said "Now I know I can face life. I can take care of myself, and if need be, of my daughters." They said she spent too much on them. She answered: "I have learned that pleasant memories are the bank account that matters." When she told me this ten years later, on Wake Island, she had so many memories stored up that she said "I doubt if I have room for any more." But another was added, while we sat at lunch in Wake's Quonset dining-hall.

The waiters were small, brown, ageless men from Guam, all

called "Boy." They caucused in the kitchen, and elected a spokesman, who approached us hesitantly, bowed, and made a breathless little speech. Madame Pandit must kindly excuse him for intruding. He intruded because everyone knew she was a Great Lady who did good things for poor people. "Guamanian boys very happy if you accept small remembrance of thanks and best wishes from the heart." He dropped a carton of *Sea Stores* cigarettes before her, and rushed off to find more aspirin for my comrade of the night before, who never got to be her seatmate.

Soon after, the interlude on Wake was over. At Tokyo dignitaries awaited her, flanked by reporters and photographers. She said what should be said by the retiring president of the United Nations, her country's most distinguished foreign representative. Then, finally, she could go to meet her new grandson.

3.

"You were born to wealth and station but . . . when you lifted up your voice in behalf of the dependent peoples . . . you made yourself the dear Ambassador to the hearts of millions of human beings who never saw your native land but will henceforth love you and look toward you with hope." So said Dr. Mordecai Johnson, president of Howard University, in conferring her first but far from last honorary degree on Her Excellency Madame Vijaya Lakshmi Pandit, Ambassador Extraordinary and Minister Plenipotentiary of the Republic of India to the United States of America, in Washington, D. C., in 1949.

Several years later, in India, in her brother's house in New Delhi, she said "My public life is over. There is no work left for which I am needed. From now on, I shall sit in the shadows." No one I have ever known would be less likely to leave the battlefield with the issue still in doubt. But in India's capital, in 1961, she weighed her words as she had not done on Wake Island in 1954.

"The first effect of people getting a little more of what they want is to increase their sense of discontent at not getting more" was truer nowhere than in India after fourteen years of independence. The Congress Party, that had won the fight for freedom, still ruled the nation. Her brother, who led the fight, was still Prime Minister, and said as he had from the beginning: "When you start not merely at Zero but at Zero Minus One, each small advance is a major victory."

This was not enough for careerists who emerged from obscurity after Independence Day in 1947. With mystical affection, the masses called her brother Nehruji, and looked to him for miracles. To a growing phalanx of casuists, he was too much the autocratic idealist, too loftily impractical, too little aware of a widening gap between planning and performance. He had yet to face a vote of no confidence, but there were allegations in Lok Sabha, India's House of the People, of misfeasance in high office, bureaucratic inefficiency, corruption down the line.

Gandhians out of power complained he had become too fond of his own image. In the coffeehouses, table orators rang changes on "After Nehru, who?" In his own Cabinet, there were ambitious Ministers who said it was long past time of retirement for veterans in the Congress hierarchy whose claim to eminence rested on having gone to jail when that was fashionable. V. K. Krishna Menon, his Minister for Defense, was notoriously caustic in this regard. Morarji Desai, his flamboyantly ascetic Minister of Finance, made no secret of his own aspiration to rise higher.

Even Delhi's bearded Sikh taxidrivers told their passengers the Communist Chinese were building a military highway from captured Tibet into India's Himalayan territories; but India's policy continued to rest on *Panchshila* and peaceful coexistence with Peking. There was disaffection in India's Armed Forces, controlled by Krishna Menon. General K. S. Thimayya had to be prevailed on not to resign as chief of staff. India's legal Communist Party won elections in Kerala, the country's most populous and most literate state. Portugal refused to discuss withdrawing from Goa, the last colonial enclave on the subcontinent. Life expectancy lengthened, the birthrate accelerated, while food production faltered.

Jawaharlal Nehru's sister was never blind to her brother's failings; nor was he. There was sad truth in an American journalist's plaint that "Sycophants wove a cordon around him, and toadies vied in eagerness to agree, no matter if he was wrong." It was also true, that he "suffered from the wordiness all around him, and the fussiness, and the ineffectuality, and the begging and the prevarication." But she could testify to falsity in another journalist's sneer that "He so dreads the eventual inevitable that he will not consider selecting, training and preparing a successor." He had in fact sent certain Congress leaders back to their constituencies, there to prove, if they could, that they still spoke for the people they represented.

One among them might succeed him; but it would have to be by democratic choice, not by conferred inheritance.

He applied the same rule to his sister and his daughter, despite a rising garboil whose instigators raised the cry of *Nehru nepotism*. His widowed daughter, Mrs. Indira Gandhi, had been a member of the committee controlling the Congress Party as early as 1953. In 1959, she was Congress president. Now his sister, Indira's aunt and onetime prison cellmate, had returned from being honored overseas by presidents and queens and dictators. By the calendar, seventeen years separated the Nehru widows. In public belief, for once not altogether wrong, they were very close. He gave no new appointment to either.

Cynics scoffed that they only bided their time. Some observers, even at a certain level in the American Embassy, said "The 'Nehru *mystique*' is yesterday's illusion." Not so, said others; "not as long as the Nehrus themselves believe in it." I cannot say what Vijaya Lakshmi Pandit thought when I argued "But there will always be work to be done, that you can do better than anyone." I only know that she is wonderfully skilled at changing subjects when she chooses. It happened to be October 19. Suddenly, she said "Why, this is your birthday!"

Why she remembered this, seven years after she wished me a happy birthday in Tokyo, is something only she could explain. What she did about it was typical of her. Moving gracefully past a Railways Minister, a Joint Secretary from Information and Broadcasting, a correspondent from West Germany, a Ford Foundation cultural advisor from Harvard, and a cluster of attachés armed with briefcases, she met her brother coming down the stairs, and turned his attention to the only person present who had no actual business there. "Today is his birthday, and he is away from his family." And her brother said, "Come along, while I talk with the children."

Like his sister, he was smaller than photographs made him appear, but had a way of being taller than those around him. Pinned to his spotless light-grey *sherwani* was the single rose-bud he always wore. Physical fitness and vital energy had been his lifelong attributes. This morning, he walked slowly, head bowed a little. His eyes were weary. When suddenly he stopped, I thought he would turn back.

Instead, helped by Hari, his body-servant, he picked small white star-shaped flowers, and placed them in a cup of leaves. I found myself holding this, and in surprise broke stride, bumping against a young couple, a bride and groom in Delhi on their honeymoon, who were sightseeing outside the Prime Minister's House when they were invited to come in. They still could not quite believe they would be able to tell their grandchildren "Once we walked with Nehruji, almost as close as we are to you."

A hundred children, scrubbed, shy, smiling, awaited him in a corner of the gardens. He went among them, singling out one and then another, asking about their parents, their schools, their ambitions; making them laugh, and laughing with them. There was no politician's pose for the populace in this. No pictures were taken for the press. They called him *Chacha,* Uncle, and for half an hour he was unaffectedly avuncular. It seemed that more than the children, he was on holiday.

When for the third time one of his secretaries said "Sir!",

he chose a lovely little girl to walk with him to a doorway at which he said as if he must remind himself: "Well, now I become a statesman." He was about to be escorted to his car when all at once he asked, "What have you done with your flowers?" I blurted, "I thought the bride should have them." He looked at her, and at her husband. They made a handsome, hopeful pair. "Of course. Of course." Then we watched him go to do his best for four hundred and sixty million hopeful people.

Not quite three years later, he was dead. One of his ministers spoke for India. "Life is out; the light is out." His sister was sixty-four. Against advice of Congress Party strategists, who had various reasons for warning her of certain defeat, she left her sinecure as Governor at Bombay to compaign for his vacant seat in the House of the People. North India's villagers remembered the Great Lady who did good things for poor people. Confounding the experts, they elected her by a large majority.

For two weeks, a party wheelhorse served as caretaker Prime Minister, while scramble for succession went on behind the arras. Then, said a Congress spokesman, compromise was reached, "with dignity and smoothness that belied fears expressed for some years." It produced a successor about whom the Western world knew nothing, and India at large knew little more. Diminutive, colorless Lal Bahadur Shastri, who had no enemies because no one had seen him as a rival, took up the burdens Jawaharlal Nehru had borne for seventeen years. Party strong-men dismissed him as expendable. Newspapers dubbed him "the Sparrow."

He named Nehru's daughter, Mrs. Indira Gandhi, to his

Cabinet, as Minister for Information and Broadcasting. It was said this was merely an act of deference.

Then in the House of the People, Shrimati Vijaya Lakshmi Pandit, Member of Parliament from Allahabad in the United Provinces, made her first speech under the new regime. It was a calm but headline-making challenge to her own party to put its house in order before time ran out. Her bill of particulars alleged indecision and double-speak in foreign affairs, false claims and hidden failures delaying progress at home.

There were contradictory interpretations of her purpose. Those who felt the sting of the lash said she simply could not realize the Nehru Era ended with her brother's death; even that she sought to shift responsibility from him, to a scapegoat not strong enough to fight back. Then what her brother had managed to postpone since Mohammed Ali Jinnah and the Muslim League ripped Pakistan away from India in 1947, began with brief but savage skirmishes in the Rann of Cutch, followed quickly by invasion and all-out war in disputed Kashmir. And as other inheritors have done when emergency called for resources unsuspected in them even by themselves, Lal Bahadur Shastri confounded his minimizers.

More Gandhian in personal humility and asceticism than his predecessor had ever been, in a space of hours he let the world know that India had renounced Gandhi's philosophy of nonviolent resistance, and rallied the unprepared nation to fight militant Pakistan to a standstill. Newspapers in India and abroad proclaimed "The Sparrow has become the Hawk!" What the press learned only after it was over was that in India's darkest hour, Shastri turned to the lamp in the shadows.

4.

There is no published record of any adverse comment Vijaya Lakshmi Pandit has ever made regarding the man who is said by many in India to have hastened her brother's death. In fact, she has never had much to say about V. K. Krishna Menon. He, not she, resented her brother's decision that made them both spokesmen for India at the United Nations. She was in the United States, pleading India's cause, when after twenty-three years away in England, he returned to India at last, and was made Minister-Without-Portfolio in the new-born nation's Cabinet. Congress leaders questioned Menon's right to sit above them. No one knew as well as she, how stubbornly her brother stiffened against uninvited advice.

Seeing scant loyalty to each other among contenders for high place, he favored the latecomer who shared his distaste for now-change-partners. Krishna Menon, a thoughtful observer said, "sees even more fools in the world than there are." His superciliousness affronted the rank-and-file. Jawaharlal Nehru seems to have felt there was need for a gadfly. "Some men of great ability," he said regarding Krishna Menon, "are victims of a sense of frustration that drives them to actions that make them personally unpopular." His sister knew how little he valued personal popularity.

India bore deep scars inflicted by professionals in uniform who acted without consulting civilian authority. Departure of British officers had left the armed forces in confusion, made worse by breakdown of organization resulting from decision by thousands to cast their lot with separated Pakistan. A strong new broom was needed; and Krishna Menon volunteered. Someone had said of him what Talleyrand said of Napoleon: "How unfortunate that so great a man should have been so badly brought up." Taking command as Minister for Defense, Menon proceeded to prove that he was no Napoleon.

Once an American President's supporters coined a slogan, *He kept us out of war,* and with it reelected him, just before war began. Krishna Menon, placating Soviet Russia and Communist China while sedulously affronting the United States, declared that thus he kept war away from India. American tanks and planes poured into Pakistan. He said India needed no such dangerous gifts. Military men who protested were retired, or sent to join Indian Army units on United Nations peace-keeping duty along the Gaza Strip. When American aircraft builders offered to sell India fighter-jets, Menon said, "India will build her own." Only a prototype was produced. Then Peking tired of pretending.

Communist Chinese troops attacked in the Himalayas. India's frontier defenders, ill-armed, ill-trained, without artillery or air support, lacking even ambulances for the wounded, crumpled and were driven back, as far as the Chinese chose to drive them for the moment. His trust in Peking pledges contemptuously betrayed, Jawaharlal Nehru looked with cleared vision at Krishna Menon, while Menon blamed everyone but himself. He had to be forced to resign, and left the highest office he would ever hold, crying he had been sacrificed to please the mob.

For the first time, India asked for military aid from the United States and the United Kingdom. Some came. Need for much more forced diversion of funds from education and food production. Taxes doubled, then tripled. Peking strategists believed limited aggression would be enough to wreck India's economy and topple its democratic government. Instead, betrayal and attack made India a nation. But it dealt a death blow to the man who created India.

He lay down, and closed his eyes. *Death*, Gautama Buddha preached in India two thousand five hundred years ago, *is no more than permission granted to other modes of life to exist, so that everything may be ceaselessly renewed. The smallest moment of life is stronger than death and cancels it.* But the millions who had utter faith in their Nehruji looked askance at his successor, Lal Bahadur Shastri. And in their hour of fear and doubt, Pakistan struck across the United Nations ceasefire line in Kashmir. Washington, having invested some three billion dollars in the good faith of a paper-ally, halted aid to Pakistan, but simultaneously cut off economic assistance to India. With what they had, India's Army and Air Force blunted the Pakistan drive, and counterattacked. Peking intervened. Shastri the Sparrow rejected Peking's ultimatum.

Now called Shastri the Hawk, he asked Vijaya Lakshmi Pandit to go to Europe as his personal envoy. She went without the fanfare that attended missions for her brother, and returned avoiding interviewers. To this day, there is dispute in Delhi as to what she discussed with De Gaulle in Paris, what negotiations she carried through in West Germany and the Netherlands. The fact remains that soon after, arms and *materiél* not stamped *Made in U. S. A.* reached the battle-front, where Pakistan's American-built war-machine slowed to a halt.

She visited forward areas, and was cheered by India's *javans,* volunteers of every caste and creed. She and her daughters worked as volunteers in hospitals crowded with civilian refugees from India's side of the cease-fire line that she had helped to establish. Food shortages set Delhi residents to digging up lawns and flower beds and planting kitchen gardens. She planted and tended hers.

She was in the United States, on another unpublicized mission, when at Tashkent in Soviet Russia on January 11, 1966, Lal Bahadur Shastri and President-Field Marshal Mohammed Ayub Khan of Pakistan signed the pact that brought uneasy armistice between neighbors who once lived with no spitefence between them. Twelve hours later, the Sparrow who became the Hawk was dead; and aspirants to succession, clamoring and contending, found neither time nor reason to lament the going out of an earthen lamp that had done the best it could.

5.

"The family," said one press report, "headed by Mrs. Vijaya Lakshmi Pandit, strongly rallied round." She flew home to India, gave no interviews, made no speeches, was inconspicuous at Congress conferences. But her presence was felt. When votes were counted, the victor was her niece, her brother's daughter.

On January 24, 1966, two days before India's sixteenth Republic Day, six days before the eighteenth anniversary of the assassination of Mohandas Karamchand Gandhi, Mrs. Indira Gandhi was sworn in as third Prime Minister of the only

Asian nation that has maintained unbroken succession of constitutionally elected government since colonialism ended in the East. Her name caused some Americans to think she belongs to the Mahatma's family. She does not; they were not related, except by belief in Nehru destiny.

Around the globe, newspapers printed pictures of the Nehru widows side by side, united, embracing, smiling. Then as she had done before, Vijaya Lakshmi Pandit returned to her corner in the shadows. For how long, no one prophesied.

"Because the cause is great," her brother wrote, "something of that greatness falls upon us." She laughs as she always has, with honest amusement, at accusation of greatness. "I have been remarkably fortunate. All through my life, loving hands have been stretched out to help me. When I have done well, there have been many voices raised in praise, and for mistakes I have received forgiveness in full measure. It is for this reason alone that I am able to carry on."

Surely she has been loved and praised, perhaps more universally than any other woman born in this century. But sixty-seven years ago no one, least of all those who loved her most, had cause to expect she would ever be known of outside of her own family.

II⊛

"I have been remarkably fortunate."

She was born on August 18, 1900, at Allahabad, capital of Uttar Pradesh, the United Provinces, once the kingdoms of Agra and Oudh. That was a year of drought and famine in the Middle Land, where 2,500 years earlier Gautama Buddha had offered compassion to all humanity. Again at the turn of another century, as they had down through the ages, the poor died miserably in ditches. But in Anand Bhavan, the fine white mansion of the fortunate Nehrus, there was luxury and happiness.

Anand Bhavan means "Home of Joy." Its ebullient lord and master, Motilal Nehru, was a barrister, so successful and sought after that it was said he earned a thousand rupees for each minute he spent in court. His son, Jawaharlal—which means "a priceless jewel"—was handsome, manly, articulate, brighter than his tutors, and already, at eleven, coveted as a future son-in-law by heads of the finest families. His father's whole life was bound up in him.

Quite simply, Motilal believed the world was made for men. He was faithful to his wife, but far from uxorious. He provided for her bountifully, but thought of her and all others of her sex as passengers traveling in a separate car hooked on behind a train for men only. The women's quarters at Anand Bhavan were an enclave apart, wherein all was Indian in the orthodox Hindu style. This was as it should be. Religion was good for women; it kept them contented in their predestined sphere.

His own domain was a Little England. Hindus were welcome, but so were Muslims, Buddhists, Sikhs, Jains and Christians. He respected his birth-faith, but had no respect for caste or creed distinctions. His guests sat on chairs imported from France, dined off Spode and told loud English jokes.

His son when small saw him toss off a glass of ruby-tinted port, and ran to the women's quarters crying *"Bapu* is drinking blood!" Motilal was hugely amused. An orthodox Hindu visitor, watching his butler serve a platter of fried eggs, protested aghast, *"Panditji,* you are not going to eat those?" Brandishing knife and fork, Motilal replied "I certainly am. And in another few moments, I am going to eat their mother, too!"

He owned the first automobile in Allahabad, a Model T Ford. When he drove it down the center of the street, even bearers of the White Man's Burden got out of the way. Asked if it was true that he sent his laundry to be done in London, he answered "No, but it is an excellent suggestion." His charities were numerous. No one who hungered left his door unfed. But above all, he lavished generosity on his family.

He was away in England, where he liked to go, when his daughter was born. He cabled from London "Call her Swarup Kumari for her mother." Swarup means "Beautiful," and Kumari is "Princess." Actually, her mother's name was

Swaruprani, but Rani means "Queen," and his play on titles amused him, while the compliment it implied did no harm to marital harmony. When he came home and found that his wife preferred to call the baby Nanhi, "Little Daughter," he said that was all right.

He favored letting women have their way in minor matters. It was natural for them to be excited about a baby, since babies were their reason for existence. However it struck him as rather odd that his son should be so charmed by the sister who now demanded attention hitherto given to him alone.

The story is that he tested Jawaharlal with a lawyer's thrust. "You needn't pretend with me. Stop worrying. She's only a girl. She'll have no claim on my estate. It is still all for you." If this happened, it would have had to be because instinct and training made her father mistrustful of anything not covered by precedent. In any event, he yielded to her brother's insistence that work piled up in his office could wait until he paid a call on Little Daughter.

He studied her, touched her cautiously, and left the women's quarters without comment. Her nurse said the long drought ended and the rains came the night she was born, and this was an omen that meant she would always be fortunate. As far as Motilal Nehru was concerned, it was luck enough for any girl to be his daughter, and his son's sister. And there were many who agreed.

2.

Her birthplace stands on hallowed ground. Allahabad is a very ancient city, although its name, from the Arabic *Illaha-*

bas, City of God, dates only from the sixteenth century, when Akbar the Great, Muslim Emperor of Hindustan, built a mosque and a fort on the site that to Hindus from time unrecorded has been *Prag* or *Prayag,* the Place of Sacrifice. It lies at the confluence of the Ganges and Jumna rivers, sacred to Hindus who believe these are joined underground by a third sacred stream, the legendary Saraswati. They call the juncture *Triveni,* the Triple Braid.

Annually, the faithful come from great distances for *Maghmela,* the bathing festival, when sins are washed away with ritual baptism. Every twelfth year, there is a *Kumbh-mela,* when never less than a million pilgrims gather for a great religious fair. Going to bathe, they pass a pillar engraved with edicts of Asoka, Buddhist Emperor of India in the Golden Age, who sent missionaries from India to Greece, Syria and Egypt three centuries before the birth of Christ.

From earliest childhood she was reminded that where she walked clinging to her nurse's hand, Rama the hero-god of the *Ramayana,* India's *Iliad,* had been reunited with his loyal brother, Bharat, after fourteen years in exile. Not far off is the Bharadwaja shrine, to which her mother took her often. Here, it is believed, Valmiki, fabled author of the *Ramayana,* prayed and wrote. And there was her own family's history to make her realize how fortunate she was, to be a Nehru.

They were Brahmins, of the Twice-Born caste, which in Hindu cosmology made them superior to kings. Kashmiri by descent, her ancestry traced to the Aryas or Aryan conquerors, "Lords of the Field," who brought the *Vedas* to India more than three thousand years ago. Imperial dynasties in India, she was told, had less claim to royal lineage. To this her father added that premier Maharajahs had less cognizance of *noblesse oblige.*

The first Nehru in India was Raj Kaul, a Kashmiri scholar-poet, so celebrated in his days that in 1716 the Moghul Emperor of Delhi, Farrukhsiar, invited him to court and gave him a benefice of land alongside a canal. People called the noble *émigrés* Kaul Nahar, the Kauls by the canal. Before long, Kaul was dropped, Nahar became Nehru, and a Pundit Lakshmi Nehru was among the first Indian barristers ennobled by the British East India Company, which ruled the subcontinent as a private monopoly until 1858.

Her father's father, Ganga Dhar Nehru, was *Kotwal,* Supreme High Commissioner of Police at Delhi, until 1857. That was the year of what the *Encyclopaedia Britannica,* though long edited and published in the United States, continues to call the Indian Mutiny—which had begun to be spoken of by Indians, in her childhood, as India's first War for Independence.

The war was lost. The victors tied selected rebels at the mouths of cannons and blew them to bits. Her grandfather, refusing further service to the British, moved with his family to Agra. Within sight of the Taj Mahal, he was halted by British soldiers, who spied a flaxen-haired little girl in his company and accused him of kidnapping an English child. She belonged where she was. Little Daughter sometimes saluted the *Kotwal*'s portrait, on the wall in her father's Little England. It showed him with fair skin, red hair, blue eyes, easily able to pass for English if he chose.

He died at Agra shortly before her father was born on May 6, 1861. When an elder son, succeeding as head of the family, was appointed to the High Court at Allahabad, the Nehrus moved there. Before he was twenty, her father had passed examinations for the bar, and had begun to prosper. According to custom his brothers chose his bride. She was, of course, Kashmiri and Brahmin. Tragically, she died very young, and her infant son survived her only a few days. Bereft, Motilal Nehru plunged into work to dull his sorrow, and showed a Midas touch. He was already richer than his brothers when they decided he should marry again, and, as before, chose the Kashmiri Brahmin maiden he should marry. She was Little Daughter's mother.

Barely fifteen when she married, not quite five feet tall, with dainty hands and feet, large hazel eyes, and flowing chestnut hair, Swaruprani Thussu was fragile but not frail, gently shy but steel-strong in her way. Motilal, seven years her senior, seemed to tower over her. But like her son and daughter, she walked taller than she was. Orthodox, as her husband was not, she was untroubled by tales that their first home, a house at the end of a lane in the city's heart, was haunted by a weeping ghost.

To Swaruprani it seemed to be more frighteningly haunted by her husband's clients, always increasing in numbers and importance. She welcomed seclusion in the women's quarters. There, on November 18, 1889, she bore a son. Motilal had lost one son. He did not propose to lose another. He told Swaruprani "I have named him Jawaharlal," and at once began arranging his future.

In that same year in London, a poor student from a village in India, who would have to make his future for himself, summoned courage to call on the great Cardinal Newman and congratulate him for supporting dockworkers who had gone on strike for better hours and pay. The meeting led Mohandas Karamchand Gandhi to his first acquaintance with *Lead Kindly Light,* a hymn Newman wrote while he was an Anglican vicar, before he became a Roman Catholic convert. Gandhi and Jawaharlal Nehru would not meet until 1916. In 1889, there was no earthly cause to surmise that their paths would ever cross.

3.

Gandhi was a *bania,* of the Vaisya caste, which ranked third in the immutable social order: the faceless majority, subject always to *Ksatriyas,* the caste of warriors and administrators, and infinitely inferior to Brahmins. He came from Porbandar on the Kathiawar Peninsula, above Bombay on India's west coast. His forebears were village grocers, until three in succession achieved ill-paid posts as minor ministers in several of Kathiawar's one hundred and eighteen petty principalities. All three, including his father, were ill-educated, and died poor.

Married at thirteen, he scraped and struggled for an education. His wife, Kasturbai, could not read or write. He found no time to teach her. As a child he had stolen coppers to buy cigarettes, and contemplated suicide by swallowing poisonous *dathura* seeds. Courage failed him just in time. Beside his father's deathbed he confessed his sins.

Christian missionaries repelled him, with their litany of *Holier than thou the benighted heathen,* but he learned the Sermon on the Mount by heart. When his brother found means to send him to England to study law, before he left his wife and her baby he took three vows: never to touch wine, meat or women. In London, at first, he was overcome by the sense of belonging that came from wearing trousers and a necktie.

He did foolish, wasteful things, and became a bit of a dandy. He cultivated a mustache, bought a chimney-pot hat that cost nineteen shillings, paid a Bond Street tailor ten pounds sterling to make him an evening suit, invested three pounds in a violin and a guinea in elocution lessons, considered taking dancing lessons but remembered his third vow, and slowly regained resignation to poverty. Thereafter he joined the Vegetarian Society, walked ten or twelve miles each day to find the cheapest restaurant, attempted to speak before crowds but failed miserably, and managed to pass the London Matriculation Tests. On June 10, 1891, then twenty years old, he was called to the bar. Two days later, he sailed for India. "Notwithstanding my studies, there was no end to my helplessness and fear."

In contrast, Jawaharlal Nehru was shielded from need for doubt or dread as completely as the Buddha-to-be, Prince Siddhartha, whose fond father decreed he must never see human misery, and imprisoned him in palaces of pleasure, behind guarded gates that shut out all unpleasantness. Jawaharlal was only three when Motilal moved the family to a fine new bungalow in a district otherwise reserved to Europeans.

At six, when for the first time he felt pain, it was only because of his father's temper. In Motilal's *pukka* British library, he had spied two fountain pens, and decided one would not be

missed. It was. His father roared, accusing everyone, until the
trail led to Jawaharlal. Motilal's silver-headed cane flailed up
and down, again and again. "Almost blind with pain and
mortification, I rushed to my mother, and for several days various creams and ointments were applied to my aching and
quivering body." But when his father came to ask if he had
learned a lesson, he stood straight and silent until Motilal sued
for forgiveness.

As was his way, Motilal attempted amends by giving what
was not asked for. His professional duties took him away for
days on end. He returned from each absence bearing gifts,
until sometimes Jawaharlal hid to avoid another package-
opening ceremony. A day came when even Motilal hardly
knew what to purchase next. Then he saw and forthwith
bought for cash a manorial establishment surrounded by gardens sloping down to the Ganges. Refurbished and enlarged, it
became the Home of Joy.

The family had lived there for a year when Swarup Kumari
Nehru was born. There were stables, tennis courts, an indoor
swimming pool, a regiment of servants. No school in India,
Motilal decreed, had enough to offer his son. Jawaharlal must
be tutored at home. Summoning a venerable Brahmin pedagogue, he commanded, "Teach the boy Hindi and Sanskrit."
This was easier ordered than performed.

Jawaharlal's Hindi would never be fluent, and his Sanskrit
remained as fragmentary as his Latin. He thought, and always
would think in English. Nor did Motilal disapprove of this
predilection. He sent the Brahmin away, and employed as
tutor a learned, eloquent, star-crossed Irish-Belgian, Ferdinand
Brooks. Brooks said "The boy has a questing mind that pur-

sues ideas, not merely ways of cloaking them with words."
Motilal confessed a twinge of jealousy. "Right from the start,
Brooks could talk to Jawa, and get him to talk as I never
could."

In time to come, the British superintendent of a prison for
Indian rebels complained to his most illustrious prisoner: "I
cannot understand your passion for reading. I finished all my
reading at the age of twelve." Brooks sharpened in his pupil an
appetence for printed pages that would never dull. When his
sister was born, Jawaharlal was so engrossed in comparing Voltaire and Nietzsche that he could not spare time to see her until the next day.

Thereafter, the bond between brother and sister strengthened with the years. Whatever he did, she must try to do. "I
cannot remember when I did not try to make him proud of
me." He rode well. Seeing her toddle out to watch her brother
gallop across the lawns, her father bought a pony and an English saddle, and terrified her mother and her nurse, but delighted Little Daughter, by setting her astride the pony, then
leading it back and forth until she and Bijli, "Lightning,"
were used to each other. Thereafter, they were friends. Sometimes she fell off; but she never let her brother see her cry.
Eventually, he allowed her to ride beside him.

4.

"I was only two, and I can't expect you to believe that I
really remember our first gallop together, but I do." Her
brother saw how his books entranced Little Daughter, and
while they rode together, recited poems he had read, by

Goethe and Swinburne and Tagore. "Of course I couldn't understand a word. But I pretended I did, and he was too kind to make fun of my seriousness." Then one day he returned from going somewhere with Brooks, and hardly noticed her, and was uninterested in riding or swimming with her.

Brooks had taken him to hear Mrs. Annie Besant, a redoubtable Irishwoman, who had progressed from campaigning for free thought and birth control in England to proselyting in India for the Theosophical Society founded by Madame Blavatsky and Colonel Henry Olcott. Brooks had expounded her mystical theories. Now Jawaharlal heard her in the very solid flesh. "I was dazed and in a dream."

Mrs. Besant had this effect on many. "She was a powerful orator, and it was a treat to listen to her," says K. P. S. Menon, India's elder statesman (not the Krishna Menon known almost too well by Americans). "It was she who first roused our minds to the anomaly of British rule in India." Her method was to begin by saying theosophy was a distillation of metaphysics understood most anciently by India's mystics.

"India, she would point out, already had a splendid civilization when primitive tribes such as the Franks, the Huns, the Slavs, the Goths, the Magyars, the Angles and the Saxons were roaming about Europe warring with one another. Then she would dwell on the present state of India, poor, ignorant, ridden by disease and superstition. She would assert there was no way of eradicating these evils unless India was administered by Indians themselves. More impressive than what she said was her manner of saying it. She would begin quietly, with her arms folded in front, and gradually warm up. When she reached the climax of her argument, her whole being would shake with emotion; her hair which had been neatly combed would stand on end, and she would look like one possessed."

Shortly before she came to Allahabad, Hindu orthodoxy had reigned briefly at Anand Bhavan, even in Motilal Nehru's Little England. Jawaharlal was thirteen, and it was time for the ceremony that linked him with uncounted Brahmin generations. He wore beneath his English clothes the thread that marks the bearer as one of the Twice-Born, when for the first time, he listened to Mrs. Besant. "I decided to join the Theosophical Society, and Mrs. Besant herself performed my initiation."

This was not what made his father shout "I'll not allow it!" Motilal saw no harm in sampling other religions. He had himself been a member of Mrs. Besant's society, briefly, until he decided he had heard enough. She amused him; yet he respected her sincerity. He had employed Brooks on her recommendation. He was sure his son, like other romantic youngsters, would outgrow cloudy mysticism when he grew a little older. But Mrs. Besant preached more than theosophy. Her politics, in Motilal's opinion, were much too heady a drug for the young, and especially for Jawaharlal.

He had watched the Indian National Congress since its formation at Bombay in 1885, when the organizer, a Scotsman and former civil servant, Alan Octavian Hume, opened the first session by calling for "Three times three for Her Majesty the Queen-Empress, God bless her!", and the cheers were given with unanimous fervor. At the time, it was predicted that the first Congress meeting would be the last.

The Congress platform expressed vague hope for establishment of a representative government in India, and perhaps, some day, of an Indian Parliament. It prayed for "fusion of all elements in the population, regeneration of the nation and consolidation of true union between Great Britain and British India." Motilal saw neither harm nor promise in that. But now radicals and extremists in the Congress shouted for *Swaraj*, Home Rule; and Mrs. Besant was their prophetess.

He was well-acquainted with the leader of one Congress faction, Gopal Krishna Gokhale, who argued for moderation in dealing with the Raj. Still Gokhale had been jailed for criminal subversion. As for Gokhale's rival for Congress control, Bal Gangadhar Tilak, his battle cry was *Action now!* At least they were men, therefore not given to feminine hysteria; thus a little less dangerous than Mrs. Besant. Yet Motilal saw in all three a tendency toward appeal to madness in the mob, that once unleashed would run wild, trampling law and order, destroying any hope for true reform. In no sense deaf or blind to India's wrongs, he felt correction must come one step at a time, through the planning and with the consent of constituted authority.

He was well aware that his conservatism was as much misread by British friends and associates as by Home Rule hotheads and rabble-rousers. "Old Motilal Nehru likes the jam on the butter on his bread too much to want tomorrow any different from yesterday!" He disdained denial. The middle road was safe and sure, and he would do all he could to keep his son from leaving it. However, since the incident of the whipping he kept his temper chained when he dealt with Jawaharlal.

Neither his son nor Brooks was made to feel it was any decision but Brooks' own that prompted Brooks to say he had decided to leave Anand Bhavan and follow Mrs. Besant. "I have never done anything positive. I must find out if I can." As they parted, with Nanhi watching and ignored, he told Jawaharlal, "The truth is, I've done badly for you. I've set you looking for what isn't there."

In this, he may have summed up his own tragedy. Obscure in Mrs. Besant's retinue, oblivious to her politics, still seeking a key to the Infinite, he was her humble devotee until she proclaimed she had discovered the new Messiah, in the person of a young man named Jeddah Krishnamurti. Then Brooks parted from her, drifted across the countryside, and before long died by drowning, under circumstances still unexplained.

5.

The departed Brooks continued to be a presence at Anand Bhavan. Even Little Daughter felt this. Some of the hours her brother had formerly spent with Brooks, in discussion and debate far too arcane for her, were spent now with her. But a little girl's wide-eyed adoration was no substitute for the give-and-take Brooks had provided. Jawaharlal was sixteen, she was not quite five, when he told their father he would like to go to school in England. Motilal, though he dreaded separation, said, "That is what I was just about to suggest," and next morning announced "We will make it a family holiday."

Little Daughter's English dissatisfied him; it had a Hindi accent. Travel abroad would correct this. They would take the child along, to see her brother settled. Her mother must go, too, to keep her out of mischief. That Swaruprani in all her days had traveled only from seclusion with her parents in

Lahore to seclusion in the women's quarters at Anand Bhavan, and trembled at the thought of crossing salt water and mingling with casteless *farangi,* mattered not at all to Motilal.

On shipboard, Swaruprani kept Little Daughter with her in their cabin, observing Brahmin orthodoxy, while Motilal and Jawaharlal drank champagne at the Captain's table. In England, at the Derby at Epsom Downs which Motilal insisted they must all attend, she walked two steps behind, head bowed, eyes cast down. But Little Daughter ran ahead, beside her brother and their father, who flourished tickets for the Enclosure and made sure Jawaharlal got a close view of His Majesty the King-Emperor, Edward VII.

His Royal Highness, Motilal reminded his son, had visited India when he was Victoria Regina's heir apparent, and Motilal was Jawaharlal's age, and there was no wild talk of Indian nationalism and *Swaraj.* Tomorrow, they would arrange Jawaharlal's enrollment at Harrow. It might be true that England's wars were won on the playing fields of Eton; but Harrow produced the men who ran things properly in peace time: Peel, Palmerston and Lord Randolph Churchill who was Secretary of State for India in 1885, and his son, young Mr. Winston Churchill, the incumbent Undersecretary for the Colonies.

At Harrow, the headmaster protested that Jawaharlal was past the usual age for entrance. Brusquely, Motilal overruled this Buzfuz technicality. In haste to be gone now that the die was cast, he commanded Jawaharlal to study sensibly, write regularly and remember he was a Nehru. Then he set about arranging for Little Daughter's education. In London, he summoned and crossexamined an assortment of English gov-

Three Generations of Nehrus

Motilal Nehru

Swaruprani, mother of Jawaharlal and Little Daughter

Jawaharlal Nehru as a child

ernesses, some of whom he frightened into tears, none of whom passed muster, until he came to Miss Cecelia Hooper.

She said she was not at all sure she could endure India, or him. He barked. She froze. He found himself offering twice the fee he had decided to pay. She said no amount of money could induce her to commit herself beyond twelve months. Chuckling suddenly, he took her on her terms. As it turned out, she would be a member of the Nehru clan for the next twelve years.

She, not Swaruprani Nehru, was in charge when Little Daughter met her first world-shaker. This was on her birthday, at Wiesbaden Spa in Germany, where her father went to take the waters *a l'Anglaise.* Invited to a party given by Kaiser Wilhelm for children of the *haute noblesse,* and singled out to be presented to His Teutonic Majesty, she curtsied because Miss Hooper said she must, but was frankly unimpressed. Much more memorable to her was her father's sudden decision, before they sailed for home, that she must be taken to Liberty's in London and outfitted head to toe in proper English fashion.

Henceforth, he informed her mother, Little Daughter would do her growing up *a l'Anglaise.* What Swaruprani Nehru thought of this, she left unsaid. She was sure that when Jawaharlal returned to Anand Bhavan, his sister would be sent back to the women's quarters and the rightful studies of a Hindu maiden. So it might have been, for any other brilliant brother's sister. But though she missed him greatly, during Jawaharlal's absence his sister made a place for herself that she was never to lose.

6.

She was seven, when her mother bore a second daughter. From Harrow, her brother cabled that though he did not yet know if he had a brother or another sister, he thought Krishna would be an appropriate name for either. Their father agreed. But though he had two daughters now, Motilal continued to call Swarup Kumari "Little Daughter." This would be his habit for years to come.

It had become a ritual for her to sit quietly in a corner in his library, while he read her brother's letters aloud. They were frequent and affectionate; but each showed more self-confidence than the last. He sent his photograph, in the uniform of the Harrow cadet corps, appending the headmaster's commendation: "Quite good capabilities for a soldier." He mentioned other Harrovians from India with pointed irony.

A Baroda princeling was good at cricket, but feared what might leap at him from inside a book. The heir to the great Maharajah of Kapurthala amused his English schoolmates with his haughtiness; he shouted that he would have their heads cut off if they ever came into his kingdom, and they ducked him in a water bucket. Jawaharlal himself played no cricket, and made no enemies.

His headmaster described him approvingly. "A very nice boy, quiet and refined, who works well and keeps his opinions to himself." He did not keep them from his father. Words his sister had never heard, over which his father growled, dotted his pages: determinism, activism, Fabian Socialism. He wrote about writers not represented on his father's bookshelves: H. G. Wells, Bertrand Russell, Harold Laski, Sigmund Freud, George Bernard Shaw. A boycott of British goods in India, concurrent with mass meetings to promote purchase only of *swadeshi,* things made in India, was denounced in the British press and in Parliament as close to outright treason. He was sorry the boycott failed. "There is, of course, no one here at Harrow with whom I can talk about it."

He moved on, from Harrow to Trinity College at Cambridge, where there were a hundred other students from India. He fraternized with few. Some of them formed a debating society. He attended its meetings, but seldom spoke. When Bepin Chandra Pal, a Bengali politician visiting England, addressed the group, Jawaharlal wrote, "The volume of noise was so terrific that I could hardly follow what he was saying."

He was much more interested in news from Bengal concerning a terrorist bomb-making factory that had been discovered after two Englishwomen were killed by a bomb meant for the local British magistrate. This resulted in a conspiracy trial. For commenting on the case, Bal Gangadhar Tilak, an orthodox Brahmin but a radical as opposed to moderates in the Indian National Congress, was sent to prison for six years. Jawaharlal asked for more details regarding this.

He wrote about a book he had read, the H. G. Wells *A Modern Utopia,* which proposed the creation by volunteers of an order of self-chosen and self-dedicated aristocrats, "something like Plato's Guardians," to assume the task of promoting social reforms. He became a Fabian Socialist, with much the same enthusiasm he expressed when he joined Mrs. Annie Besant's Theosophical Society. "He seems to think," Motilal growled to Little Daughter, "that I am in need of education and he is providing it."

However much her brother's wide-ranging letters taught her father, they were her first introduction to ideas and events that set her mind roaming and searching. "I was terribly young, but even so, being made to wonder was a long step towards wanting to find answers. I'm sure my brother didn't realize he was my teacher. I didn't realize it myself until a good deal later."

Her father's friend Gopal Krishna Gokhale spoke in England explaining the purposes of the Indian National Congress. Her brother went to hear Gokhale, and reported that he was "not merely moderate but almost apologetic." This capsuled dismissal touched off his father's temper. Gokhale, Motilal wrote angrily to his son, was one of the few sane men in politics in India, and not to be jeered at by young upstarts.

Her brother's reply said he understood that their father must take the British side, but he, Jawaharlal, was under no such obligation. Motilal roared. He swore to Little Daughter that he would cut off her brother's allowance, order him home, take a cane to him if need be, to clear his muddled head. The storm blew over; or rather, was blown away in a new typhoon set off by her brother's mention that he toyed with the idea of seeking a post in the Indian Civil Service.

This would keep him in England three years longer, but the end-result should satisfy his father. A fifth of all the higher I. C. S. careerists employed by the Raj were Indians. Their income and tenure were guaranteed, as long as they stayed out of politics. The British treated them almost like gentlemen, as long as they did not object to being called *babus*.

Motilal answered scathingly. Some of his best Indian friends were in the I. C. S. They served India well, and deserved respect. On the evidence, he took leave to doubt that Jawaharlal had the balance, the practicality, the sense of responsibility, that Indians in I. C. S. must have if they were not to deserve being patronized as *babus*.

Answering in his own good time, Jawaharlal said his father might very well be right. He would continue in the law. But he hoped it was clear between them that he made this choice by his own free will. So saying, he continued with precise details of Alberto Santos Dumont's flight through the air in a machine he had invented, two hundred and fifty yards in twenty-one seconds. Next time the family saw him, he said, he might drop in by air, just to spend the weekend.

Motilal stopped reading, crumpled the page, and stared at nothing while Little Daughter studied him. Perhaps she could make him laugh. Her brother liked the songs at Harrow, especially "Jerry You Duffer and Dunce" and "When Grandpapa's Grandpapa Was In the Lower Lower First." He had sent copies of them, and she had memorized the words, while Miss Hooper played the music on her father's imported piano. She began to sing. Her father commanded "Stop that noise!"

To this day, she confesses ruefully "I simply cannot carry a tune." That afternoon, she ran weeping to the women's quarters, only to be tracked down by Miss Hooper, who said it was time for her mathematics. She loathed mathematics, and said so violently. There was no escape. She muttered over compound fractions, until her mentor said helplessly "We'll try again tomorrow," and proceeded to history.

Here Miss Hooper ventured on quaking ground. Jawaharlal's example had given his sister a habit she has never lost, of asking "Why?" and "Why not?" Her own father's father, the *Kotwal* whose portrait she passed whenever she went foraging in her father's library, had suffered ruin and insult during what Miss Hooper called the Indian Mutiny in 1857. Her English-written textbook chronicled a series of victories over rebels of her race. She was expected to take joy in this.

So she might have done, but for her brother. He had penciled marginal question-marks in many volumes on their father's shelves. In some, there were slips on which he scribbled contradictions. She followed trails he had marked, and came to an Englishman's recital of punishments meted out when the Mutiny was crushed: forty rebels blown to bits at cannon mouths on the parade ground at Peshawar, an unrecorded number hanged without trial in the Sikander Bagh at Lucknow, "perhaps two thousand" slain with cold steel after they surrendered and were disarmed.

One English writer said "The English threw aside the mask of civilization and engaged in a war of such ferocity that justice became a dirty word, and reason and humanity feminine frippery"; but another said "The natives of India gratefully accepted the Queen's proclamation transferring government of India to the Crown as the charter of their lives and liberties, and a suitable opening to a new order."

7.

Something was wrong somewhere. As this conviction strengthened, Little Daughter read farther afield from the gospel as Miss Hooper taught it, until one morning she announced herself as counsel for the defense reopening a case that had been closed with a verdict of "Murder most foul" a hundred and twenty-four years before she was born. The case was that of the Black Hole of Calcutta.

For generations, English teachers had taught Indian pupils that on a June night in 1776, their forebears imprisoned one hundred and forty-six English men, women and children in a dungeon in Calcutta, only eighteen feet by fourteen. Only twenty-three, the English said, emerged alive next morning.

But Little Daughter had come upon a record of subsequent inquiry, which established the actual number of prisoners at sixty-three, and declared their incarceration was a mistake for which their own countrymen shared the blame, and that even a charge of criminal negligence could not have been sustained by a responsible British magistrate. Miss Hooper is said to have noted mildly that the writer making these statements was Indian, and therefore possibly prejudiced. Little Daughter is said to have asked, "Are the English never prejudiced?" and to have entered in evidence Mountstuart Elphinstone's monolithic *History of India*. First published in 1841, reprinted regularly, it was referred to as a compendium of unquestionable facts. Her father's copy was the edition of 1905, with additions by Englishmen he had known.

"Akin to the indolence of the Indians," said Elphinstone, "is their timidity. However the most prominent vice of the Hindus is their want of veracity. Hindus are fitted for intrigue and cunning. Patient, supple, insinuating, they glory in flattery and importunity. But their great defect is a want of manliness. Their slavish constitution, their blind superstition, their extravagant mythology, the subtleties and verbal distinctions of their philosophy, the languid softness of their poetry, the effeminacy of their manners, their love of artifice and delay, their submissive temper, their dread of change, the delight they take in puerile fables, and their neglect of rational history, are so many proofs of the absence of the more robust qualities of disposition and intellect throughout the mass of the nation."

She knew two men: her father and her brother. Most of the servants at Anand Bhavan were male, but that was a different matter; their lowly caste excused their weaknesses. But she could not, and would not, accept Mountstuart Elphinstone's contemptuous dismissal of such men as her father, and her brother, as "deficient in courage, simplicity, and integrity." Miss Hooper, herself at sea between the Scylla of what she knew and the Charybdis of textbook authority, said it was time for mathematics. Her pupil disagreed.

Her brother had underlined a sentence in a book by Baron Meston, who was once lieutenant-governor of the United Provinces. "Before A. D. 1000, the art of contemporary narrative hardly existed in India." Alongside, he had queried "What about the *Vedas?* The *Ramayana?* Kalidasa? Babur the Tiger's memoirs? The *Bhagavad Gita?*" She knew the *Ramayana* only from stories her mother had told her. The other references were wholly new to her. This called for more long hours in her father's library. She was determined that when her brother returned, she would be ready to talk with him about any discovery he had made, to which he guided her unknowingly.

Columbus, seeking islands, was blind to continents. Not so Little Daughter. Whatever byway opened up, she must explore it. Thus she came to a new understanding of caste, which hitherto had been a fact of life that always was. *Caste,* she learned, was from the Portuguese *casta,* adapted by the English. The proper word for social divisions was *varuna,* which meant "color." *Sudra,* the appellation of the lowest strata, actually meant "black." Then there had been a color-line before the British came.

Brahmins, her far-off ancestors, and *Kshatriyas,* the warriors and clan-leaders who conquered and became kings, were whites; they came from Persia and Mesopotamia into Western India, probably fifteen centuries before the Christian Era, with their higher culture and deadlier weapons, and met dark-skinned earlier inhabitants and subdued them. What the world called *caste* had been initially an arrangement to insure race purity. For Brahmins particularly, there was a continuity of unmixed blood which bearers of the White Man's Burden in India could not claim for themselves. But no history by any Englishman took cognizance of this.

The English authors of a dozen books in her father's collection expatiated on their discovery of paintings in the Ajanta Caves, done twenty centuries ago, still a bright-colored panorama of the ancient past; and of excavations at Harappa and Mohenjo-daro, the Camp of the Dead, revealing an Indus River civilization that flourished and died at least a thousand years before Julius Caesar reigned at Rome. Must India's history be only what was written in English by Englishmen?

She thought not. Her best authority to the contrary was her most trusted guide: her brother. "The past of India," he wrote, "is a long, long one, lost in the mists of antiquity; it has its sad and unhappy periods, which make us ashamed and miserable, but on the whole it is a splendid past of which we may well be proud and think with pleasure." But her authorized textbooks, which were gospel to Miss Hooper, said nothing of any importance occurred in India, except for Alexander the Great's invasion in 326 B.C., which was a failure, until Sir John Mendenhall as emissary for Elizabeth the Virgin Queen arranged with Akbar the Great, in A.D. 1605, for an East India Company trade monopoly.

Suddenly, she stumbled upon the works of Thomas Babington Macaulay, who had been a brilliant student in his times at Trinity College at Cambridge, where Jawaharlal studied now. Like her father when he prepared a case, Little Daughter appraised the credibility of the witness, his qualifications as an expert.

In 1834, by virtue of an India Act he helped to write and push through Parliament, Macaulay became a member of the Supreme Council for India, although he had never been there. He noted frankly that the excellent salary this guaranteed him, £10,000 per annum for five years, would enable him to amass a fortune of £30,000 for doing very little. Altogether, he spent twelve months in India, during which, according to his English biographer, "he vindicated the liberty of the press, established the equality of Europeans and natives before the law, and inaugurated the system of public education." Remarkable, if true. But Little Daughter was less and less convinced by English praise of Englishmen.

Like Mountstuart Elphinstone, Macaulay decried the dishonesty of Hindus, with particular reference to their unchristian habit of avoiding taxes if they could. He praised Lord Cornwallis, "the first English nobleman of rank to become

Governor-General of British India," for initiating a method that mitigated this evil. This was done by creating a class called *zamindars*: tax-farmers who purchased exclusive right to collect taxes in their districts and remit the revenue to the Raj, less a percentage for their trouble.

Her brother had penciled, "See Cornwallis in the American Revolution." This led her to an English historian's brief resume. It appeared that in 1781 Lord Cornwallis had put American rebels to flight until the French came to their rescue. Then, overwhelmingly outnumbered and surrounded at a place called Yorktown, Lord Cornwallis had been forced to surrender, but did so with honor, and to show his invincible spirit, ordered his bagpipers to play *The World Turned Up-Side Down* while his soldiers marched out to lay down their arms.

Madame Ambassador Vijaya Lakshmi Pandit would hear a rather different version when she mentioned Cornwallis and Yorktown in the United States. She would learn very few Americans knew that Cornwallis had gone from defeat in the Colonies to impose a curse on India. That, her father said when Little Daughter asked him about the *zamindars,* was what Cornwallis did.

Zamindar powers had become hereditary. The inheritors extorted more and more from the peasantry, remitted less and less to the government, loaned rupees to landowners at usurious interest, so they could pay their taxes, and then confiscated their lands for failure to repay the loans. In cold fact they were feudal barons, and the people in their grasp no more than serfs. But Motilal Nehru said it helped no one to blame Cornwallis for a system by now so integral that excising it would tumble the whole structure of the Raj, the ruling power in British India.

Time, he said, takes care of what surgery will not cure. Consider that Cornwallis had also fostered laws that virtually excluded "natives" from even the least part in India's administration, and the East India Company refused to hire them except as servants, called *peons,* and *babus,* petty clerks. But eventually there were simply not enough English willing to go to India, to fill all the posts prosperity created. Necessity mothered concession. Then it was that Indian gentlemen in black coats, *vakils,* lawyers, like himself, produced a middle class, something unknown in India before them. Princes and *sahibs* laughed at them at first; then they began to win cases, and the laughter quieted.

Some of them started newspapers. Their editorial frankness annoyed the Viceroy, Lord Lytton. In 1878, he tried to muzzle them with a Vernacular Press Act that imposed rigid censorship. Englishmen themselves protested this, and Lytton was forced to rescind it. And the result? Young Rudyard Kipling came from the British-owned *Civil & Military Gazette* in Lahore, to write for the Indian-owned *Pioneer* in Allahabad, because it had more readers and paid better; and young Mr. Winston Churchill, as a very junior cavalry officer whose mess-bills and polo ponies ran him into debt, also sought employment as a correspondent for the *Pioneer,* writing about battles with Pathans in the Khyber Pass, and thus embarked on a career as an author, which in turn got him into English politics.

Little Daughter, said Motilal, must realize that proper progress is made one step at a time. "You may live to see the *zamindars* vanish like the dinosaurs. No good change ever comes quickly." She asked "Why doesn't it?" He studied her, then said little girls who thought too much overburdened their gentle minds, and instructed Miss Hooper to see to it that Little Daughter spent less time with books and more with her mother and baby sister in the woman's quarters. But even during exile, books were piled around her.

8.

When her own daughters made her a grandmother, Vijaya Lakshmi Pandit would lecture them out of her childhood experience. "You must get your children to read and read, read anything and everything. I think the best thing that happened in my own peculiar education was that I developed the habit of reading, and the hunger for more. In the modern world there are so many distractions, so many shortcuts and bypaths. Books keep you from getting lost."

Another and even more impelling habit became a part of her. "Heaven guard your children from any easy success. Let them plod and dig, and grow within themselves. Don't make it easy. *Iron's the tonic the spirit needs.* Discipline, from inside. None of us will ever live long enough to learn as much as there is to be learned. The human being who says 'Now I know enough' is self-reduced to a cipher."

She was only eleven, but far along in her "peculiar education," when King George V and Queen Mary came to see their Star of Empire, stepped ashore through a rococo marble Gateway to India erected at Bombay, and proceeded in imperial progress to a great *durbar* at Delhi. There Motilal

Nehru joined the cheering that followed the announcement of plans to build a new city adjoining Old Delhi, where the last Hindu ruler, Prithwaraja, was put to death by Mohammed Ghor, the Muslim conqueror, in A.D. 1193. Establishment of a New Delhi was in fact a British proclamation: *We are here to stay.*

She was twelve when Lord Hardinge, the Viceroy, was target for a bomb which exploded in the golden *howdah* of the elephant on which he and Lady Hardinge rode to see the progress toward completion of the palace they would occupy in New Delhi. Her father spoke of this as the shocking act of a fanatic. In the books she read there were people called fanatics by the governments they tried to overthrow, but called heroes if their acts as individuals were followed by great change.

She tried her best to understand about India, yet she knew little more of the India outside the boundaries of the Home of Joy than imagination could add to contradictions in what had been written, and to views expressed by her brother in letters from which her father read to her less and less often.

One person might have told her much; her father's body-servant, Hari, an elfin creature, by birth an Untouchable. To the orthodox, his kind were pariahs, condemned to lifelong punishment for sin committed in past lives. It was therefore a sin to lift or permit the rise of Untouchables from their pre-destined earthly Purgatory. But Motilal Nehru lived by no rules other than his own. When Hari stood hungry on his doorstep, he took him in, gave him a home and sent him to school.

Hari repaid his benefactor by lying and stealing. Caught and thrashed, he ran away, but soon crept back, and was allowed to stay. When she sought him out, he put his work aside. "My duty," he said, "is to sing and dance for little children." Himself no bigger than a child, he capered and told fantastic tales. She forgot her load of puzzlement for a while. Then she remembered, and poured out questions. He was suddenly uncommunicative, refusing to say more than "There are things out there about which Motilal Nehru's fortunate daughter need never concern herself."

Clearly, he prayed she would never have to leave the peace and security that was her Nehru birthright. So did her father. Watching her from his Little England, Motilal Nehru shook his leonine head. More and more, the stir and ferment of change closed in around the Home of Joy. He gave thanks that at last his son was coming home.

9.

In seven years, Jawaharlal had spent only three weeks in India. In England, he had taken on an English milord's elegance, the studied casualness of a Cambridge *litterateur;* had downed champagne when Old Harrovians foregathered; had watched Emmaline Pankhurst and her suffragettes chain themselves to lampposts in Trafalgar Square; had become a student of Garibaldi's liberation campaigns in Italy. He had gone to Ireland to watch the Sinn Fein badger the British, and made the acquaintance of Saif-ud-Din Kitchlew, a Muslim radical who would be India's first recipient of the Stalin Peace Prize. He had arrived at only three certainties: that he had no desire to be a barrister like his father, that truth, like the world, is round, not flat, and that "I have become a queer mixture of the

East and West, out of place everywhere, at home nowhere."

His sister saw a stranger. He told their father, while she listened in her corner, that he had passed his Inner Temple tests and examinations for the bar "with neither glory nor ignominy." He had no present ambitions, social, professional or political. To an Allahabad professor who invited him "to meet a few groups of keen students trying to think," he replied by asking "What about the groups inside me?"

She had imagined walking by his side. Now she felt unwanted, unneeded. As her mother had foreseen, her father's time and thought were transferred back to Jawaharlal. At first, "I indulged myself in the sin of self-pity." Then she put on ladylike aloofness. On Sundays, starched and prim, she went with Miss Hooper to services at Holy Trinity, the Anglican church across the road. Her mother frequently sent flowers for its altar, and gifts of fruit for the English vicar.

He was a gentle and godly man who saw no incongruity in preaching against Hindu paganism to a congregation largely Indian. His Bishop set his course. "When India shall have become wholly Christian it will not be surprising if it shall appear that the bright day has been hastened, not alone by the sublime efforts of missionaries with their pure Gospel from the Occident, but also, though in an inferior degree, by those grosser and weaker efforts from the very body of the Hinduism of the Orient. It is one of the historical glories of Christianity that, for its greater triumphs, it not only marches to victory by virtue of its own irresistible potency, but that it transmutes all that is good in the hostile ranks to minister to the final achievement."

Returning from Holy Trinity, she often went with her

mother to a Hindu shrine that had been a place of prayer for twenty centuries, as Indian in her *sari* as she had been *pukka* British an hour before. Always, she lived between two worlds, and had the best of both, and still was, like her brother, not altogether at home in either.

Bibi Amma, her mother's widowed sister, lived in shadows in the women's quarters. Married very young, she was still young and childless when her husband died. It could never have occurred to her to resist the tradition that sentenced her to lifelong seclusion. Gentle, devoted, uncomplaining, she was an object lesson to Little Daughter. Marriage could end for her, and for her sister, as it had for Aunt Bibi Amma.

Already, her father had arranged her betrothal to a boy she had never seen, then invalidated the arrangement, before she was told of it. Any day she might be informed that a new betrothal had been negotiated. Her mother and Aunt Bibi Amma thought this should be soon. Nor did she shrink from marriage. But she had begun to wonder if it must be all that life could offer. It had not been for her new-found heroine, Mrs. Sarojini Naidu, who visited often at Anand Bhavan.

Like Aunt Bibi Amma, Sarojini Naidu had married young. But after marriage, she worked beside her husband, a medical officer, in dirt-poor villages in Hyderabad. In 1908, King Edward VII gave her the Kaisar-i-Hind gold medal, for saving lives by organizing flood relief. Her first book of poems had been translated in several languages. Her husband rose to Major General's rank, but she continued her independent career, with his full approbation.

Now she was a leader in the Indian National Congress. Dynamic, confident, she would never let orthodoxy make her another Aunt Bibi Amma. And her presence and example took her young admirer farther toward a road not yet discerned. From her, Little Daughter heard for the first time Rabindranath Tagore's parable of the lamp in the corner. She heard, too, his *Janagana-mana,* Morning Song of India, that had been sung for the first time during the Congress meeting at Calcutta on December 27, 1911.

> Thou art the ruler of the minds of all people, dispenser of India's destiny.
> Thy name rouses the hearts of the Punjab, Sind, Gujarat, and Maratha, of the Dravid and Orissa and Bengal; it echoes in the hills of the Vindhyas and Himalayas, mingles in the music of the Jamuna and Ganges, and is chanted by the waves of the Indian Sea.
> They pray for thy blessings and sing thy praise. The saving of all people waits in thy hand, thou dispenser of India's destiny.
> Victory, victory, victory to thee.

In 1950, Janagana-mana would be adopted as Free India's national anthem. In 1913, it could not be sung in public. It had a ring of revolution. Hearing it, Motilal Nehru frowned. He might have done more than frown if he had heard Sarojini Naidu telling Little Daughter about Jhansi-ki-Rani. *This hoary India of ours would waken to the flash of the valorous Rani's sword!* So a poem in Hindi says. To Swarup Kumari, the young Queen of Jhansi was India's Joan of Arc.

She was born Lakshmi Bai. She was able to read when she was five. For two hours every day, she practiced writing by setting down over and over in their proper sequence the thousand

and one names of the Hindu divinity, Ramachandra. Married young to Jhansi's Rajah, at twenty she was a childless widow. The Raj decreed that since he left no male heir, her husband's territories lapsed to British ownership. She resisted. An English historian said "She considered herself aggrieved because she was not allowed to adopt an heir." Those who even today place flowers on her tomb think this was less than the truth.

Her saga began on May 10, 1857, when Indian soldiers serving the East India Company were accused of mutinous intent and stripped of their uniforms. Rescued by their comrades, they marched to Delhi and called on the last of the Moghul monarchs, Abu Zafar Siraj-ud-din, to lead them in driving the British out of India. He was eighty, and had no heart for war. Zinat Mahal, his young Queen, came out of *purdah* to lead the fighting in his stead.

Near Allahabad, another woman, the Begum Hasrat Mahal, wife of the deposed King of Oudh, raised revolt in behalf of her young son. But Jhansi-ki-Rani's sword flashed brightest. Women followed where she led. They and their children fought in her army. Her capital was besieged, and finally overrun. She escaped to Gwalior and inspired beaten troops to a desperate last stand. She died in battle leading a forlorn-hope charge. The conquerors were chivalrous. Their General reported to London "She was the best and bravest man the rebels had."

The *chhatarri,* the modest marble monument that marks the spot at which she was hurriedly cremated lest her body fall into the hands of the victors, is near a shrine to St. Jude, Patron of Impossible Causes, at which more Hindus than Christians pray. What Jhansi-ki-Rani fought and died for in

1858, was still an impossible cause when Little Daughter rode her pony along the riverbank at Anand Bhavan, declaiming Jhansi-ki-Rani's exhortation to her soldiers at Gwalior, imagining that the riding crop she waved above her head was Jhansi-ki-Rani's flashing sword.

Her father saw this as girlish play-acting. Her brother said "Not only women play-act." He saw himself as a pretender. In his father's law offices, and in court, he did what was expected of an England-polished barrister. Earning large fees was easy. Caring enough was not. Eleven years older than his sister, he had not outgrown what his father feared in him, but ignored in Little Daughter.

10.

She told Miss Hooper she would read no more romances written for little English *Memsahibs*. She wished she had been born a boy. "They can do what they please and go where they please." Her hair distressed her; it was thick and curly, but would not grow long. She was too plump; her cousins called her "Fatty." She wanted to learn to dance, like English boys and girls. Her mother said this was unthinkable for a well-born Hindu maiden. Then her brother came to her, saying "It is much too long since we settled the situation of the universe."

As they had before he grew up and away from her, they held long, serious conferences. "That is, my brother talked, I listened." The First World War had begun in Europe. He had his own view of it. "To us Hindus," he said, "this is the *Kali-yuga,* the cycle that began in 3102 B.C., and now approaches its end; which is to be marked 'by confusion of classes, overthrow of established standards, cessation of religious rites, and the rule of cruel and alien kings.' " He spoke with the faint self-mockery he had come to wear as a shield. "It has been truly said, that when war breaks out, the people involved go mad. Wait a bit, and we shall have the madness here in India."

Madness or not, soon the British called on India "to prevent German tyranny from spreading to the East and engulfing the world." By law, the Royal Indian Army was constituted solely for defense of the subcontinent. No unit had ever fought overseas. Now the Raj sent Indian troops to every front from France to Mesopotamia. Concurrently, the Raj made it clear that talk of change in British India was tantamount to treason.

This, Jawaharlal told his sister, was not altogether unjustified from the British point of view. Muslims in India looked to the Sultan of Turkey as the Khalif of Islam. Turkey's entry into the war on Germany's side created a tug between loyalties. Many England-educated Hindus were frankly pleased by German victories. Jawaharlal said "If I sympathize with any country concerned, it is France."

He had begun to attend Indian National Congress meetings. The first of these was at Bankipore in Bihar. Returning, he said it struck him as more of a social affair than a political rally, "very much an English-knowing, upper-class tea-party." He had heard loud pledges of "Loyalty to Britain!" These came mostly from ruling princes and their adherents.

Since 1818, the Raj had asserted paramount rule over all of India's titled rulers. Before the Crown superseded the East India Company in power over the subcontinent, Maharajahs,

Rajahs, Nawabs, Ranas and Nizams were regarded as archaic survivals, useful mostly in saving administrative expense. After 1858, their status improved. They were "breakwaters in the gale," encouraged to "develop as enlightened despots." They held titular sway over a quarter of India. Their subjects formed more than one-fifth of the population. There were five hundred and sixty-two of them, mighty and minor and minuscule, of whom a hundred and nine were considered important enough for admission to the Chamber of Princes.

Queen Victoria had pledged "We shall respect the rights and dignity and honor of the Native Princes as our own." King George V had reaffirmed Lord Canning's promise that "The integrity of the princely states shall be preserved," by declaring a royal guarantee "ever to maintain the privileges, rights and dignity of the Indian Princes, who may rest assured that this pledge is inviolate and inviolable." If Germany triumphed, the princes might lose power and place. Reasonably, then, the Chamber of Princes was unanimous in support of the Empire.

There was markedly less enthusiasm in the middle classes, on which the heavier financial load was placed, or among the masses who became a reservoir of expendable man power. One morning, Indians were informed that they had voluntarily presented a gift of a hundred million pounds sterling to His Majesty the King-Emperor. Not long after, another similar gift was announced to the givers after it had been paid over. Before the Armistice in 1918, nearly a billion English pounds were deposited with the Bank of England, as contribution paid in war taxes by Indian peasants, few of whom had ever heard of Germany. Two hundred and ten thousand Indian soldiers were sent abroad. Altogether, India was to provide nine hundred thousand men in uniform, and four hundred thousand for the Labor Corps.

All were listed as volunteers. India's Punjab alone furnished three hundred and fifty thousand of these. At Anand Bhavan, Jawaharlal told his sister that in fact, Punjabi *zamindars* were ordered to supply fixed quotas of recruits from among their tenants and landless debtors. Press-gangs roamed the Punjab, filling the quotas with no questions asked. Punjabi Sikhs were warriors, as they had been since their sect first faced religious persecution in the fifteenth century. But one of their bearded legion, Baba Gurdit Singh, chartered a Japanese ship, the *Komagata Maru,* and filled it with Sikhs who said "This is not our war."

They sailed from Calcutta to Vancouver, British Columbia, where Canadian police refused to let them land. The *Komagata Maru* was chivvied back to Calcutta. Its passengers, driven ashore, fought British police at Budge Budge. A good many were killed, the rest herded back to the Punjab. Soon after, some of them appeared in press-gangs recruited by Punjabi *zamindars.*

Before the war, German observers including the German Crown Prince had traveled freely in India, had listened to proponents of India's freedom, and appear to have believed that a few German victories in Europe and the Middle East would touch off revolution in British India. Toward this end, expatriate Indians in Europe were formed into a Committee for Free India, financed from Berlin.

Word filtered through to Anand Bhavan regarding Dr. Champakaraman Pillai. Bitterly anti-English, recklessly a revolutionist, he was hunted with a price of £100,000 on his head, but escaped to Germany, and there became a submarine officer. Under his guidance, a German U-boat shelled British installations along the Indian Ocean. In far-off San Francisco, one hundred and five Indian revolutionaries were arrested. The American prosecutor alleged that "For more than a year prior to the outbreak of the European War, Hindus and German agents in San Francisco were preparing openly for war with England. Men were recruited and sent to India. Military expeditions were organized from America and Siam. Arms and ammunition were smuggled through China and Japan. The whole conspiracy was a well-defined effort to create a revolution in India."

The Raj declared, "The conspiracy was started in 1912. It had for its object freedom by mutiny, whereby the English were to be driven out of India and the country governed by the people themselves." The whole truth about the conspiracy, which undoubtedly existed, has never been told, and probably never will be. Even Jawaharlal heard only rumors; and his sister heard only the essence of these.

There was no secrecy regarding a parallel conspiracy in Ireland. The British Indian press told much regarding Sir Roger Casement, who opposed enlistment of Irishmen to fight for Britain, went to Berlin to seek assistance for Irish rebellion, attempted to recruit Irish prisoners-of-war for a Liberation Army, and finally landed in Ireland from a German submarine, and was captured, tried for treason and hanged.

Then in Dublin on Easter Sunday in 1916, two thousand Irish civilians declared war on the *Sassenach*. Before their ammunition ran out, they had killed one hundred and sixteen

British soldiers. Fifteen of their leaders were executed. Then the British offered to discuss Irish Home Rule. No offer of the sort was contemplated for India. *Agents provocateurs* infiltrated Indian regiments overseas, mixed with Indian prisoners-of-war, were busy in Afghanistan and among Pathan tribesmen on India's North West Frontier; but officially if not in fact, the Raj dismissed these activities as in no way reflecting the feelings of true Indians.

11.

In 1965 the Irish Republic would pay its highest tribute, a state funeral, to Sir Roger Casement, hanged and buried in England fifty years before. In 1966 Free India's first flagship, I.N.S. *Delhi,* would sail to Cochin, his birthplace, bearing the ashes of India's Roger Casement, Dr. Champakaraman Pillai, who died in forgotten obscurity in Hitler's Germany in 1934. In 1916 Motilal Nehru told his son, while Little Daughter listened in her corner, that Home Rule could never possibly come to India. "There is no India to accept it!"

Her brother said there was indication that Indians could unite as one in what was happening at Lucknow, where the Congress and the Muslim League had held joint sessions, thanks to the efforts of a Muslim lawyer, Mohammed Ali Jinnah. Their father scoffed. "I know Mr. Jinnah. As a barrister, he's one of the best. But since he began talking 'Indian nationalism,' he's a changed man. My guess is he'd like to be India's Robespierre, but only if he could be absolutely certain no Danton or Marat will bob up to share the glory. Don't let me see you taking Mr. Jinnah for a model!"

She doubted if her brother would ever be a copy of anyone, even of their father. In any event, little more was said regarding Jinnah, though as the future unfolded, the fate of India would rest on Mohammed Ali Jinnah and Jawaharlal Nehru. At this time, her father was concerned about her brother's growing interest in another London-educated barrister turned Indian politician, Mohandas Karamchand Gandhi.

Jawaharlal had talked more and more with her about Gandhi since newspapers had reported Gandhi's arrival in India, by way of London, in early 1915. The press had paid little note to his inclusion in that year's birthday honors, as a recipient of the King-Emperor's Kaisar-i-Hind medal "for services to the British Empire." Within a year, he was being headlined because of his rising notoriety as a new force in the Congress.

One of her father's friends said "With the coming of Mahatma Gandhi, Mrs. Annie Besant became a back number who still strove to be in the forefront: a waning star, vying in vain with the rising sun." Her brother had been Mrs. Besant's convert, when he was thirteen. At twenty-seven, he was charmed by Gandhi, though they had yet to meet. He said one evening "I am going to Lucknow for the Congress meeting." To his sister's protest, "But this is Christmas Week," his sardonic answer was, "And if we were Christians like our masters, we would be shooting Germans while we tell each other it is the season of peace on earth, goodwill towards men."

Their father said, "I suppose that fellow Gandhi will be at Lucknow." Her brother said, "I hope so." Grimly, Motilal dismissed them. "I have a brief to prepare." The brief, she soon learned, was against that fellow Gandhi.

Her father lectured her often about the golden opportunity her brother endangered, if he involved himself with Gandhi. He had only to follow in his father's footsteps to do as well or better. As for Gandhi, he began his career as a lawyer by losing his first case, in Small Causes Court in Bombay, and when he gave up trying to earn a living in the city and retreated to his village in Kathiawar, he earned less in a year than Motilal Nehru's retainer for a single brief.

Let it not be said that Motilal Nehru looked down on Gandhi for reasons of origin, caste or failure to grow rich. What he objected to was Gandhi the rabble-rouser. The man had caused trouble in South Africa as recently as November 1913, when he organized and led a protest march of indentured Indian laborers from Natal into South Africa's Transvaal. He rallied them with a word he coined: *Satyagraha*, which he translated as meaning "Holding onto truth."

Her brother thought it was thrilling, "that a community of poor, downtrodden, ignorant workers and a group of petty merchants, far from their home country, should take up this brave attitude." To their father, what Gandhi preached and practiced was destructive to law and order, which were his household gods.

He agreed with Gopal Krishna Gokhale who advised Gandhi when he reappeared in India that he had better spend a year rediscovering the country from which he had been absent so long, before he presumed to meddle in its politics. Gokhale said Gandhi had taken his advice. But in Motilal Nehru's opinion, he had learned nothing much, since he now proposed *Satyagraha* in India. Nor was Motilal alone in opposition to the apostle of civil disobedience.

Moderates in the Congress Party were so little taken with Gandhi that he failed to garner enough votes for election to a minor committee, and had to be appointed to it by the presiding officer. To Motilal, this savored of backroom bartering, which he abhorred. Muttering over his notes, suddenly he burst out at Little Daughter. "Your brother says Gandhi has what the others lack. 'While they talk, he acts!' Acts how? *Satyagraha?* Incitement to anarchy?" Wisely, she was silent.

She worried less when her brother returned from Lucknow saying that in person he found Gandhi disappointingly unimpressive. Gandhi had appeared in a village lawyer's uniform: long tailcoat over his *dhoti,* rumpled turban askew on his head, seeming "medieval and revivalist, and very distant and different and unpolitical." His language "was almost incomprehensible to an average modern." Eventually, Jawaharlal confessed to his sister that quite possibly Gandhi failed to impress him because "I was a bit of a prig with little to recommend me," while to Gandhi, "the spruce young barrister from Allahabad, English in dress, Inner Temple in manner, must have seemed not worth bothering about."

His father may not have been as perceptive as his sister. Laying aside his brief against Gandhi, Motilal spun a web for which he had ancient precedent. Rajah Suddhodhana, father of Prince Siddhartha who was to become Gautama Buddha, feared idealism in his son might draw him into rash venturing, and decided a wife and the responsibilities of marriage would bind Siddhartha to his heritage. Suddhodhana summoned sixteen lovely princesses, from among whom Yasodhara was chosen as Siddhartha's bride. Motilal canvassed Kashmiri Brahmin families, and selected Kamala Kaul, whose father was a respected businessman in Delhi. That she bore the same name as the founder of the Nehru clan was fortuitous coincidence. Her own family's name had originally been Atal. She was only a year older than Little Daughter, tall, slim, and lovely. Little Daughter approved of her. So did Jawaharlal. It was their father who delayed the wedding.

It troubled him, that Kamala had lived in orthodox seclusion. He told her father it would be best for all concerned if she came to Allahabad to prepare herself for marriage to his son. She would live with an aunt, but spend much time at Anand Bhavan, until she and the Nehrus understood each other. Dubiously, Kamala's father assented. At once, he was called on for further concession.

Kamala's English was limited. Jawaharlal's wife must be able to converse with him, or at least to listen intelligently. She could study with Miss Hooper. Possibly Motilal had a second string to his bow. Little Daughter also had things to learn. It would be good for her to have an exemplar, committed to the duties that would be hers when he chose a husband for her.

As usual, he had his way. Kamala came to Allahabad, and entered her novitiate as a Nehru-to-be. She saw little of Jawaharlal, and was never alone with him. She spent many hours with his sisters. Little Daughter studied Kamala's carriage, and copied it: The lobe of the ear always in line with the ankle, head high, hands never uncontrolled. Under Kamala's instruction, she dieted, and lost pounds. So did Krishna, at nine almost a miniature of her sister.

Astrologers cast horoscopes. The wedding date was set for *Vasanta Panchami,* the March day that heralds the birth of spring, when students garland their books and wear yellow, in tribute to Saraswati, patroness of the arts and sciences and of speech and learning. War in Europe and Egypt and the Middle East gave the Raj reason for tax increases that tightened the purse strings even of premier Maharajahs. But Motilal's preparations would have taxed a Moghul Emperor's treasury.

A week before the wedding, he assembled more than a hundred guests, family connections, friends and business associates, and marched them aboard a special train he had chartered, stocked with food and drink, for the trip from Allahabad to Delhi. Hundreds more joined them there. The houses he rented could not accommodate everyone. He had tents set up in gardens he had leased, creating what the press called Camp Nehru.

Festivities continued for ten days, during which Little Daughter made a new discovery. She expected her brother to be admired, and Kamala was the year's most beautiful bride. But in her first public appearance, she herself experienced, for the first time, the warming glow of admiration mixed with envy. At sixteen, she was suddenly slender, and strikingly attractive.

A dozen fathers whispered to their staring sons, "I will pay a call on her father." She was well aware of this, and confesses its effect. "I became absolutely impossible. I was, as the Americans say, spoiled rotten." Still all centered around her brother. Back at Anand Bhavan, their father set builders to work on a separate house for Jawaharlal and Kamala, and then took charge of their honeymoon.

12.

The honeymoon was in fact a family pilgrimage to Kashmir, the ancestral homeland. Motilal made it a royal procession by special train to Lahore, by Frontier Express to Peshawar near the Khyber Pass, by motor cavalcade to Srinagar and the Dal Lake and the Gardens of Shalimar. A new Camp Nehru was ready in a private grove, with Hari and a staff of servants bustling between tents and *shamianas,* bright-colored marquees shading room-sized areas floored with Persian carpets. Here as much as at Anand Bhavan, there was luxury and ease. But though Jawaharlal was devoted to Kamala, she felt, and so did his father and his sister, his restlessness.

Very soon, he set off to climb to the Amarnath Cave, a holy place to Hindus who believe it is visited annually by a pair of immortal doves. Amarnath is three miles above sea level. Pilgrims sometimes make the tortuous ascent inching along on their knees. Jawaharlal, running recklessly across a high snow-field, plunged down into a deep crevasse, and was extricated with difficulty.

This was kept from his father as long as possible. When he learned of it, he was stern. "You are no longer free to run around looking for excitement. You have a wife. You must think of her, and of the son she will give you." Jawaharlal said soberly, "You are right." But his sister saw how his eyes still strayed to the mountains.

Her mother and Aunt Bibi Amma said it was already past the time when a husband should have been chosen for her. She

did not dissent. But though her father set the time and circumstance of her brother's marriage, he put off a decision regarding hers. Wiser even then than he surmised, she guessed the
truth he would have shouted down. "A daughter is too precious to be handed over in haste to anyone, however good. At
least, that is how my father felt."

He watched from his *pukka* British tea table, set out beside
the stream that flowed through Camp Nehru, while she
drifted away from Kamala and Krishna, stepped from stone to
stone to reach a little island, sat down on a grassy bank and
opened a book of new poems by Sarojini Naidu, read a little,
then laid the book aside and dreamed. Suddenly, he was calling to her, quietly for him. "You must not move! You must
not move!" Hearing, she obeyed, though now she saw what
he had seen.

An arm-thick cobra writhed toward her. Helpless, her father and brother and mother and sister and sister-in-law stood
frozen while the cobra coiled and raised its distended hood
above her, swaying as it tensed to strike, deadly fangs darting
inches from her face. Then very slowly, it sank down. In a
moment, it was gone.

She rose, smoothed her *sari,* and picked up her book. Unhurriedly, she went to face her father. Neither spoke. Nothing whatever was said about the cobra by anyone, until that
evening a mendicant *sanyasi,* a holy man by self-appointment,
materialized from the woods and recounted what occurred that
day while he, he said, was many miles away.

Naga, King of Cobras, he reminded the Nehrus, spread his
hood above He-Who-Was-About-to-Become-the-Buddha, beneath a *bo* tree near Banaras, at the hour of the Enlighten-

Motilal Nehru at age 58

A family picture of the Nehrus

The child Jawaharlal with his parents

Ganga Dhar, grandfather of Jawaharlal and Little Daughter

ment. Cobras repeat this act of withheld death, he averred, when they encounter those whom the gods have marked for special service to mankind. This Nehru girl would surely rise some day to height and fame.

Motilal paid the fortune-teller and sent him away. Prophecies, he said, were no more to be relied upon than cobras. No one questioned this dictate. Next morning, he said it was time they got back to Allahabad, where he and Jawaharlal had law business waiting. No one argued against his decision. But before long, he was confronted by another prophet, who could not be silenced, paid off and dismissed.

In North Bihar, in the Himalayan foothills, early in 1917, British owners of indigo plantations at Champaran were suddenly confronted by the unbelievable. An intruder named Mohandas Gandhi had organized work stoppage on their properties. Served with orders to leave the district, he refused to go. Haled before a British magistrate, he stated a case against the landlords so cogently that charges against him were withdrawn. Authorities named a committee of inquiry, and made Gandhi a member—an act of recognition the Raj would soon regret. The committee's findings produced the Champaran Agrarian Act, which redressed grievances against which Gandhi had been the first to raise a voice that could not be stilled.

News of this brought on new crisis at Anand Bhavan. Motilal Nehru had no quarrel with reform by due process of law. But Gandhi claimed victory for "the first direct object lesson in civil disobedience," and Jawaharlal applauded what in his father's view was nothing less than open incitement to rebellion. As if Motilal had not enough to plague him, his well-ordered, private world was further shaken by desertion.

Miss Hooper announced she was leaving the Nehrus, to be married. Grumbling, but magnanimous in loss, Motilal arranged the wedding, and gave the bride away, at Holy Trinity across the road. Little Daughter and her sister were bridesmaids in English frocks. Father and son, by tacit stipulation, postponed discussion of Gandhi during reorganization of the household, now reduced by one.

Then on November 19, 1917, what Motilal had prayed for occurred. His son became a father. Kamala bore a daughter, not a son; but whereas Prince Siddhartha named his son Rahula, signifying *Chains,* the man who would some day be spoken of as Siddhartha's avatar named his daughter Indira Priyadarshini. The second name said much. Its meaning is *Dear to the sight.* It can also be interpreted as *One who sees to the good of others.* Within sight of Anand Bhavan, there stood and still stands one of the pillars bearing edicts of Asoka, the Buddhist Emperor, carved in stone in 259 B. C. "King Priyadarsi [*sic*] wishes members of all faiths to live everywhere in his kingdom. He honors men of all faiths. By acting otherwise, one injures one's own faith. Concord alone is commendable."

All his life, in his letters, and when they talked alone, Jawaharlal Nehru called his only child *Dear to the sight.* "If I had been a son, not a daughter," she has said, "I could not have helped my father in the ways I have." That when she said this she added "The political world would have been much more sensitive to the situation and wary of it, in terms of perhaps a male successor," has its irony in view of history's decision. But in 1917 this was far beyond the horizon.

13.

Indira Priyadarshini's birth was followed by warning from doctors that her mother showed symptoms threatening onset of serious illness. Her father, acutely conscious of his own unfailing health, showed a side of himself seen previously only by his mother and his sisters. "His gentleness and understanding in the sickroom were infinite, and his patience was unlimited." Touched behind his shielding bluster, Motilal Nehru missed what was not clear to his son until too late.

"I was far more grownup than she was," Jawaharlal said of Kamala in his *Autobiography*. "Yet with all my appearance of worldly wisdom I was very boyish, and I hardly realized that this delicate, sensitive girl's mind was slowly unfolding like a flower. There were many petty quarrels over trivialities. We both had quick tempers, sensitive natures and childish notions of keeping our dignity. She gave me strength, but she must have suffered and felt neglected."

News that the Czar had fallen, completing what began when Lenin and Trotsky launched the Russian Revolution in the month of Indira Priyadarshini's birth, fed spreading flame in India. Bal Gangadhar Tilak founded a Home Rule League. Mrs. Annie Besant immediately formed a rival organization. "The price of India's loyalty," her manifesto declared, "is India's freedom." The Raj interned her. Motilal Nehru agreed that this was contrary to British justice, but would not go further.

Jawaharlal cited the case of Sir Roger Casement, hanged for demanding Ireland's freedom as the price of Irish loyalty.

"Was that not true courage, which mocked at almost certain failure and proclaimed to the world that no physical might could crush the invincible spirit of a nation?"

His father saw no relevance to the issue in India. "All this talk of 'Indian nationalism'! You will note that Mohammed Ali Jinnah has stopped talking 'Indian nationalism.' I hear he has gone or is going to settle in England. Why do you suppose he would do that, unless he has finally realized that 'Indian nationalism' is fool's fire, and he has the sense to stop running after it?" Jawaharlal suggested, "Possibly Mr. Jinnah feels someone else has captured the center of the stage, and he cannot recapture it." His father asked, "Gandhi the Mahatma?" The answer was in growing throngs that heard Gandhi declare *Swaraj* was not enough; India must have *Purna Swaraj,* total self-rule.

This was going too far for Mrs. Besant, whose most perfervid oratory had never gone beyond demand for Home Rule in Dominion status. Neither she nor Bal Gangadhar Tilak, however, could stem the drift of their former followers into Gandhi's camp, where the shout was *Inquilab Zindabad!* Long live the revolution!

Casualty lists from Indian regiments fighting overseas lengthened constantly. So did communiqués explaining British defeats. Disaster in Mesopotamia was blamed on collapse of medical and commissariat services, for which authorities in India had assumed responsibility. Austen Chamberlain resigned as Secretary of State for India. His successor, Edwin Montagu, announced that reforms in India would be considered. What these might be was not specified.

In the Khedda district of Gujerat in Western India, Gandhi

launched his second test of civil disobedience. For four months, he led peasants in *hartals,* work-stoppages, and mass demonstrations. Certain concessions were granted. The victory was small, but Jawaharlal told his father, and his sister: "Gandhi has a method of action which is open and straight and may be effective. No one else has done as much."

Then on August 20, 1917, in the House of Commons, Edwin Montagu announced policy for India. "The British Government and the Government of India, on whom the responsibility lies for the welfare and advancement of the Indian peoples, must be the judges of the time and measure of each advance, and they must be guided by the cooperation received from those upon whom new opportunities of service will thus be conferred and by the extent to which it is found that confidence can be reposed in their sense of responsibility."

His sister asked Jawaharlal what meaning he found in a statement that seemed to her to say nothing. He said it meant only that the British would never learn, and told the story of a stranger who once appeared in India. "He made himself notable immediately because he wore copper plates tied around his waist and on his head he carried a lighted torch, while he strutted with staff in hand looking down his nose at all around him. Asked the reason for his strange attire, he said his wisdom was so great that he was afraid his belly would burst if he did not wear the copper plates around it, and he carried the light on his head because he pitied the ignorant around him, who lived in such darkness until he came."

The sardonic parable did not amuse their father. "The British," he reminded them, "are fighting a war." Jawaharlal said "Not our war." Next morning, Hari the Untouchable re-

ported that Motilal had slept the night through on the hard
floor beside his bed. He continued to do this for some time,
saying he wished to experience something of the fate that
awaited his son, if Jawaharlal went much farther along Gandhi's road. "But your bed will be on stone, in a prison cell."

Finally, in last resort, he did what not even the Viceroy
would have thought of doing at that time. From his Little
England, he dispatched not an invitation but a command, for
Gandhi to come and face him. And surprising all the Nehrus
but Jawaharlal, Gandhi came.

14.

Sarojini Naidu called him "Mickey Mouse." His disciples
were shocked, but he laughed. He had large ears, he was
perky, he possessed an incurable and often bewildering opti-
mism, and no person or problem overawed him. He would not
wholly discard Western garb, and strip to homespun *dhoti* and
loincloth, until 1921, when "He made himself poor like a
peasant and the people made him holy and called him *Bapu*";
but there was much of the peasant in his manner. He was
shrewd, patient and firm. His voice belied his mild exterior.

"It was courteous, and full of appeal, and yet there was
something frightening in it," Jawaharlal had reported in the
past to Kamala and to his sister. "Behind the language of
peace and friendship there was power and the quivering
shadow of action." Now he told them, "Father found him an
excellent witness, and began to like him while questioning
him."

There is neither East nor West, / Nor Border, nor Breed,

nor Birth, / When two strong men stand face to face, / Though they come from the ends of the earth. Kipling's paean to a border tribesman and the British Colonel's son whose horse he stole was published when Jawaharlal was a child. He was thirty, when his life's course was set at last, by confrontation at Anand Bhavan, where quite literally his Kashmiri Brahmin father and the *bania* from a Kathiawar village contended for his soul.

In the women's quarters, his sister taught Kamala the recipe for *rasam,* a peppery South Indian dish, while his mother watched over Indira Priyadarshini. In his Little England, Motilal Nehru tried his most important case, with no thought that the verdict would some day cause him, his son and Gandhi to be bracketed, perhaps irreverently but in the minds of millions not incorrectly, as "Father, Son and Holy Ghost."

No antagonists could have been more oddly matched. An observer who knew both, and admired them equally, said of Motilal Nehru, "He was one of the most gracious aristocrats I ever met. In his looks and bearing, in his gait and speech, he showed that he was the product of a thousand years of Hindu civilization, impregnated, for a few hundred years, with Muslim influence." He faced Gandhi armed for cut-and-slash.

"I have heard," he had told his son, "of saints and supermen, but have never had the pleasure of meeting them, and must confess a feeling of skepticism about their real existence." He had contempt in reserve. "Politicians," he said, "are men who have failed at everything useful." But Gandhi differed from any politician he had known.

His cross-examination went back to 1893, when Gandhi, for a fee of a hundred pounds plus expenses, left India to argue a case for an Indian merchant in South Africa. There he found that all Indians, no matter what education or affluence they attained, were classed as an inferior race and labeled "Coloureds." They could not walk on public footpaths, or go outdoors after nine at night without special permits, or own property except in restricted ghettos. If they came as indentured laborers, and did not return to India at the end of their term of servitude, they must either sign new indenture papers or pay an annual tax amounting to twelve pounds sterling for a family of four—whose total income on the average was twelve shillings a month.

He did not need to involve himself. Settling the case that brought him from India was a simple matter. But another Indian national asked for help. With a first-class ticket, wearing English clothes, Gandhi boarded the train from Durban for Pretoria. He was ordered out of a car by its only other occupant, a white man. "Coloureds," he was told, could travel only in the baggage van.

He said he would not leave voluntarily, but offered no resistance when a constable shoved him out onto the platform. The train steamed away. He shivered through a wintry night, then was able to board another train to Charlestown, where he took the stage for Johannesburg.

His ticket entitled him to ride inside. He was told Coloureds must travel outside, or walk. As far as Pardekoph, he rode atop the stage. There he was ordered off. He refused to move. The driver boxed his ears, and tried to haul him down. He clung to the sidebars. Passengers intervened because they were in a hurry to be on the road. He was allowed to continue his journey. When he reached Pretoria at last, he could find lodging

only in a house so poor that not even Coloureds were turned
away.

He called a meeting of Indian immigrants. Not many came.
He proposed forming a Natal Indian Congress, and offered his
legal services without charge. Only three of those present, a
barber, a clerk and a shopkeeper, were willing to risk offending
their white masters. From this unpromising beginning, his
doctrine of *Satyagraha* spread, until thousands followed him in
demonstrations and protest marches. But after twenty years,
Indians in South Africa were still without civil rights. Then
what, Motilal asked, did Gandhi think he could do for Indians
in India?

Reforms were pledged when Mrs. Annie Besant was released from internment. There had been none. Reforms were
pledged again when Montagu succeeded Chamberlain. The
Congress and the Muslim League asked for limited self-
government, with parliamentary power of the purse and control of the executive, arguing reasonably that "A contented
India is the greatest and surest asset of the Empire." But the
Empire said "We will give you no more than we decide you
deserve, and you will not get that much if you go on annoying
us with your mischief."

What magic did Gandhi claim to possess that would move
the immovable, change the unchangeable? The magic, Gandhi said, was in the soul of the masses, yet unawakened. Did
Gandhi seriously believe the illiterate, superstitious, caste-
divided mob could improve on British government of India?
Gandhi polished his steel-rimmed spectacles, and nodded.

Motilal broke off their duel. Gandhi left as he arrived,
alone, after telling Jawaharlal "Don't push your father too far.

Don't cause him pain." His own eldest son, Harilal, had deserted him, become a drunkard, abandoned wife and family, converted to Islam, changed his name to Abdulla. Jawaharlal knew of this. So did his sister.

She had found it hard to understand why he was so drawn to an odd-looking, humble *bania* who ate only fruit, nuts and raw vegetables, and walked in patched tennis-shoes. What he had tried to do for their father gave her a new opinion. Her brother said "He possesses an amazing knack for reaching the hearts of people." He had reached hers. Before long, he reached many more.

15.

Beginning in 1917, a commission headed by Mr. Justice Rowlatt had conducted star-chamber inquiries into "the question of sedition and the course of criminal conspiracies." Three months after the Armistice of 1918, these inquiries produced the Rowlatt Acts, which empowered magistrates to try political cases without a jury in certain areas, authorized provincial authorities to intern suspected political troublemakers without trial or specific charges and made possession of a seditious document "with intention to publish or circulate it" grounds for arrest and imprisonment. All India called these acts the Black Bills.

Even Motilal Nehru said "They are lawless laws, transgressing constitutional propriety." He could not, however, bring himself to approve of Gandhi's proclamation: "Once the Black Bills become law we offer *Satyagraha.*" He and those who joined him in *Satyagraha Sabha,* Gandhi said, would disobey the Black Bills if these were applied to them, but resistance would be passive. He called for national observance of a day of mourning, in nonviolent protest. "You cannot," Motilal told his son and daughter, "have challenge to law and not have violence."

March 30 was to be *Satyagraha Day*. The date was changed, to April 6, too late for word to reach organizers in Delhi. There on March 30, every Indian-owned establishment closed. Walkout of workers forced closing of British offices, shops and factories. Hindus and Muslims marched together in the Chandni Chowk. In the Jumma Masjid Mosque, a Hindu priest addressed a Muslim congregation.

British authorities sent soldiers and police to disperse *Satyagraha* demonstrators. There was a rattle of gunfire. Men, women and children were wounded. On April 6, in cities and towns and villages, military and police detachments fired on unarmed marchers, who fought back with sticks and stones. There was riot and arson in Lahore. Europeans were attacked. On April 8, Gandhi was arrested. News of this exploded rioting in Bombay and Ahmadabad. At Amritsar in the Punjab, city of the Golden Temple of the Sikhs, two Congress delegates were jailed. Demonstrators paraded, demanding their release. Several marchers were killed.

At Anand Bhavan, Hari the Untouchable scurried bringing newspapers. Headlines appeared to prove the case Motilal had maintained. Civil disobedience was out of hand, and Gandhi could not halt the violence. If Jawaharlal had gone with Gandhi, almost certainly his name would now be somewhere on the lists of jailed, wounded or dead.

Then more news came from Amritsar. There on April 13,

the Hindu New Year's Day, thousands gathered for memorial services in the Jallianwalla Bagh, a public park surrounded by high walls and tenements, described in subsequent testimony as "resembling a very large swimming-bath with perpendicular sides." According to Winston Churchill, "The crowd was not armed, except with bludgeons, and it was not attacking anybody or anything." However General Reginald Edward Harry Dyer rushed to the scene, with sixty-five Gurkhas from Nepal, birthplace of Buddha, and twenty-five Muslim Baluchis from the North West Frontier. He also brought two armored cars, which were too wide to get through a narrow entrance.

Dyer made do without them. He cried warning, once, for the throng to disperse. There was no way out past his troopers blocking the exits. He shouted "Fire!" Ninety marksmen blazed away pointblank. He ordered "Cease firing!" only "when my ammunition was almost exhausted." By then, three hundred and seventy-nine men, women and children had been killed, and more than twelve hundred wounded.

Dyer marched his men back to barracks, leaving the dead and wounded where they lay. Later, he admitted "The mob could have been broken up without firing," but said he would have continued the attack "but for the restricted space." His purpose "was to strike terror into the whole of the Punjab." To this end, he considered it essential to show no sign of weakness by giving aid to the wounded.

He asked for no defense. Born in India, in the Punjab where he now commanded, he had been a Royal Indian Army careerist since 1885, had won the C. B. for action against Iranian border raiders during the First World War, had written a book about his campaigns, and was regarded by his peers as the flower of British military knighthood. Nor did his peers appear to see anything wrong in what he did at Jallianwalla Bagh.

"Some say," the British historian, Lord Elton, sums up in his *Imperial Commonwealth,* "that to condone Dyer's action it is only necessary to have had some experience of the April sun in the Punjab, and of commanding a handful of soldiers among a vast mob seething with revolt. Others that what he did was fully justified, since only instant and ruthless action could have saved the Punjab, and perhaps India, from bloodshed on a much more terrible scale."

On an earlier page of *Imperial Commonwealth,* Lord Elton recounts verbatim the officially enshrined story of the Black Hole of Calcutta, which Jawaharlal Nehru as a boy, and then Jawaharlal's sister, had found to be something less than accurate. His Lordship calls it "an outrage that had to be avenged," and gives thanks for good out of evil. "The Black Hole ensured that the British would become the next rulers of India." He does not note that massacre in Jalllanwalla Bagh ensured that India's own people would replace the British as rulers of their country.

"The deepest resentment was caused by the apparent assumption through a good deal of the subsequent controversy that Indians were an inferior race." This "apparent assumption" went so far, in fact, that to pass through a lane in Amritsar, where allegedly an English *Memsahib* had been assaulted by persons never identified, all Indians of whatever creed or quality were compelled at bayonet point to crawl.

This was too much for Rabindranath Tagore. Retired to his *ashram* near Calcutta, he had been an unlighted lamp in the

shadows during much of the *Swaraj* crusade. He scorned imperialism as "the organized gregariousness of gluttony," yet
accepted the courtesy title of *Sir,* conferred by the King-
Emperor, following award to him of the Nobel Prize for litera-
ture. Now in a letter to Lord Chelmsford, published from end
to end of India and in England's Opposition press, he renounced his title, in protest against "the enormity of measures
taken by Government in the Punjab."

The time had come, he said, "when badges of honor make
our shame glaring in the incongruous text of humiliation, and
I for my part wish to stand, shorn of all distinctions, by the
side of those of my countrymen who, for their so-called insig-
nificance, are liable to suffer a degradation not fit for human
beings." The Raj had more important problems than a Hindu
poet's indignation to contend with.

A king had been murdered in Afghanistan, just when Britain prepared to reward him for arresting German agents and
escaped prisoners-of-war, and for rejecting Bolshevik overtures
after the Russian Revolution. His nephew and successor either
could not or chose not to stop Afghan Muslims who attacked
in the Khyber Pass, seeking vengeance on the British for ending the Caliphate in Turkey.

The First Afghan War, begun in 1838, ended in 1842
when seven hundred British and four thousand Indian troops,
with twelve thousand camp followers, attempted to get back to
British India from Kabul, and one sole survivor managed to
reach safety at Jalalabad. The Second Afghan War made a
hero of Lord Roberts, Rudyard Kipling's "Bobs," but ended,
like the one before, in British withdrawal from Afghanistan,
and bitter echoes in England of *But what good came of it at*

last? / Quoth Little Peterkin. / Why, that I cannot tell, said he, / But 't was a famous victory.

The Third Afghan War introduced a new method for subduing the lesser breeds. British planes bombed Jalalabad and Kabul, killing many civilians. Most of the fighting was done by Indian troops, many of them recently returned from fighting for the Empire against the Turks in the Middle East, some of them Muslims from the Punjab press-gangs, now required to kill or be killed by their Islamic brethren.

General Dyer was shocked, and so were his brother officers, when he was recalled from command of a brigade in the Khyber to face a board of inquiry on which there were as many Indians as Englishmen. At Amritsar, the Congress completed purchase of Jallianwalla Bagh and established a martyrs' memorial. Jawaharlal Nehru, on the night train from Amritsar to Delhi, was pointedly ignored by "a red-faced Englishman in pyjamas with bright pink stripes," who told another Englishman there was only one way to keep the Wogs in their place. It was Dyer, on his way to judgment.

The board of inquiry filed two reports, one English, the other Indian. Dyer was asked to resign. Lord Elton says, "He was warmly supported by many members of both Houses of Parliament, and by a powerful section of the British press." Finally, it was ruled he could no longer serve in India. Even this was affirmed by the House of Commons only after angry debate, and by a narrow margin. The House of Lords appended a resolution deploring Dyer's dismissal as "unjust," and as "establishing a precedent dangerous to the preservation of order in the face of rebellion." In a libel suit growing out of aftermath, a Mr. Justice McCardie decreed that "General

Dyer, in the grave and exceptional circumstances, acted rightly, and was wrongly punished."

Lord Elton laments, "His career was broken." His punishment may have been eased a little by presentation to him of a purse of £26,000, raised in England by popular subscription, and a golden sword "as a testimonial from English ladies."

Long before he heard of this, Motilal Nehru's faith in British justice was as dead as Dyer's targets in Jallianwalla Bagh. At fifty-eight, renouncing the gains of forty years, he dismissed his British clients, informed former British guests they were no longer welcome in his home, withdrew Krishna from an English-managed school, and joined his son and Gandhi in the fight for freedom.

16.

There were no family conferences at the breakfast table: *Can we afford? Do you really think we should?* Motilal sold off his horses, closed his stables, reduced his regiment of servants to a corporal's guard of old retainers, who would starve if he turned them into the streets, and only then told his wife and daughters what was expected of them. It was not much. They were to put their jewelry away, and wear *saris* of the rough handspun cloth called *khadi,* which Gandhi had made the uniform of civil disobedience; and they were not to worry.

Jawaharlal told Kamala little more than that he was finished with practicing law, and would be away from her even more than in the recent past. "Unkindness to her would almost have been better than this semi-forgetful, casual attitude." But his final realization that "A country's progress can be mea-

sured by the status and progress of the women of the country"
would be a long while coming.

He was no more ready than his father to see the women
they loved and sheltered brought into any proximity to un-
washed peasants, sweating politicians and the British police.
To son and father, Mrs. Annie Besant was a special case. So
was Sarojini Naidu. Gandhi praised a woman who had joined
his following, "that remarkable lady, Gangabehn Majmun-
dar." But she was widowed, unorthodox, wealthy in her own
right, with no family responsibilities. Gandhi's own wife,
Kasturbai, was seldom seen and never spoke in public.

India's women have since suggested that perhaps men excluded them from the freedom crusade in the 1920's because
men themselves were not yet really sure, and therefore, man-
like, avoided trying to explain, what they were fighting for.
There was none of the concerted conviction in India that produced the American Declaration of Independence. Not even
Gandhi had called for complete separation from the Empire.

He believed in the masses; but in plain truth the masses had
yet to join what was initially a middle-class movement of lawyers, doctors, merchants and traders. There was ingrained suspicion of these *Swaraj* promoters. To India's peasants, they
had fattened on crumbs that fell from the table at which
Sahibs and *Memsahibs* dined; if they wanted change, it was
only so they could displace the British. The poor would have
new masters, but would still go hungry.

The people knew what to expect from the Raj, and from the
Maharajahs. The Chamber of Princes in its reply to Congress
talk of independence said a *Vakil Raj,* a rule by lawyers, would
never be tolerated. The peasantry feared the princes; lawyers

were known in the villages as the agents of princes and *zamindars* and moneylenders. Why, then, make misery worse by inviting the anger of the anointed? Why follow this *vakil* from Kathiawar, Mohandas Gandhi?

"When they know him," Jawaharlal told his father, and his sister, "they will follow him." This would happen, he said, because no one, *vakil* or villager, could see and hear Gandhi without believing in him. "There are no rough edges or sharp corners about him, no traces of vulgarity and commonness. Having found an inner peace, he radiates it to others, and marches through life's tortuous ways with firm and undaunted step." But Gandhi's methods, he admitted, sometimes bewildered him.

Gandhi laid down a rule. "The task dictated by duty, caring nothing for the fruits of the action." He preached mystically that the spinning wheel of ancient India would weave a fabric of liberty. At the same time, he called for surrender and sacrifice that even Rabindranath Tagore rejected as "a philosophy of negation and nihilism." Tagore's was one of many condemnations of Gandhi for "expecting his followers to treat hanging as a way of life."

Lala Lajpat Rai, whose followers called him the Lion of the Punjab because of his roaring tirades against the Raj, that had gotten him exiled from India for eleven years, turned now to a crusade against Gandhi's strategy of nonviolent noncooperation, which he denounced as "unreal and utterly impractical." Orthodox Hindu members of the Congress rebelled against Gandhi's pronouncement that "I regard Untouchability as the greatest blot on Hinduism." Mohammed Ali Jinnah, since 1916 the permanent president of the Muslim League, suddenly reversed his stand in support of Hindu-Muslim solidarity.

He had brought the Muslim League into joint sessions with the Congress, and was credited with originating the slogan, *Musulman-Hindi ki jai!* Hail to Muslim-Hindu unity! But emergence of Gandhi and Jawaharlal Nehru as Congress leaders was more than he could bear. Scornfully rejecting "Hindu pacifism," he broke with Congress and left the country, to practice law in England, "so disgusted with developments in India that he did not even take time to dispose of his property before departing."

It seemed to many that Gandhi, having loosed a whirlwind, left it to others to endure the gale, while he meditated in his *ashram*. He took no part in Congress' investigation of the massacre in Jallianwalla Bagh, conducted by the Nehrus, father and son, and their friend and fellow barrister, Deshbandhu Das. Walking the lane along which men he and his father knew had been forced to crawl like animals to reach their homes, questioning survivors of the massacre, Jawaharlal had no word to give from Gandhi. Nor did Gandhi appear at Congress sessions at Amritsar, over which Motilal presided.

Then Gandhi acted, in his Gandhian way. In a letter to Lord Chelmsford, the retiring Viceroy, he set August 1, 1920, as the day on which he would ask all India to unite in a non-cooperation program. With the letter, he returned the Kaisar-i-Hind and Zulu War medals the British had given him. In effect, he declared nonviolent war. And at Amritsar, Congress delegates raised a shout soon heard from Peshawar to Travancore, from Bengal to Bombay: *Mahatma Gandhi ki jai!* Hail to Gandhi the great-souled!

17.

At Anand Bhavan, there was another prophecy concerned with a cobra. This one had lived for years in a compound where firewood was stored. It was well-behaved, and so much an accepted resident that when a new servant was engaged, no one thought to mention it. Encountering the cobra, the new servant killed it, and boasted of his deed. Hari the Untouchable drove him into the street, and warned him not to come back. But other servants said someone in the Nehru family would suffer for the slaying of the cobra. Hearing of this from Hari, Little Daughter silenced the superstitious whisper. Her father, her brother, in fact everyone in the family, had quite enough to think of, without being told of dire prophecies.

She watched strangers come and go, who in other days would have been halted at the gates. Among them was a tiny creature, no taller than Swaruprani Nehru. His white Congress cap was too big for him. His shyness was not altogether explained by his humble birth into the *Kayastha* sub-caste of petty scribes and clerks. Orphaned in childhood, he had swum a river to reach the nearest school, and gone hungry while he gained an education. In his only gesture of pride in self, he had added Shastri to his patronymic, Lal Bahadur, because it was a name long associated with scholarly attainment.

When Lal Bahadur Shastri succeeded her brother as India's Prime Minister, American correspondents were no more at loss than writers for India's own newspapers for details about his beginnings. There were no photographs taken in his youth; his family could not afford such luxuries. Vijaya Lakshmi Pandit searched her notably retentive memory, and reminded him of their first meeting, at Anand Bhavan, forty years before. He in turn recalled how he looked from the fringe of crowds, at her father, her brother and her, the fortunate and beloved Nehrus.

In those days, her father and brother worked day and night to further Gandhi's strategies. Motilal Nehru took no cases, except in defense of Congress members arrested under the Black Bills; for these, he accepted no fees. Jawaharlal gave all his time to recruitment and training of Congress organizers, and to spreading Gandhi's message. "He is humble yet clear-cut and hard as a diamond," Jawaharlal told his sister, "and pleasant and soft-spoken but inflexibly and terribly earnest." She thought how truly this also described her brother.

"I realized more than ever how cut off we were from the people and how we lived and worked and agitated in a little world apart from them," he said long afterward. From her view, and from Kamala's, he had in fact gone from them, into the world outside. He hardly saw them, or his daughter, until Vijaya Lakshmi intercepted him hurrying to a Congress rally, and told him "Kamala is very ill."

Conscience-punished, he took Kamala and small Indira to Mussoorie, a health resort in the Himalayan foothills. Even there, he was taken from them by the cause he lived and breathed. A delegation from Afghanistan was at Mussoorie. They came to accept terms dictated by the British, victors in the Third Afghan War. Fighting continued, on the North West Frontier. Wazir and Tochi tribesmen must be subdued before the Raj could turn full attention to *Swaraj* disturbances. If trouble east and south forced withdrawal of troops from the Khyber, Afghan forays might resume.

He was ordered to give his word he would have no contact with the Afghan delegation. He said he came to Mussoorie only because his wife was ill and needed rest and quiet; he would, however, talk to anyone with whom he chose to talk. He was ordered to leave the district forthwith. He refused to leave, and was threatened with arrest.

When news of this reached his father and sister at Anand Bhavan, Motilal Nehru did what he would never have done in his own behalf, appealed to former British associates to intercede for his son. As she had been sure he would, her brother rejected intervention. The police, however, insisted on releasing him. Returning to his hotel, he found Indira being carried in the arms of one of the fierce-looking Afghans. They sent fruit and flowers to Kamala, and told Jawaharlal "We have lost, but somehow we think you will win." Kamala said it was time to end their holiday and did not show her knowledge that he ached to be back where noncooperation had begun. Very soon, he was in the villages, rallying Muslims, as much as Hindus, to join in support of Gandhi.

On the banks of the Jumna, two hundred landless peasants begged him to come and see how they lived. He told his sister "I was filled with shame and sorrow: shame at my own easy-going and comfortable life and our petty politics which ignore this vast multitude of semi-naked sons and daughters of India; sorrow at the degradation and overwhelming poverty of India. Their faith in us embarrassed me and filled me with a new responsibility that frightens me."

Gandhi preached that poverty ennobled spiritually. Her brother saw nothing noble in hunger and misery. "The wind is blowing in the villages," he said, "and through the mud huts where dwell our poverty-stricken peasantry; and it is likely to become a hurricane if relief does not come to them soon. All our political problems and discussions are but the background to this fact, that too many of us have preferred to ignore."

What he said and did exposed him to increasing personal risk. Gandhi's manifesto spelling out his doctrine was interpreted by authorities as a call to arms. "When there is only a choice between cowardice and violence I would advise violence" was quoted out of context. "A mouse hardly forgives a cat when it allows itself to be torn to pieces by her" was cited as a subtle threat. "It is possible for a single individual to defy the whole might of an unjust Empire to save his honor, his religion, his soul, and to lay the foundation for that Empire's fall or regeneration" was taken as incitement to treason.

Jawaharlal, now known as Gandhi's chosen messenger, was kept under constant surveillance by police and agents of the British C. I. D. Near an isolated village, he was halted by soldiers on a bridge. Firing broke out farther on. Suddenly he was surrounded by fleeing, terrified, unarmed villagers. Putting himself between them and rifles leveled by the soldiers, he managed to convince their officer he would gain no promotion by emulating Dyer at Amritsar.

On another occasion, he arrived too late. Servants of a *zamindar* convinced a number of credulous peasants that Gandhi wanted them to loot the holdings of another *zamindar*. They burned and destroyed, shouting *Mahatma Gandhi*

ki jai! Too late to halt the havoc, Jawaharlal appeared and arraigned the looters for bringing shame and disgrace on the
freedom crusade. The guilty wept like children. Before they
could disperse, police surrounded them. A thousand, ten times
as many as had been involved, were arrested and imprisoned.
He could do nothing, even for the innocent.

18.

"I am vain enough in some ways," he told his sister. "But
there could be no question of vanity with those simple folk.
There is no posing about them, no vulgarity, as in the case of
many of us in the middle classes, who consider ourselves their
betters. They may be dull and uninteresting individually, but
in the mass they produce a feeling of overpowering pity and a
sense of ever-impending tragedy."

A sense of Damoclean danger to him as their most-beloved
haunted his wife, his sisters, his mother and, above all, Motilal.
Still they let him go his ways with no word spoken to dissuade. Associates in the Congress were less understanding.
One of them said, "You are so aloof, I'll bet you haven't a single friend!" His only answer was, "I like to open my heart before a crowd."

Unlike Gandhi, he stepped down from above. He did this
without self-consciousness, and never patronized. However,
his sister recalls that he made no attempt to emulate Gandhi's
asceticism. He was always fastidiously clean; his white Congress cap was starched, worn like a part of him. Where he
could, he traveled by automobile, and carried food and water
with him. He was likely to speak of things and places villagers

had never heard of, but pleased them by taking it for granted he talked with friends. He was not a firebrand; emotional display embarrassed him. "In sum, he was the classic hero of Indian mythology: rich, high-born, handsome, brilliant, who renounced the world's pleasures to devote himself to strangers who had none of what had been his birthright."

He said in later years, "Scratch a Hindu and you'll find a Buddhist." Hinduism had reabsorbed Buddhism almost two thousand years before, while like Christianity, Buddhist belief went abroad from its birthplace. But a legend grew, of which he as much as his sister was aware. Prince Siddhartha was Jawaharlal's age, when he began his wanderings in search of a cure for misery and fear. What Jawaharlal taught was as revolutionary as Gautama Buddha's teaching of love and compassion, in India's Dark Ages five centuries before the birth of Christ.

It began and ended with "You can be free." More and more, this was accepted not as a politician's promise, but as gospel, made so by its source. Legend would grow through the years: that he was more than mortal. It would become a joke, to the very wise and sure. Neither he nor any other Nehru indicated awareness of it. He only said, "I feel at home in the dust and discomfort, the pushing and jostling of large gatherings, although their want of discipline sometimes irritates me."

His sister rejects a claim sometimes made for her, that she tugged against custom and circumstance, yearning to go with him into the other world he was discovering. She had at this time made her own discovery. She was deeply in love.

III❀

"Loving hands have been stretched out to help me."

Ranjit Sitaram Pandit, arriving uninvited at Anand Bhavan, told Krishna Nehru, then thirteen, "I came to meet your sister, and perhaps to marry her." He did not arrive altogether unknown. He had published an article in the *Modern Review*. Jawaharlal read and liked it. So did his sister. It was brought to Gandhi's notice by his secretary, Mahadev Desai, who had been Ranjit's friend when they were in Oxford. Gandhi recalled that in his youth, Ranjit's father had been kind to him.

More than this was in his favor. He hailed from Gandhi's homeland, Kathiawar, where his father was a leading barrister. At thirty, he was successful in his own right, practicing law in Calcutta. His birth-language was Marathi, but he was fluent as well in Hindi, Urdu, Persian and Bengali. Studies at Oxford, the Sorbonne and the University of Heidelberg made him equally at home in English, French and German.

He played the violin, sang, was good at tennis, cricket and polo, swam expertly and was a big-game hunter. He enjoyed translating Sanskrit plays and poems. He was handsome, gay, extremely likeable and as confident as he was unorthodox. What was worth doing was to be done immediately. Arriving one day, he proposed the next, and on the third was accepted.

Vijaya Lakshmi Pandit has never forgotten that he told her when he asked her to marry him: "I've traveled many miles and crossed many bridges to come to you. But in the future, you and I must cross our bridges hand in hand." *A daughter is too precious to be handed over in haste to anyone, however good.* But her eyes told her father he had no choice.

He must, in fact, have welcomed a decision that for once was not his own. A new wave of arrests had begun. All the Nehrus knew both Jawaharlal and Motilal might be arrested at any moment. Unless everything was hurried, this could occur before they saw Swarup Kumari married.

Motilal commanded the astrologers to waste no time in casting horoscopes. Obediently, they fixed on a date not far ahead: May 10, 1921. At once, days of lavish Nehru open-handedness returned. Again for a while, Anand Bhavan was truly the Home of Joy. Tents and *shamianas* were set up in the gardens. Motilal hired more servants, and laid in stores of food. Meanwhile Swaruprani took charge of arrangements that even Motilal admitted were outside his province.

Shyly assisted by Aunt Bibi Amma, she planned her daughter's trousseau. This, it was decided, must include a hundred *saris,* which meant a hundred and one; there must be an odd number for good luck. Color and texture of the bridal *sari* called for many conferences, in which Kamala and Krishna cast their votes. Customarily, Hindu brides wore pink, peach or red, though if the marriage took place in the spring, the *sari* could be green or yellow. Finally, decision was unanimous. Swarup Kumari would wear shell-pink brocade.

Then a letter came from Gandhi. Not only were he and Kasturbai coming to the wedding; he would be happy to give the bride away. Motilal barked "No!" Not even the Mahatma could deprive him of his parental prerogative. But Gandhi's further suggestion struck him as reasonable. Gandhi took it for granted that Swarup Kumari's wedding *sari* would be of *khadi,* the symbol of noncooperation with the British. Swaruprani, for once unsubmissive, said, "If she must be dressed like a villager's child, there will be no wedding." Motilal stormed. The Nehru women were silent, and by silence forced a compromise. *Khadi* it could be, if the stuff could be dyed shell-pink. Motilal sighed with relief. Then he learned the depths of feminine subtlety. Every length of *khadi* sent to be dyed was returned with word that the cloth was too coarse to take the dye. Motilal blustered, to no avail.

Then a package arrived, addressed in Gandhi's familiar handwriting. He sent six yards of *khadi* almost as fine as silk: "For Swarup. Spun by Kasturbai with her love." Off this went to the dyers, to come back a glowing golden orange, the color of sunrise. Swarup Kumari said she would wear it happily, with pride. Blessing her, Motilal fled from the women's quarters, to cope with the problem of where to put all the guests who had invited themselves to the wedding.

The Congress executive committee voted to attend en masse, at his expense, and hold a policy meeting afterward. Congress rank-and-file, hearing of this, came in hope of getting a glimpse of their leaders. Word spread in the villages, that a Nehru daughter was being married, and the Mahatma

would be at her wedding. This brought villagers in throngs.
They were sure the Nehrus would share the wedding feast
with them.

Motilal said "No" to no one. There might not be another
day like this, for him. Krishna was not yet fourteen. He was
sixty, and not well, and in his mind prison and the grave had a
single yawning entrance. But when May 10 dawned, no one
at Anand Bhavan was more busy and gay and outgiving.
"Wherever you looked, there he was."

2.

The day began very early for the bride. Tradition decreed
she must do nothing for herself. She was waited on by seven
unmarried maidens. Milk instead of water was poured over her
in a ceremonial bath. She was rubbed with scented oil. The
palms of her hands and the soles of her feet were tinted with
henna. Her curly hair was brushed until it shone. Aunt Bibi
Amma, assisted by Krishna and Kamala and small Indira
Priyadarshini, served her from a tray of food sent by Ranjit.
That, too, was traditional: The groom shares his wedding
day's first meal with his bride.

In old days, he would have appeared riding a white horse,
preceded by a band and an elephant painted with many-
colored designs. He came with his mother, older brother and
sisters, in a decorated automobile. Received with gifts of flowers and lights and incense, the Pandits sat together in a row.
Swarup Kumari appeared only long enough to garland Ranjit
with flowers.

Suddenly, there was noise at the gates. Hari the Untouchable scurried to find Jawaharlal, begging "Come quickly!" He faced a detachment of police. Why had they put a cordon around Anand Bhavan? The Englishman in command said "You know what day this is!" The Nehrus have always said they had quite forgotten, until the police reminded them, that exactly sixty-four years before, on May 10, 1857, what the British called the Indian Mutiny had begun.

Gandhi's presence, Congress leaders and rank-and-file gathered together, hundreds of villagers camped close by, had put the Allahabad authorities on edge. All bearers of the White Man's Burden had been ordered not to go out unarmed. All available soldiers and police patrolled the city. The wedding day that was also an unforgotten anniversary could end in another Jallianwalla Bagh.

Jawaharlal calmed the police commandant. "You have my word that if there is any violence, it will not be caused by anyone who is here to see my sister married." The police drew back a little, but stood guard while the ceremony went on.

Hindu priests sat crosslegged in a circle around the wood fire over which vows must be made if they were to be eternal. The long rites ended with the chanted admonition that concludes: "In wisdom and humility may you both serve the community for a hundred years." Then Ranjit took his bride to his brother and mother and sisters, to be accepted into the family. Their acceptance began with conferring the new names they had chosen for her. Since Ranjit meant "Victor," they named her Vijaya, for "Victory." They added Lakshmi, for "Fortune." She need not use the names unless she chose, but they would always call her by them.

In their orthodox belief, she was born anew at the moment

of her marriage, into a life so entwined with her husband's that if he died before her, she would retire into seclusion for the rest of her time on earth. Ranjit's grandmother, Gopika, had been the last woman in her village to perform *sati* or *suttee*, self-cremation of a widow on her husband's funeral pyre. A shrine commemorated her voluntary immolation. The Pandits expected Ranjit's bride to bind herself to the past they cherished, and believed she did so when she said that as long as she lived, she would bear no name but Vijaya Lakshmi Pandit.

She slipped away with her attendants, took off the Gandhi *sari*, donned one chosen by her mother, of heavy gold tissue embroidered with gems. The girls arranged strings of pearls across the back of her head, up and down the part in her hair, across her brow. They braided her hair with a gold cord, fastened it with jeweled pins, and put on her finest earrings, necklaces and bangles. This was for the wedding photograph. Then Vijaya Lakshmi and Ranjit went to Gandhi to receive his blessing, before departing for Calcutta and a round of parties.

Orthodoxy was left behind. They were amusing and amused, extravagant, forgetful of any trials or troubles but their own. Looking back at herself when young, she would tell her daughters one day, "I was the ghastly sort who faced a crisis by dissolving into tears. Your father called me a second-hand Christian martyr. I was never upset or angry enough to try and remedy a state of affairs. I just sat and suffered. I had to cure myself of that habit. The cure took time."

They were in Europe, on their honeymoon, when Edward Prince of Wales was dispatched to India to show himself to his future subjects. The government of King-Emperor George V believed the presence of his son "would excite the imagination of the masses with their traditional reverence for royalty, and bind closer the ties between India and the British Crown." His progress was anything but triumphal. The Congress boycotted all functions connected with his visit. When he landed at Bombay, he was greeted by rioting that continued for three days. Fifty people were killed and at least four hundred injured. Arrests filled the jails. Deshbandhu Das, president-elect of the annual Congress session, sent a message from his cell. "The whole of India is a vast prison."

The evening of December 6, 1921, returning from a Congress meeting, Jawaharlal found police searching Anand Bhavan. They had warrants for him and for his father. Next day, Motilal was sentenced to six months' imprisonment "for being a member of an illegal organization." Jawaharlal received the same sentence, "for distributing announcements of a demonstration against the Government." Indira Priyadarshini watched the proceedings from her grandfather's arms. It was her first experience in the prisoners' dock, but not her last.

From prison, Motilal sent a letter. "It is now my high privilege to serve the motherland by going to prison with my only son. I am fully confident that we shall meet again at no distant date as free men. Continue nonviolent noncooperation until *Swaraj* is achieved. Enlist as volunteers in your tens and hundreds and thousands. Let the march of pilgrimage to the only temple of liberty now existing in India—the jail—be kept in an uninterrupted stream, swelling in strength and volume as each day passes."

During December 1921, and January 1922, thirty thousand *Swaraj* pilgrims were imprisoned. Motilal and Jawaharlal, two

of Jawaharlal's cousins and fourteen others, were crowded into
an old weaving shed in Lucknow District Jail. They were
there when Vijaya Lakshmi and Ranjit Pandit returned from
their honeymoon.

3.

Her brother said "I think prison has made a man of me."
He "found a strange relaxation in washing his own and his father's clothes." He indulged his fondness for gardening, took
exercises to keep fit, taught himself to brew tea and fry eggs.
"There is much to learn, much to do." But their father was
the more contented prisoner.

Men of sixty seldom change habits or opinions. He had
changed both totally. His reasons were complex. Quite probably the Indian journalist, Frank Moraes, guessed shrewdly
when he said Motilal "was too fond a father not to know how
his son would like him to behave." He left no doubt of the behavior he expected from his daughter. She was to spend no
time or tears on him, or on her brother. She was Vijaya
Lakshmi Pandit now, not Swarup Kumari Nehru. Her duty
was to her husband and her home. She agreed. They set up
housekeeping in Calcutta. He returned to his law practice. He
had not, thus far, taken any part in the *Swaraj* crusade. He
was not cut out for political struggles, and knew it. So did she.
But she missed nothing of what went on where the storm was
darkening.

In mid-February, 1922, in Chauri Chaura village in the
Gorakhpur District of the United Provinces, not far from
Allahabad, police fired on villagers, who retaliated by setting

fire to the local jail. Twenty-two policemen, trapped inside, were burned to death. Gandhi, aghast, called for immediate cessation of civil disobedience, Motilal Nehru protested this retreat from action he had supported reluctantly in the beginning. Belatedly admitting that no statute on the books made Jawaharlal guilty of any punishable offense, authorities released him, but kept his father in prison. He went first to his wife and daughter, then hurried on for a strategy conference with Gandhi.

Before they could meet, Gandhi was arrested and sentenced to six years' imprisonment by a British magistrate who said, "There are probably few people in India who do not sincerely regret that you have made it impossible for any government to leave you at liberty." Sarojini Naidu, reporting this to Vijaya Lakshmi, said Gandhi took with him into prison a copy of the Sermon on the Mount, that had been sent to him by some American schoolboys in California.

She had heard "Blessed are the meek" preached by the Anglican vicar when she went to Holy Trinity with Miss Hooper. She reread the Beatitudes now. She saw no meekness in her brother, when he came for a brief visit. He smiled less often, spoke more sharply to the point. At no time did he ask her, or her husband, to walk beside him. He asked them only to be with Kamala and Indira when they could.

After six weeks of freedom, he was rearrested, on charges of criminal intimidation, extortion and sedition. He refused to defend himself, or even to plead "Not guilty" and thus give a color of legality to his trial. His sister brought his daughter, now the age she had been when she went to England to see

him entered at Harrow, to watch British justice as it had come
to be administered in British India.

In what was more drumhead courtmartial than trial, he was
convicted, sentenced, hustled away to a cell. Together, when it
was permitted, his sister and his daughter went to see him.
Mrs. Indira Gandhi says today "My childhood memories begin with the searching of homes and persons, the arrests and
visiting my father and other members of the family in prison"; and saying this, explains much about herself. Her father
and six others, including Gandhi's son, Devadas, and
Mahadev Desai, Gandhi's secretary, who had been Ranjit
Pandit's friend at Oxford, were confined in a jail within a jail.
They had a spinning wheel like Gandhi's, and worked it as he
did, symbolically. They cultivated a vegetable garden in the
prison yard, watering it with water drawn up from the well in
a leaking bucket, by thrusting their shoulders against a wood-
en yoke, as peasants did if they were too poor to own a bullock.

"Most of all," Jawaharlal told his sister, "I miss the sound
of women's voices and the laughter of children. And it suddenly strikes me I have not heard a dog bark in a long time."
That was the extent of his complaint. Celebrating his thirty-
third birthday in prison was completing a page, so he might
go on to the next chapter. "More and more I look on life as an
adventure of absorbing interest."

More and more, she made his philosophy her own. Yet still
she was the listener, not a participant. Released on January 31,
1923, he was immediately elected president of the Allahabad
Municipality. Discussing with her a proposal "intended to
correct the treatment of prostitutes," he said "The world

would be a very different place if we could abolish prostitution and lying and cruelty and oppression and the thousand and one ills that flesh is heir to, by passing resolutions and appointing committees." She was still his pupil, who longed to be a partner.

He was elected secretary of the All-India Congress. Coincidentally, British authorities offered him a lucrative appointment to Education Minister of the United Provinces. He told his sister "The coincidence is not exactly an accident," and said "No, thank you" to the British, and accepted the Congress post. He was surprised when Kamala asked to be given Congress work, and "far too busy to see beneath the surface and . . . blind to what she looked for and so ardently desired." So his wife and his sister waited in their corners. Thus far, there was no work for women in the fight for freedom.

4.

In March, 1924, she bore her first child. She had hoped for a son, but Ranjit Pandit hoped for a daughter, and had chosen her name: Chandralekha, which means "The Crescent." The night Chandralekha was born, a crescent moon shone in the sky. With her baby daughter in her arms, Vijaya Lakshmi went to Anand Bhavan. Her mother was ill. So was Kamala. Jawaharlal, jailed for the third time, contracted typhus. Released "for reasons of health," instead of recuperating at home he returned to Congress duties. In mid-January, Gandhi had been released "on commutation of sentence." Motilal Nehru appealed to him. "Help me convince my son of the folly of monkey-tricks such as living on parched rice and traveling third-class."

Her father had given up all ease and luxury, but as for her brother "There is no point in primitiveness when it is unnecessary. It hurts me." Gandhi promised to do what he could. "But as you know," he confided to Vijaya Lakshmi, "your father has a very stubborn son." She smiled, but only for a moment. Far more important than her brother's idiosyncrasies was the news she must give him: that doctors said Kamala was in the advanced stages of tuberculosis. She should, they said, be taken to Switzerland for treatment. Gandhi told him "Your wife must be your first concern." His sister helped in convincing him. In March, 1926, Vijaya Lakshmi and Ranjit Pandit sailed with Jawaharlal, Kamala and Indira. They were joined in Europe by Motilal and Krishna, now nineteen.

All the Nehrus went to Moscow, to watch the celebration of the tenth anniversary of the Russian Revolution. While they were there, Leon Trotsky was expelled from the Communist Party, now ruled by Joseph Stalin. In Brussels, at the Congress of Oppressed Nationalities, they met Madame Sun Yat-sen, one of the Soong Sisters, widow of the Father of the Chinese Revolution, and heard her opinion of her sister's husband, Chiang Kai-shek, who had just established his Kuomintang government in China. They also met, but took little note of, a lean, secretive Indo-Chinese with waxen skin and a wispy beard, who called himself Nguyen-Ai-Quoc. When they heard of him again, he was called Ho Chi Minh.

In London, they encountered an expatriate countryman

who would have strange impact on the lives of Jawaharlal Nehru and Vijaya Lakshmi Pandit. His name in full was Vengalil Krishnan Kunji-Krishna Menon. His father, like Motilal Nehru, was a rich and respected barrister who had expected his son to follow in his footsteps. Like Jawaharlal, seven years his senior, he had been a boyhood convert to Mrs. Annie Besant's theosophy. Unlike Jawaharlal, he had left his studies to follow her.

He did Boy Scout work in Southern India, until in 1924 Mrs. Besant sent him to study in England, with the understanding that in six months he would return to India to teach in the university she had founded at Adyar. Still in England three years later, he said he had "no intention of returning to India in a hurry." He was in so little haste that he postponed return until 1947, when independence was *un fait accompli.* In London, he edited books, gave lectures, acquired a cult of Indian students awed by his cold brilliance, raised funds for the Indian League and wore asceticism and intellectual arrogance as if they were shining armor.

Under South India's matriarchal system, his proper name was his mother's, Vengalil. Menon was a caste-suffix, indicating he came of a lineage of accountants and supervisors. But no Brahmin was more patronizing. Jawaharlal, jesting, said, "I am getting rather fed up with my name. It is always being misspelled and mispronounced. The other day a B.B.C. announcer got hopelessly muddled over it and went on ha-ha-haing." V. K. Krishna Menon was never amused by slights, however inadvertent. He, not they, set a color bar between himself and bearers of the White Man's Burden. Jawaharlal appears to have accepted him at first as a zealot whose immediately proffered allegiance could do no harm, and might possibly have some value. This acceptance was enough for Krishna Menon.

He began a flood of letters written as if he were Jawaharlal's Ambassador-at-Large. Vijaya Lakshmi was not asked, and did not volunteer, her estimate of the voluntary exile who made no secret of contempt for "those who demand a share in freedom's fruits merely on the basis of a term in jail." As for Krishna Menon, he ignored her until, much later, she stood in his way. Jawaharlal, Kamala, Indira and Krishna sailed for home. Motilal was prevailed upon to stay a while in London, where Vijaya Lakshmi and Ranjit Pandit spent a season of escape from India's realities. "We were still not used to austerities, to wearing coarse clothes and buying India-made goods no matter how poor in quality, when all our lives we had had the best. It seemed to me, young as I was then, that everything gay and lovely had been cut out of my life."

London shops were full of luxuries. Laughing diners crowded London restaurants. There was a gala automobile show. "Ranjit and I, in a holiday mood, ordered a Rolls-Royce, without for a moment considering what might become of it if it was shipped out to India. The police, when they came to search a house, took what they liked. A car like that would be the first thing they'd take. But we thought of nothing but the joy of being free to be foolish. Ranjit was still a member of the Bar Association, and played a lot of cricket and tennis. He bought some sports equipment for the club at home. Then a letter came from India. We couldn't return the sports things. But we canceled the order for the Rolls."

They could have remained in London. Ranjit had no

political-activities black marks against him, that might militate against his chance to prosper professionally in England. Mohammed Ali Jinnah, who had, was nonetheless easily able to earn high fees from English clients. Ranjit would have been welcomed by any of a dozen law firms. His wife was very much an asset. London society found them romantic, charming, a great catch. Without undue immodesty, they realized all this.

What awaited them in India? They had cut their living costs there, so they could contribute more to the Congress treasury. He had neither aptitude nor training for active Congress service. But he was powerfully drawn by the same magnet that drew Jawaharlal and then his father to cast their lot with Gandhi. He read in Vijaya Lakshmi what she felt, but did not say: that for good or ill, they belonged in India.

They were foolishly extravagant for one last London evening. Then they sailed for home.

5.

Among their *bon voyage* gifts was a book someone bought because of its title, apparently without bothering to look inside its cover. *Mother India,* by Katherine Mayo, an American journalist, was the year's best-seller, in the United States and in England. In its praise, the London *New Statesman* said it revealed indisputably "the filthy personal habits of even the most highly educated classes in India—which, like the degradation of Hindu women, are unequaled even among the most primitive African or Australian savages." The reviewer concluded: "Katherine Mayo makes the claims for *Swaraj* seem nonsense and the will to grant it almost a crime." They read *Mother India* with fascinated incredulity.

Few books, in fact, have succeeded more completely in creating an indestructible scarecrow out of rags and tatters of half-truths, held together by threads of titillating shock. Forty years after the first of its forty-odd editions, and in that time revised only to the extent of substitution of *Hindus* where originally it read *Indians,* it continues to hold an honored place on library shelves, to be consulted by students and many of their instructors, to be quoted as gospel by guides of tourist groups and to condition the thinking of Congressmen voting on aid to India, industrialists contemplating investment there, and Peace Corps volunteers deciding where they wish to serve.

In 1929, its impact on Vijaya Lakshmi and Ranjit Pandit confirmed what Katherine Mayo said she expected. "I am fully aware," she wrote, "of the resentments I shall incur; of the accusations of muckraking; of injustice; of material-mindedness; of lack of sympathy; of falsehood perhaps; perhaps of prurience." What comment she made in words, Vijaya Lakshmi Pandit will not say; but her vocabulary is known to include pyrotechnics not recommended in the Manual of Protocol.

In childhood, she flustered Miss Hooper by presuming to question Mountstuart Elphinstone. She could cry "Liar!" now from her own hard-learned knowledge. "The British administration of India," said *Mother India,* "be it good, bad or indifferent, has nothing whatever to do with conditions there . . . Inertia, helplessness, lack of initiative and originality, lack of staying power and sustained loyalties, sterility of enthusiasm, weakness of life-vigor itself—all are traits that are truly characteristic of the Indian not only of today, but of long-past history. His soul and his body are indeed chained in slavery. But he himself wields and hugs his chains and with violence defends them."

She thought of her husband, her brother, her father. "The whole pyramid of the Hindu's woes," said Katherine Mayo, "material and spiritual—poverty, sickness, ignorance, political minority, melancholy, ineffectiveness, not forgetting that subconscious conviction of inferiority which he forever bares and advertises by his gnawing and imaginative alertness to social affronts—rests upon a rock-bottom physical base. This base is, simply, his manner of getting into the world and his sex-life thenceforward." And what of herself? *Mother India* declared "Childbearing and matters of procreation are the Hindu woman's one interest in life, her one subject of conversation, be her caste high or low."

If she had flung the book over the ship's rail, no one who has known her would wonder. Instead, she read more; and reading, grew more and more determined that as far as she could, however she could, she would do her part in disproving a catalogue of libels. "Given men," said a woman she would never meet, "who enter the world physical bankrupts out of bankrupt stock, rear them through childhood in influences and practices that devour their vitality; launch them at the dawn of maturity on an unrestrained outpouring of their whole provision of creative energy in one single direction; find them, at the age when the Anglo-Saxon is just coming into the glory of manhood, broken-nerved, low-spirited, petulant ancients; and need you, while this remains unchanged, seek for other reasons why they are poor and sick and dying and why their hands are

too weak, too fluttering, to seize or hold the reins of government?"

As for Gandhi: "A creed through centuries built into weak,
ignorant and fanatic peoples is not to be uprooted in one or two
hundred years; neither can it be shaken by the wrath of a single prophet, however reverenced." And as if she challenged
Vijaya Lakshmi Pandit from the page: "The . . . chapters
of this book state living facts of India today. They can easily
be denied, but they cannot be disproved or shaken." They
could be; and they were. Vijaya Lakshmi Pandit, she vowed
to herself, would find some way to be among the shakers and
disprovers.

In India, Gandhi's review of *Mother India* was headed *The
Drain Inspector's Report*. In London, the *Times,* the Thun-
derer, austerely declined to publish a letter of rebuttal signed
"by ten prominent Indians then visiting Europe," with the
explanation that it was an established rule "to decline all letters criticizing publications other than those for which the
Times itself was responsible." The rule did not deter publication of letters signed *Pro Bono Britannica* and *Friends of General Dyer,* which expressed approval of the fact that Americans were finally learning what Englishmen had known all
along.

Gandhi said, "No serious American can possibly be taken
in by Miss Mayo's scurrilous writings." In this, for once, he
was wrong. He was, however, right when he added, "The
general public that has already been affected by *Mother India*
will never read refutations however brilliantly attempted."
Nine Indian writers published point-by-point contradictions.
None were read abroad.

Charges were leveled, that British opponents of change in India had subsidized the Katherine Mayo polemic. These were never substantiated. However, belief would not down that *Mother India* had further purpose than its author's stated desire to inform Americans who until then knew regarding India only that "Mr. Gandhi lives there; also tigers." Credibility of the accuser was appraised in terms of the past record.

Her first book, a study of Y. M. C. A. dealings with American soldiers in France during World War I, was titled *That Damn Y*. Her second, *Isles of Fear*, made a positive case against granting independence to the Philippines. In October 1925 she was in London, arranging with the Colonial Office for her first visit to India. According to the English publisher, Jonathan Cape, "I first heard of *Mother India* in January 1927, when I met Miss Mayo in New York. She told me that a book on India on which she had been engaged for some time was nearly finished."

Rather clearly, this allowed for something less than extensive research. Still others than Vijaya Lakshmi Pandit found it strange, that Katherine Mayo recorded no meetings with Congress leaders other than Gandhi, frankly said she had only brief talks with him, made no mention of Jallianwalla Bagh, said nothing whatever about Motilal or Jawaharlal Nehru. She quoted lengthily from the Abbé Dubois, but neglected to note that he wrote in 1807. Claiming exhaustive interviews with women who spoke for India, she gave no place to such of them as Princess Amrit Kaur of the premier House of Kapurthala, who left her palace, became a Christian, then walked India's roads as Gandhi's disciple; or Kamaladevi, famously gifted and beautiful, who renounced secluded luxury to rally women with the challenge "If you want your rights you must work for them." She seemed never to have heard of Sarojini Naidu, who was on the way to America to confront her, when Vijaya Lakshmi and Ranjit Pandit landed at Bombay.

Headlines in India read *Our Unofficial Ambassador Goes to Undo Mayo's Mischief.* In the United States, the American publishers of *Mother India* put forth *After Mother India,* by Harry H. Field, to whom Katherine Mayo's preface expressed indebtedness "for a helpfulness, both in India and here, beyond limit or thanks." Sarojini Naidu, intending rebuttal of *Mother India,* found herself called on instead to answer charges lodged by its defender, who ranked it in historical importance with *Uncle Tom's Cabin* and Darwin's *Origin of the Species.*

His *After Mother India* quoted an affidavit by a woman living in Los Angeles, which avowed that after her husband was killed during rioting against the visit of the Prince of Wales, in Bombay in 1921, Mrs. Naidu came to her as Gandhi's emissary and "very frankly asked my price for refraining from ever discussing or advertising the affair in America, and from myself returning to America. Under no condition, said Mrs. Naidu, would they be willing that the American public should learn that they were killing people so promiscuously that even a white face cost a man's life."

The accusation stunned Sarojini Naidu, who said Gandhi and all his followers would let themselves be killed rather than be guilty of killing or of condoning it, and that color had nothing to do with the freedom crusade, "any more than caste or creed." But whatever she said, *Mother India* went on selling, turning a scarecrow into stone. It had, however, roused many women of India, beginning with Vijaya Lakshmi Pandit, to determination they would disprove its thesis not by words but in action.

6.

At Anand Bhavan, in the room in which she was born, on her sixth wedding anniversary, she gave birth to her second daughter, who by Ranjit Pandit's choice was named Nayantara, "Star of the Eye." Twenty-nine years later, Nayantara published in the United States her book of memories, which she dedicated "To my parents, Vijaya Lakshmi and Ranjit Pandit, who have made all good things possible."

She wrote, "The future for a woman in my mother's opinion began with marriage and children. It might end in any one of all the fascinating vistas modern times held out to women, and in fact, if a woman had had the good fortune to be educated at considerable expense to her parents, it had better end in one of those vistas. This could mean anything from original accomplishment and recognition, to solid hard work in some sphere that might pass unnoticed all one's life. Ultimately, the future of the conscientious citizen meant work."

The vista for Vijaya Lakshmi Pandit in 1929 was a view from far off. Frequently, she heard of dispute between her father and her brother. Jawaharlal threatened to resign as Congress secretary, rather than accept the policy Motilal supported, which was summed up in a sentence: "We have some chance of winning Dominion status; we have none, of winning total independence." Neither would compromise. During one argument Motilal exploded as furiously as he had when he caned his son for taking a fountain pen without per-mission. He ordered Jawaharlal to leave his house, and Jawaharlal was about to go, when he realized Kamala beside him. Ill, fragile, loyal, she clasped his hand. *Whither thou goest, I will go.* And Motilal, staring at them, relented. Still he insisted the Congress must adopt the report he had fos-tered, which intimated that unless the British Government gave India a constitution and Dominion status within a year, the Congress would revert to insistence on full independence.

"It is," Jawaharlal told his sister, "an offer of a year's grace and a polite ultimatum." So the authorities interpreted it. There were conspiracy trials in the Punjab and Bengal. A young revolutionary, Jatindranath Das, went on a hunger strike in prison, and died after fasting sixty-one days. His death gave *Swaraj* a martyr. Gandhi, touring the United Prov-inces, speaking to crowds of a hundred thousand, preached *Daridranarayan,* "God that resides in the poor." Lord Irwin, who would become Viscount Halifax, proclaimed from the Viceroy's palace "We are in India to keep our tempers." It was said he always prayed before making important decisions. Vijaya Lakshmi Pandit recalls that Gandhi said "What a pity God always gives him the wrong advice."

She learned that at Lucknow, her brother was ridden down and beaten by mounted police. Her concern eased when he told her he regarded the incident as a test. "The bodily pain was quite forgotten in a feeling of exhilaration that I was physically strong enough to face and bear the blows. And a thing that surprised me was that even while I was being beaten, my mind was quite clear and I was consciously analyz-ing my feelings."

His sister analyzed hers. Her third daughter, born in October 1929, was named Rita, which is a word for "Truth." The choice had particular meaning. Chandralekha and Nayantara were names out of the past. Gandhi's appeal for truth in the present was an augury for the future. While Americans mourned their market crash on Black Friday, in India a day not of mourning but of determination commemorated the tenth anniversary of the massacre in Jallianwalla Bagh. There was thunder in the distance.

Meeting at Lahore, the Congress prepared to elect a new president, to succeed Motilal Nehru. Three provincial committees voted for his son. Five preferred Vallabhbhai Patel. Ten nominated Gandhi. Final choice might well determine whether Congress leaders accepted Lord Irwin's suggestion of a summit conference in London, or rejected what the Viceroy intended as an olive branch. Neither Vijaya Lakshmi nor Ranjit Pandit had a vote in the matter. On all sides, they were told "The choice will not be another Nehru."

Vallabhbhai Patel, a barrister from Ahmadabad, had been a scoffer at "the vaporings of Gandhi"; then, like Motilal Nehru, joined but did not always see eye to eye with him. Strong, somber, a skilled organizer, he had rallied peasants near Bombay to resist punitive land-tax assessments, and forced authorities to reconsider. For this and other victories, he was called *Sardar,* Leader. Many in India today begin complaints against their government with "If Vallabhbhai Patel had lived." In 1929, many said that if Gandhi chose not to head the Congress, the choice would be Vallabhbhai Patel. But his conservatism was held against him by a radical wing led by a bespectacled, cherubic, violent young Bengali, Subhas Bose, who frankly said, "I, not Jawaharlal Nehru, should lead against the old men who have run the Congress too long already."

His father felt, but his sister was not so sure, that Jawaharlal risked a fall by raising his voice almost as insistently as Subhas Bose, against consideration of anything less than total independence. Joining with Gandhi, Motilal Nehru carried through a resolution to accept the Round Table Conference proposal, on condition that representation would be predominantly Congress, that the conference would be based on full Dominion status, and that there would be immediate amnesty for political prisoners in India.

Jawaharlal opposed retreat from demand for independence, "even in theory and even for a short while." His father exploded typically. But Gandhi wrote to him saying, "Resist me always, when my suggestion does not appeal to your head or your heart." Hearing of this, Vijaya Lakshmi longed to be at Lahore. Her mother was there. Leaving the womens' quarters at Anand Bhavan, Swaruprani Nehru went to see, for the first time, her husband and her son before the crowd.

Lord Irwin was viceregally unconcerned by decision impending at Lahore. The train on which he traveled from Hyderabad to Delhi was damaged by a bomb set off by a time fuse. He was unhurt, and joked in a *pukka* British way about the clumsiness of "your amateur terrorists," when he met with Gandhi, Motilal Nehru, Mohammed Ali Jinnah of the Muslim League, Sir Tej Bahadur Sapru and Viththalbhai Patel, brother of Vallabhbhai. He had said before meeting Gandhi that they should be able to get on famously. "We are both deeply religious."

He had been Viceroy for three years, but boycotts, strikes, demonstrations and riots had not disturbed his equanimity or opened his mind. In his first speech in the House of Commons, in 1910, he assumed that Egyptians were "a black people," and drew several comparisons between "superior" and "inferior" races. "While we on our side most emphatically disclaim any attempt permanently to hold down the black races, we do at the same time insist that if our position in those countries is to be maintained, it can only be as it is at the present moment, by maintaining the position and fulfilling the functions of a superior race." Five years as ruler of British India taught him very little.

In 1941, by then become Viscount Halifax and Britain's Ambassador to the United States, visiting Lady Astor's girlhood home in Virginia, he mused pensively, "I regret there are no slaves. This would be my hour for visiting my slaves. I should talk affably with them, I should visit the sick and aged and read the Bible to them, and when gross impropriety or misconduct demanded it, I should correct them; and every now and then, I should pat a little head. Finally I should make them all sing spirituals with me." In Delhi in 1929, he talked affably, quoted the Bible, patted heads, and finally put the Empire in jeopardy.

What he said, and how it was said, could very well decide who would head the Congress, what course the Congress would adopt. He chose to begin by asking as if the subject were rather amusing, "I suppose you want to begin about your political prisoners?" To his pained surprise, the answer was

"No." They wanted assurance first that Dominion status for India was the fixed purpose of the London Round Table Conference.

He hardly hesitated. "I cannot give you any such assurance. Dominion status must depend on how you conduct yourselves." Gandhi rose. So did the others. At this moment, the crusade for *Swaraj* was transmuted into a revolution for independence. The question was only who should command in the field. And Gandhi had made his choice.

"Jawaharlal Nehru," he told Congress delegates and thirty thousand watchers at Lahore, including Swaruprani Nehru, "is undoubtedly an extremist thinking far ahead of his surroundings. But he is humble and practical enough not to force the pace to the breaking point. The nation is safe in his hands. His appointment as the captain is proof of the trust the nation reposes in its youth. Jawaharlal alone can do little. The youth of the country must be his arms and his eyes. Let them prove worthy of the trust."

7.

At Lahore on the last day of 1929, Motilal Nehru, as retiring Congress president, passed the gavel to his son; and with it, a legacy not as he had planned, of wealth and ease, but one of toil and trial. Presidency of the Congress was the highest post an Indian could hold in India. Gandhi was sixty. Motilal Nehru was sixty-eight. Jawaharlal Nehru was forty. They had placed the future of India on his shoulders.

The throngs that had shouted *Mahatma Gandhi ki jai!* now shouted *Nehruji ki jai!* Riding a white horse, he led a procession that would have done honor to a king. His mother, weeping happily, garlanded him with flowers. His father said, "The one thing I am proudest of is that Jawaharlal is my son." What neither father, mother nor brother realized was that they were about to find cause for pride as well in the wife and mother they once called Little Daughter.

Ranjit Pandit watched her while she read reports of the drama at Lahore. "Success often comes to those who dare and act; it seldom goes to the timid who are afraid of consequences," her brother said in accepting his election. "We play for high stakes, and if we seek to achieve great things, it can only be through great dangers." The dangers multiplied. Thirty thousand saluted the tri-color flag he unfurled, and departed spreading the chant: *Inquilab Zindabad!* Long live the revolution! All of India's people were called on "to launch a program of civil disobedience, including nonpayment of taxes." January 26, 1930, was designated as India's first Independence Day.

On January 26, numberless crowds intoned a pledge in unison: "We believe that it is the inalienable right of the Indian people, as of any other people, to have freedom and to enjoy the fruits of their toil and have the necessities of life, so that they may have full opportunities of growth. We believe also that if any government deprives a people of these rights and oppresses them, the people have a further right to alter it or to abolish it."

In their quiet, comfortable home, Vijaya Lakshmi and Ranjit Pandit looked at one another in long silence. Sometimes since, she has said he "was almost dragged" into giving up his law practice, moving with her and their three daughters back to Anand Bhavan, and dedicating the remainder of his days to the struggle in which he had been only remotely involved during the first eight years of their marriage. Those who knew them say the decision was entirely his own, and that his reasons were part of a love story the author of *Mother India* could never have understood.

8.

The new year, her father wrote to Indira, had dawned "with the air dark with the shadow of coming events." For Motilal Nehru, it began with an act of faith and sacrifice. With Jawaharlal's complete approval, he gave Anand Bhavan to the cause, to house a Congress hospital and the All-India Congress Committee. Today, it is a national monument, sometimes called India's Mount Vernon.

The family moved across the road, into a smaller house, Spartan in its furnishings. Everyone had daily tasks. There was no more going between enclaves. "It is only the kings and princes, who have nothing in them but their kingships and princedoms," her brother told Vijaya Lakshmi, "who have to put on their liveries and uniforms to hide the nakedness underneath." He had gotten into a habit of uttering quotable remarks. She knew why. People had taken to calling him *Bharat Bushan,* Jewel of India, and *Tyagamurti,* Embodiment of Sacrifice. She decided something should be done about this. At the breakfast table, she said with eyebrow quirked, "O Jewel of India, please pass me the butter." He frowned, then smiled, then laughed aloud, as he did less and less often. Kamala joined gently in the game. So did Indira. "O Embodiment of

Sacrifice, is it time for me to go to school?" His mother was
not amused, but he thanked Vijaya Lakshmi for making fun
to make him laugh. "You must keep reminding me that the
only time I get in trouble is when I let the grownup in me get
the better of me."

He was on the brink of realization, and revealed this by
quoting Nikolai Lenin. "He said, 'No nation can be free
when half the population is enslaved in the kitchen.'" Again,
he said "It is very interesting how extraordinarily difficult it is
even for intelligent people to give up old ideas and accept new
ones. Even the radicals, who imagine themselves very advanced, often stick to old and exploded ideas, and shut their
eyes to changing conditions." He was not quite ready to say,
as he would within a year: "See the women of India, how
proudly they march ahead of all in the struggle! Gentle, yet
brave and indomitable, see how they set the pace for others!"
His sisters, his wife, his daughter, his mother, still waited in
the shadows.

Then suddenly, without prior consultation with Jawaharlal
or Motilal, Gandhi announced he would postpone civil disobedience if the British would concede "the substance of independence" by meeting eleven demands. These were for total
prohibition of alcohol, revision of the rupee exchange rate, a
fifty percent reduction in land taxes, abolition of the salt tax, a
reduction of at least fifty percent in military expenditures, a
similar slash in salaries of civil servants, a protective tariff
against imported cloth, a bill giving preferential status to India
shipping, release of all political prisoners not condemned for
murder or attempted murder, abolition or control of the Crim-

inal Investigation Department and issue of firearms for self-defense, under popular control.

Jawaharlal and Gandhi had parted ways before, and would again. "You are going too fast," Gandhi chided. "You should have taken time to think. I do not mind your hasty acts as much as I mind your encouraging mischief-makers and hooligans." On another occasion: "The differences between you and me appear so vast and so radical that there seems to be no meeting ground between us." A meeting ground had been found. But to the Nehru family circle, Jawaharlal said Gandhi's miscellany was a jumble that had nothing whatever to do with independence. He could not in conscience support the Eleven Points.

The salt tax, Gandhi declared, was most burdensome on the poor, "for salt is the one thing they must eat more than the rich," and "The tax constitutes therefore the most inhuman poll tax the ingenuity of man can devise." In a letter to Lord Irwin, addressing him as "Dear Friend," Gandhi pointed out that the Viceroy's salary was twenty-one thousand rupees per month, while the average income of his Indian subjects was a quarter of a rupee per day. Lord Irwin failed to see what this had to do with the case.

"If you cannot see your way to deal with these evils," Gandhi wrote, "on the eleventh day of this month I shall proceed with such workers as I can take, to disregard the provisions of the salt laws. It is, I know, open to you to frustrate my design by arresting me. I hope that there will be tens of thousands ready, in a disciplined manner, to take up the work after me, and, in the act of disobeying the salt act, to lay themselves open to the penalties of a law that should never have disfigured the statute book."

Lord Irwin, it was reported, prayed after reading this. Whatever guidance he received, his formal answer went no farther than a statement of regret that Gandhi contemplated "a course of action which is clearly bound to involve violation of the law, and danger to the public peace." In effect, he thus made salt the catalytic agent of revolt.

Just after sunrise on March 12, 1930, Gandhi and seventy-eight followers set out from the Sabarmati Ashram near Ahmedabad, for the seaside village of Dandi two hundred and forty-one miles away. He carried a lacquered bamboo staff, an inch thick, fifty-four inches long. A horse was offered, but he refused to ride. Young people in his following lagged, complaining he walked too fast. "The modern generation," he said, "is delicate, weak and much pampered." In every village, recruits joined a column that to British authorities had the look of an army.

Motilal and Jawaharlal, homeward bound from a Congress session, met Gandhi and the salt-marchers at Jambusar. Gandhi said "We are marching in the Name of God." They walked and talked with him for some time, then resumed their journey to Allahabad, where there was Congress paper work to be done. "I wanted to go with him," Jawaharlal said, "marching along as he was, staff in hand, like a shepherd with his flock, with firm step and a peaceful but undaunted look." It would be a matter of regret always, for him and for Vijaya Lakshmi Pandit, that they were not with Gandhi when he reached the sea, and "made salt" against the law by picking up a crude lump cast up on the beach near Dandi.

As he did this, Mrs. Sarojini Naidu cried, "Hail, Deliverer!" The symbolic salt was auctioned to the highest bidder, for sixteen hundred rupees, or about as much as Lord Irwin earned in two days; the money went to feed the hungry. Expecting arrest, Gandhi named a Muslim, Abbas Tyabji, to succeed him. Should Tyabji be arrested in his turn, Mrs. Naidu would succeed. This was the first appointment of a woman to command in the independence struggle.

Arrest of Gandhi was delayed, but on April 14, in Allahabad, the Nehrus were wakened by police who came to arrest Jawaharlal. He was sentenced to his fourth term in prison, having been at liberty not quite seven years. He named his father to replace him as Congress president. Aging and ill, Motilal hid his illness, accepting burdens beyond his strength.

The night of May 5, 1930, Gandhi was roused from sleep and taken to jail. Tyabji was arrested. Sarojini Naidu led, when two thousand five hundred volunteers, including many women, marched to the Dharsana Salt Works, a hundred and fifty miles north of Bombay. She warned her followers they would be beaten. "But you must not resist; you must not even raise a hand or ward off a blow." American correspondents reported what transpired, without pointing out, as Indian observers did, that the Dharsana Confrontation had certain elements of the American Battle of Lexington and the shot heard 'round the world.

Four hundred Surat policemen, commanded by six British officers, halted the salt-marchers, "then rushed at them raining blows with steel-shod *lathis*." Men and women "simply walked on until they were struck down." Police "commenced savagely kicking fallen men in the abdomen and testicles." A

British officer seized Sarojini Naidu's arm. "You are under arrest." She shook off his hand. "I will come, but don't touch me." Her dignity affronted him. "Don't try the 'lady' on me!"

What she had tried in fact changed India's history. "Women left their sheltered homes in thousands and took their place beside their menfolk. Many hundreds were arrested and imprisoned. From this period derives the spirit of emancipation and equality which henceforth was increasingly to insure feminine progress in India." Foremost in the fray were the Nehru women, led by Vijaya Lakshmi Pandit.

9.

There was no more waiting in shadows. Only Aunt Bibi Amma remained a captive of tradition. Vijaya Lakshmi, Kamala, Krishna, and then Swaruprani, went into the streets to picket foreign cloth shops. Vijaya Lakshmi and Krishna shocked their mother by wearing trousers instead of *saris*. These were more practical and comfortable, they said, when they lay down across a doorway so people would not enter and buy British goods. Kamala insisted on going with them.

Motilal shuddered and muttered, but did nothing to impede his womenfolk. Like India, like the Raj, he saw a force unfettered, whose pent up strength no man had realized. His son was equally amazed and proud, when news reached him in prison that Kamala was in the thick of action at Allahabad. "She made up for inexperience with her fire and energy, and within a few months became the pride of Allahabad."

His daughter, too, was in the streets, leading the Monkey

Brigade. "I wanted to be a member of Congress," Mrs. Indira Gandhi recalled, when at forty-nine she became Prime Minister of the Republic of India. At twelve, "The Congress turned me down. They said I would have to be eighteen or twenty-one, or something like that. So I said, 'I'll have an organization of my own.' My father didn't even know about it until everything was arranged."

The *Ramayana* tells how Sita, Rama's wife, was abducted by the King of Ceylon. Rama could not cross from India to rescue her, until the King of the Monkeys came to his aid. Monkeys built a bridge, which Rama crossed to victory. "I suppose in some ways we really behaved like monkeys." So it must have seemed to the British and their police, for the real work of the Monkey Brigade was unsuspected.

"We didn't have loudspeakers, so I'd shout a sentence, and others would relay it. We wrote notices, addressed envelopes, made flags, took water to marchers, carried messages." Police surrounding a suspected house paid no heed to urchins at play. "A boy would memorize a message, that would be passed along from child to child until it reached its destination. The police would talk about when there'd be a raid, who was about to be arrested. Children playing hopscotch nearby were ignored. They'd get the news to the people concerned."

Nayantara Pandit, Tara to her family, was three, and there was chocolate cake for tea, when police came to arrest her father. Chandralekha, Lekha at home, was six. Rita was in her crib. Their mother quieted them. Their father, she said, was glad to go to prison. "Arrest was to be voluntarily courted and imprisonment gladly accepted. It was not an evil to be reluctantly borne. It was accompanied by a great deal of laughter and mutual back slapping. It made friends of total strangers, Spartans of soft-living comfort-lovers."

As long ago as Rita can remember, "We were brought up to feel that freedom was one's undeniable right, and responsible people should take action to achieve it. Going to jail was most acceptable." That it could be as acceptable to India's women as to their men, even welcomed and courted by them, was something realized too late by those most adamant against revision of the *status quo,* who thought the rising tide could be halted if they made war on women.

Purdah came to India with the conquering Muslims. Increasingly over the centuries, Muslim example plus their own religion's orthodoxy enlarged the army of Hindu women who lived secluded from a world ruled by men. There was bitter truth in Katherine Mayo's allegation in *Mother India,* that "By sheer force of a vicious custom, even the most ignorant and worthless men have been enjoying a superiority over women which they do not deserve and ought not to have."

The very poor could not afford seclusion; women did men's work, equally with their menfolk, lest they and their children starve. The very rich proved their wealth by observing *purdah* when it was convenient. Between low and high, there were many millions of women who accepted existence in curtained privacy as religiously as Swaruprani Nehru and Aunt Bibi Amma. It is one of the ironies of British history in India, that in a space of months the Raj succeeded in erasing forever a custom that had enchained India's women since before Boadicea.

Processions only of women marched in cities, towns and along back-country roads. Leaving their homes in thousands, they put themselves in the forefront where police and soldiers blocked the line of march. Kamaladevi Chattopadhyay, in 1966 director of the All-India Handicrafts Board which continues Gandhi's cottage industries, is said to have rallied women to join her, interposing between men surrounding Gandhi, and British cavalry about to ride them down, with the unflamboyant remark: "It is harder to murder women than men." Ordered to charge, British troopers refused to obey; and Kamaladevi was, and is, a national heroine.

"Generally," Jawaharlal Nehru said in his *Discovery of India*, "the attitude of the women was more unyielding than that of the men." There was cause for this, that Vijaya Lakshmi Pandit understood, although when her brother explained it he referred to a rule from which she was the exception. "They came mostly from the middle class, accustomed to a comfortable, sheltered life, but suffering from the many repressions produced by a society dominated to his own advantage by men. The call of freedom therefore had a double meaning to them. The enthusiasm and energy with which they threw themselves into the struggle had their springs no doubt in the vague and hardly conscious, yet nonetheless intense, desire to rid themselves also of domestic slavery."

The Nehru women had never suffered domestic slavery. No tradition trammeled them. With no need to strive for escape, their dedication was quite truly for the sake of others, not for their own. This did not lessen their sacrifice. Vijaya Lakshmi was helping her father with Congress letters, when the police came for him. "Aren't you a little late in arriving?" he asked. "I've been expecting your call for weeks." When he was led away, Swaruprani Nehru stood tearless, her palms pressed together in the gesture signifying "We are as one."

He was put in a cell with his son and son-in-law. Prison officials offered special privileges, but although he was sixty-nine and afflicted by heart trouble aggravated by asthma, he would accept no favors, and commanded Jawaharlal and Ranjit Pandit to say nothing about his failing health when the Nehru women were allowed to visit them.

Rita Pandit was wide-eyed in her mother's arms. Lekha Pandit led small Tara by the hand. Swaruprani Nehru, coming from a sickbed, walked with smiling steadiness. Indira hid concern for her mother. Kamala Nehru, too, insisted nothing should be said about her worsening illness. They found the men they loved shut in a stifling-hot little shed, set in the center of a circular enclosure a hundred feet in diameter, ringed by guarded walls fifteen feet high. Prison officials had kept their pets there until more room was needed for political prisoners. The place reeked. It was called the Khuttaghar, the House for Dogs.

Motilal, Jawaharlal and Ranjit Pandit were determinedly gay and casual. They had planted flowers outside the door, and obtained permission to sleep in the open, under guard. Ranjit had improvised a miniature golf-course. The three prisoners talked loudly. Still their womenfolk could hear voices from beyond the wall. In the prison's quarters for women, woman warders shouted and cursed at imprisoned women, some of whom the Nehru women knew.

Arrest of women continued. According to Frank Moraes, Jawaharlal Nehru's biographer, the Raj "took a perverse pleasure in making conditions of jail life for women political prisoners unduly harsh. Girls of 15 or 16 were often sentenced to two years' rigorous imprisonment for merely shouting slogans or gathering in assembly." Ordinances invoked by local authorities included one providing for punishment of parents or guardians, if their children or wards took part in demonstrations. Still women and their children paraded together, waving Congress flags, inviting arrest. Women in *saris* dyed saffron, the color of sacrifice, picketed British shops.

On August 13, Vijaya Lakshmi learned and told the others at Anand Bhavan that Motilal and Jawaharlal had been taken under guard from Naini Jail to a place near Poona, to confer with Gandhi regarding Lord Irwin's offer to discuss a truce. Then word came that their men had joined with Gandhi in refusing to meet with the Viceroy except on preconditions: acceptance of Gandhi's Eleven Points, and confirmation of India's right to secede from the Empire. They were taken back to Naini Jail. But suddenly, the Raj decided to be kind.

Motilal was released, "in consideration of his age and physical condition." A month later, having served his six months' sentence, Jawaharlal was freed, under warning: *Go and sin no more.* Ranjit, remaining in prison, sent word to Vijaya Lakshmi that he was enjoying opportunity to complete a translation, long laid aside, of a set of love poems in Sanskrit. "My version will be addressed to you."

With their daughters, she joined Jawaharlal, Kamala and Indira at Mussoorie in the hills, where Motilal recuperated, nursed by Swaruprani. Women's voices and children's laughter eased Jawaharlal's prison-tautened nerves. With Indira, Lekha and Tara, he play-marched in flowering gardens. Lekha carried a Congress flag, and led in singing the Congress song, *Jhanda uncha rahe hamara:* Keep our flag flying high.

His sister hummed along with the singers, lulling Rita to

sleep. "I was careful not to sing out loud, for fear of spoiling the harmony." Seeing Lekha play-act, as she had at the same age when she imagined herself as Jhansi-ki-Rani, she feared for her children, growing up in a time when even little girls were punished for loving the dream of freedom. But decision about their future was postponed, while their father remained in prison.

Holiday for Jawaharlal was brief. With Kamala, he started back to Anand Bhavan. Three times en route, their car was stopped by police officials. Each in turn served orders issued under the Criminal Procedure Code, forbidding him to speak in public. But two thousand peasants awaited him in Allahabad. He spoke, urging them not to pay taxes while the civil disobedience campaign continued. That evening, accompanied by Kamala, he went to repeat this speech to a larger crowd.

His father and mother and sisters and Indira, returned from Mussoorie by train, awaited his homecoming. Within sight of Anand Bhavan, his car was stopped by police. Kamala was permitted to proceed. He was taken back to Naini Jail. He had been at liberty eight days. When Kamala and Vijaya Lakshmi told Motilal the news, he sat with head bowed for a long moment. Then he straightened. "I am going to be well, and do a man's work!" Then he was on his feet, an old lion roaring bravely.

Jawaharlal's forty-first birthday was only three weeks off. Motilal called for public readings, on November 14, of the speech that led to his arrest. For listening, more than five thousand men and women were arrested. They went to jail singing the Congress song. Some were flogged. Learning of this in their cell, Jawaharlal and Ranjit Pandit fasted in protest, for seventy-two hours. The floggings stopped.

On New Year's Day, 1931, Vijaya Lakshmi told her father Kamala had been arrested. "She said, 'I am happy and proud to follow in the footsteps of my husband.'" Concern for her, the first of the Nehru women to be jailed, sent Motilal to tell his son they must find some way to arrange her release and prevent its repetition. "He seemed unaware of the dismay his own appearance caused. His once-erect frame was shriveled and bent. He had aged shockingly. Yet he insisted he was per-fectly well."

At Anand Bhavan, Vijaya Lakshmi told him Lord Irwin had ordered release of Gandhi and members of the Congress working committee. Soon Kamala, Jawaharlal and Ranjit Pan-dit were freed. They hurried to Motilal's bedside. So did Gandhi. "I wish," he told them, "that I could die in an India that is free." They attempted reassurance, but he said, "I shall not be here to see *Swaraj*."

Doctors decided he must be taken to a hospital in Lucknow for X-ray treatment. He protested. "I would rather die here where I have known so much happiness." Only to please Gandhi, with whom he once contended for his son, he con-sented to go to Lucknow. There, on February 6, 1931, while he slept, he died.

He was wrapped in the Congress flag. Ranjit Pandit and Hari the Untouchable drove the car in which he was taken home to Anand Bhavan. Jawaharlal sat beside his bier. Along the Ganges river bank, where he lay in state, a great throng passed silently. At dusk, Jawaharlal lighted his funeral pyre. "The stars were out and shining brightly when we returned lonely and desolate."

10.

The lamp in the corner said "Light me." Very soon, an observer said of Vijaya Lakshmi Pandit: "She little realizes the degree to which her father lives on in her." At Karachi, entering Congress politics for the first time, she spoke in Gandhi's behalf.

He came to the annual Congress session under a cloud. In meetings with the Viceroy, at which her brother was not present, he had reduced his Eleven Points to six: amnesty for all political prisoners, cessation of repressive persecution, restitution of confiscated property, reinstatement of civil servants dismissed for *Swaraj* activities, revocation of the Salt Monopoly Act and the ban on picketing foreign shops, and official inquiry into allegations of police brutality.

"I have, believe me," he assured her brother, "surrendered nothing vital. There is no loss of principle involved." Jawaharlal disagreed, and events confirmed his doubt. Authorities found a loophole in the Gandhi-Irwin agreement. Amnesty, they decided, did not extend to prisoners against whom no formal charges had been lodged. One of these, Bhagat Singh, an activist Jawaharlal knew and respected though his record put him outside the Congress pale, was hanged. "The corpse of Bhagat Singh," he told Gandhi, "will stand between us and England."

In England, Winston Churchill, campaigning for election to the House of Commons, told the West Essex Conservative Association, "It is alarming and nauseating to see Mr. Gandhi, a seditious Middle Temple lawyer, now posing as a *fakir* of a type well known in the East, striding half-naked up the steps of the Viceregal palace in India, while he is still organizing and conducting a defiant campaign of civil disobedience, to parley on equal terms with the representative of the King-Emperor."

In India, Gandhi's leadership touched nadir. Arriving at Karachi, he faced black-flag demonstrators chanting, "Go back, Gandhi! Your truce has sent Bhagat Singh to the gallows!" He addressed fifty thousand Hindus, Muslims and Sikhs. There were no shouts of *Mahatma ki jai!* Undeterred, he put before the Congress a resolution pledging abolition of Untouchability. The millions who had been called Untouchables, he said, must henceforth be called *Harijans*, Children of God.

Orthodox Hindu delegates said, "Now he has gone too far!" Intellectuals complained, "We are trying to put a nation together, and Gandhi tells us liberating Untouchables from cleaning latrines is more important than independence for India!" Jawaharlal said, "Your way of springing surprises on us frightens me." But Vijaya Lakshmi went among peasants from the villages, saying she believed abolition of Untouchability was right and just. When they voted, the commitment closest to Gandhi's heart was won, though by a narrow margin.

"The Karachi conference," said the *Central Press,* "ends as an even greater personal triumph for Gandhi than any previous Congress has seen." Vijaya Lakshmi Pandit claimed no credit. But Gandhi said, "You cannot stop now"; and Ranjit Pandit said, "Gandhiji is right." He, not she, decided that Lekha, now seven, should be sent away to school at Poona, and Tara, four, and Rita, two, should go with Lekha, so their mother could be free to work full-time for the Congress. She protested. Nothing mattered as much as being with her children. But Lekha voted with her father.

"Don't worry, Mummie," she said. "We'll be all right. I'll look after Lekha and the baby." When the three little girls boarded the train, Lekha unfurled her Congress flag. "It's to keep the police away!" Watching them carried out of sight, their mother wondered when she would see them again. The odds were that it could not be soon.

A new Viceroy, Lord Willingdon, replaced Lord Irwin. He frankly loathed the Congress, and called Gandhi "that little man." Under his hard-line policy, eighty thousand were jailed, while Hindu-Muslim separatism was encouraged. Two Muslim leaders, Khan Abdul Gaffar Khan and Dr. M. A. Ansari, Kamala Nehru's physician, joined Jawaharlal and Gandhi in attempting to dissuade him from what they believed was an invitation to massacre. He was coldly polite, but unconvinced.

Three British magistrates were killed in East Bengal, where terrorist shootings were followed by Hindu-Muslim rioting. In a political prison camp near Calcutta, Muslim guards fired on Hindu *detenus,* killing several. Gandhi, departing for the London Round Table Conference, said, "I go with God as my only guide," and learned in London that British strategy centered on a scheme to let Muslims vote only for Muslims, Hindus only for Hindus. Jawaharlal spoke out against this. So did his sister.

At Allahabad, Jawaharlal was served with orders fobidding him to attend public meetings, write anything that might be published or circulated or to travel outside the municipal limits. He told his sister and then informed the district magistrate that he would spend Christmas Day at Anand Bhavan, but would leave the following morning for Bombay, where Kamala lay bedridden.

The authorities saw subterfuge in this. Gandhi, they knew, would reach Bombay from England on New Year's Day. On Boxing Day, December 26, British police took Jawaharlal from the Bombay train, and back to Naini Jail. They handled him roughly, complaining that because of him they were kept from being at home exchanging gifts with their families. He was arraigned on January 4, 1932. The same day, Gandhi and Vallabhbhai Patel were arrested, to be held without trial under an 1827 ordinance just resurrected. It would be invoked against many more.

At Anand Bhavan, Swaruprani Nehru joined her daughters and Kamala and Indira in preparing and sending out leaflets bearing Gandhi's message from prison. "Infinite is God's mercy. Never swerve from truth and nonviolence, never turn your back, and sacrifice your lives and all to win *Swaraj*." Not even Indira let tears show in her eyes, when word came that her father had been sentenced to two years' rigorous imprisonment, plus six months to cover the fine he refused to pay.

A letter from him said, "We live in an upside down world, and it's no use expecting life to be easy. It is not a simple matter adjusting to such a world, especially for those who are sensitive. It is not normal for most of us, to spend our lives in prison cut off from our families and dear ones. It certainly should not be normal for intelligent human beings to spend all their time and energy killing each other off. It isn't normal either for some people to starve and others to get indigestion from overeating. All this is very abnormal and wrong, but it is happening."

His letters were read and reread. His sister collated them in sequence. "Our age," one said, "is an age of disillusion, of doubt and uncertainty and questioning. We can no longer accept many of the ancient beliefs and customs; we have no more faith in them, in Asia or in Europe or America. So we search for new ways . . . Sometimes the injustice, the unhappiness, the brutality of the world oppress us and darken our minds, and we see no way out. And yet if we take such a dismal view we have not learned aright the lesson of life or of history. For history teaches us of growth and progress and of the possibility of an infinite advance for man." He might well have added, "and for women."

All the Nehru women were in the fight. Kamala, ill and shaken by fever, went into the streets night after night to join demonstration marches. A family friend found her at the head of a column halted by police, and brought her a blanket against the damp cold. Returning an hour later, the friend found her shivering in her thin *sari*. She had wrapped the blanket around an old woman of the Untouchables, who stood beside her.

Swaruprani Nehru marched beside Kamala and her daughters, while Indira mustered her Monkey Brigade. Word

spread: "Motilal Nehru's widow leads. Come follow her."
Vijaya Lakshmi and Krishna were served with orders to stay at
home, and keep their mother with them, for a month, or face
arrest. They went ahead with arrangements for celebration of
Independence Day, January 26. A Congress leader should preside. But all the Congress leaders were in jail. Their mother
said "I will preside."

Neither they nor Indira nor Aunt Bibi Amma could dissuade her. She had never faced an audience. They prayed for
her, until they realized she held the crowd and the watching
police enthralled. Speaking softly as she always did, she told
how Motilal Nehru said while he lay dying "I wish I could
die in an India that is free." She told women in the throng
"None of us may live to see India truly free. But what we do
may win freedom for our children."

When she finished, there was no sound but womens' whis-
pering. The watching police made no move. But next morning
they came for Vijaya Lakshmi and Krishna. Women political
prisoners were allowed to take nothing more to jail than six
saris and some underclothing. They were packed and ready.
As the police van took them away, their mother and Indira
pressed palms together in the gesture signifying "We are as
one."

11.

Voltaire has noted that in Europe's Dark Ages, "it was a
great consolation to find in the cloisters a secure retreat against
tyranny; there was hardly a monastery which did not contain
admirable beings who did honor to human nature." This

could have been written regarding men and women imprisoned in India. By the fact of being jailed, India's women proved to their men and to themselves that they could bear an equal load. Men and women could not share in political action, then in enduring prison, without a breakdown of caste divisions. United resistance to foreign rule negated orthodoxy's restrictions imposed on women; brotherhood and sisterhood, and Untouchability, could not exist side by side.

From his cell, Jawaharlal wrote, "A small *purdanashin* gathering of women assembled to meet my wife. Apparently she addressed them. Probably she spoke of woman's struggle for freedom against man-made laws and customs (a favorite topic of hers) and urged the women not to be too submissive to their menfolk. There was an interesting sequel to this. A distracted husband wrote to Kamala and said that since her visit, his wife had behaved strangely. She would not listen to him and fall in with his wishes as she used to, but would argue with him and even adopt an aggressive attitude." In their prison, Vijaya Lakshmi and Krishna began to learn of a new kind of *purdanashin*.

They were weighed. Their suitcases were inspected. There were no women's quarters, only a walled yard in which political prisoners were jumbled together with seasoned criminals of all kinds. Entering the yard, the sisters were greeted by women who had marched beside them a few days before. Their tiny cell was shared with two women whose sins had no connection with politics. It was filthy. Vermin crawled everywhere. Firmly, Vijaya Lakshmi took charge of housecleaning. The scarlet ladies giggled, then sobered and joined lustily in sweeping and scrubbing.

The Nehru sisters waited three weeks for their trial. During that time they developed lasting friendships. "What does it matter if she does have a squint?" Vijaya Lakshmi Pandit demanded years later regarding a veteran of the *bagnios,* who said she had reformed and asked for honest employment. "She was with me in jail." She and her younger sister heard appalling tales, some of which were true. A vista opened, that sickened and saddened her. "Something has got to be done," she said. What that might be, how it might be accomplished, she did not pretend to know.

On the first visiting day, their mother arrived in a rented *tonga,* a rattletrap two-wheeled cart. Police had confiscated Jawaharlal's automobile, and Ranjit Pandit's, to cover fines they would not pay. Swaruprani brought delicacies from Anand Bhavan, which Aunt Bibi Amma had helped her prepare. Her daughters asked if she minded if they divided these with their cell-mates. She said, "Of course not. Next time I'll bring more," and presided daintily at an impromptu picnic.

They told her they had decided to refuse to take any part in their trial, or allow anyone to plead for them. She approved. With Indira, in the courtroom, she watched proudly while they faced the British magistrate and were sentenced to "one year of rigorous imprisonment." When she came to see them next visiting day, she was brusquely dismissed by guards. Vijaya Lakshmi and Krishna were gone, and for some days no one would tell her what had become of them.

They had been hauled off, with six other women, to Lucknow. There they were told they would be locked in unheated cells from 5 P. M. to 5 A. M. They could write only one letter every two weeks, and it would, of course, be censored. Before they could write to their mother, she appeared, having traveled six hours by train. She had never traveled alone before, but said everyone was kind to her.

Her sari was *khadi,* and white, the color of mourning, but she smiled brightly. She brought flowers, and good news. Women, she said, were now taking the lead in Congress work, replacing their menfolk away in prison. There were great plans for National Week. She could stay with them only a little while. She must hurry back to Allahabad, where she was chairman of an organizing committee.

They watched her leave, and prayed for her. In a few days, the prison grapevine brought a report that in a police *lathi* charge, she had been beaten and badly hurt. Rumor said she was dying. But on Visiting Day, she entered their cell, again bringing flowers; smiling, gently indomitable. She said matter-of-factly that Aunt Bibi Amma had said she should stay at home, "but of course I didn't."

She had taken her place where, of course, a Nehru should be, at the head of a procession. It moved along, until police barred the way. Someone brought a chair from a nearby house, and urged her to sit down and rest. Police arrested several men and women around her, but "They wouldn't arrest me." Then, suddenly, the police charged, flailing with ironshod *lathis.* She was knocked to the pavement, and beaten with heavy canes. She lost consciousness. When the street was cleared, a British officer found her lying in a ditch.

"He used to come to have dinner with your father, and tell English jokes. He recognized me, and insisted on taking me home in his car, though I would much rather have walked."

Jawaharlal learned what had happened days later, from a weekly newspaper, the only reading matter allowed to him in Naini Jail. "The thought of my frail old mother lying bleeding in the road obsessed me, and I wondered how I would have behaved if I had been there."

A month passed before, still bruised and bandaged, she was well enough to visit him. As she had done with her daughters, she did with her son: calmly refusing to promise she would not risk herself again, commanding, "Take care of yourself and I will take care of me." He said helplessly, "The weight of my imprisonments is not mine. It is borne by my mother, my wife, my sisters."

In Lucknow Jail, while eleven months dragged by, his sisters formed and taught classes in reading, writing and sewing. Most of their pupils were under sentence for criminal offenses. Some were Untouchables, who put up unfriendliness as a barrier against the Brahmin ladies. "It was a good education in patience, getting them to accept us, and in learning that what is well-meant is not necessarily welcomed."

In Naini Jail, their brother realized his health was deteriorating, and set about improving it. Kashmiri Brahmins, unlike others of their faith and caste, ate beef. Motilal Nehru had been a hearty trencherman. His son, contrarily, had no great fondness for meat. Now he became almost a vegetarian. He gave up smoking, and devised a regimen of exercises.

"One that pleased me particularly was the *shirshasana*: standing on one's head with palms of the hands, fingers interlocked, supporting the back of the head; elbows on the floor; body vertical, upside down. I suppose physically this exercise is very good; I liked it even more for its psychological effect. The slightly comic position increased my good humor and made me a little more tolerant of life's vagaries."

Twenty-eight years later, in his private rooms in the Prime Minister's House in New Delhi, he still stood on his head each morning, regarding his reflection in a full-length mirror. "I find it is good for my soul. It reminds me to laugh at myself occasionally. I might add that I have always had a horror of people who are inescapably and unchangingly sane and sober."

It was not easy to be anything but sane and sober, to the point of angry frustration, in solitary confinement. "The British," he said later, "are a subtle people, in some ways. They knew I am incurably gregarious. They let me have someone to talk to only on rare visiting days. If I cannot talk, I write. They limited my ink and paper." Twenty-two years from this time, an American editor who asked him to contribute an article to a collection titled *Perspective of India* reported "He replied, 'Do you want me to go to jail?' 'Of course not!' I said. 'But what do you mean?' 'The only time I have to write,' he said, 'is when I am in jail.' "

In Naini Jail in 1930, despite his jailers, he put together one page at a time of what may be the longest-remembered of his several books. For three years, he wrote letters to his daughter that were at the same time fatherly guidance, philosophical dissertation and a history of the world as seen from a prison cell in India. The first was headed *For Indira Priyadarshini on Her Thirteenth Birthday,* and began "On your birthday you have been in the habit of receiving presents and good wishes. Good wishes you will still have in full measure, but what present can I send you from Naini Prison? My presents cannot be very material or solid. They can only be of the air and of the mind and spirit." This letter ended "Goodbye, little one, and may you grow up to be a brave soldier in India's service."

What he wrote was beyond the ken of his jailers, who let his letters pass uncensored. It had great meaning to his daughter, and to his sister. V. K. Krishna Menon, who otherwise accorded scant praise to Vijaya Lakshmi Pandit, wrote in 1939 that it was she who collated the letters and arranged for their publication, in 1934, as *Glimpses of World History*. Implicit throughout is a theme summed up in the last of his letters. "The past is past and done with; we cannot change it; the future is yet to come, and perhaps we may be able to shape it a little."

At Anand Bhavan, Vijaya Lakshmi did the best she could to progress her brother's hope. Meanwhile he was moved from Naini Jail to Bareilly Prison, then to another prison at Dehra Dun in the Himalayan foothills. There his cell's barred window framed a panorama of unreachable snow-crowned peaks. He recalled his honeymoon with Kamala in Kashmir. Now tuberculosis had ravaged her bright young beauty; she was under treatment at Calcutta; she had given so much, and been given so little.

"All of us," he wrote, "have our choice of living in the valleys below, with their unhealthy mists and fogs, but giving a measure of bodily security; or of climbing the high mountains, with risk and danger for companions, to breathe the pure air above, and take joy in the distant views, and welcome the rising sun."

12.

Swaruprani Nehru and Indira went to visit Ranjit Pandit in the Allahabad District Jail. They were insulted and turned away. His sisters, in their prison, were ill-fed and granted no medical attention. Krishna contracted malaria. There was no medicine. But suddenly they were informed they would be released next day. "Time off for good behavior, and from now on you'd better watch your P's and Q's!" Guards escorted them to Allahabad, and set them free on the railway station platform.

Hurrying to Anand Bhavan, they found their father's Home of Joy dark and apparently deserted. Then Hari the Untouchable—now by grace of Gandhi and assistance from Vijaya Lakshmi a Child of God—came scurrying out of the night, to tell them their mother had gone to Calcutta, to be with Kamala. There would be no Calcutta train until tomorrow. They entered what had been their father's Little England. All that remained was echoing emptiness.

Motilal Nehru's Home of Joy, which he ceded to the Congress, and Jawaharlal's house as well, had been sequestrated by the Raj. The plan was to sell these properties to satisfy levies imposed on father and son. However some clerk stumbled on a record showing Jawaharlal had inherited some railroad shares. These were seized, along with his automobile and Ranjit Pandit's. These seizures satisfied the Raj, but not its servants.

Motilal Nehru's once *pukka* British drawing room had been stripped from ceiling to floor. "The police took the carpet," Hari said. It was Persian, fine enough for a museum. "They took it away and sold it. They said it was to pay the fine. They have come many times to take many things. They always say it is to pay the fine."

Twenty-one years afterward, Her Excellency Madame Vijaya Lakshmi Pandit, High Commissioner of India to the United Kingdom, dined in stately English homes whose owners showed her Persian carpets, Tibetan screens, priceless Gandhara sculptures, which they said happily were purchased for a penny to the pound, from dealers in Indian objets d'art. She was too much the diplomat, by then, to mention that their cheap-bought treasures were loot from Anand Bhavan.

In 1933, she brought her mother and Kamala home to Allahabad, got them settled, then went to see her daughters at Poona. Together for the first time in months, mother and daughters were determinedly gay; but realization hung over them that no next meeting could be planned with any surety. She told them "It will be a bit lonely sometimes, but if you remember there is a war on, and how many little girls and boys have had to leave their parents, you won't mind."

Before she left them, to return to Allahabad, she said again, "Soon we shall be home again." Shrugging off aching loneliness, she began bringing Congress paper work up to date. Then Krishna told her, "I met a man in Bombay and we're in love and want to be married." Customarily, their brother should have been the one to be consulted, as head of the family; but consulting him was impossible. Prison security regulations had been tightened. The *Swaraj* crusade was in another crisis stage. Jawaharlal, Gandhi and all other Congress leaders were involved.

Since 1909, the Raj had divided Hindus and Muslims in

separate electoral blocs. Now Gandhi's resolution pledging abolition of Untouchability was turned into a weapon against the Congress. The Raj proposed to create a third bloc, wholly of Untouchables. This meant in effect that Untouchability would be perpetuated. The move could wreck Congress solidarity; for orthodox Hindus might welcome it, and in so doing, repudiate the Gandhian program.

Gandhi said, "If this is done, I must fast unto death." This invoked a last resort as old as India. Sitting *dharna,* fasting to protest injustice or to prove a point, calls for starving on a wrongdoer's doorstep, until the wrong is righted, or death frees the faster and brands his enemy a murderer. Quite calmly, Gandhi made it clear that he would win or die. On the fifth day of his fast, he collapsed. On the sixth, British authorities released him unconditionally, and tabled the plan to separate Untouchables from Congress. Jawaharlal had said, "I felt annoyed with him for choosing a side issue for his final sacrifice." Now he told Vijaya Lakshmi, "Once more, Gandhi has sensed what would save the Congress." Then they heard that their mother had gone alone into a marketplace, and in deliberate violation of Brahmin orthodoxy, voluntarily accepted food from the hands of an Untouchable.

No act of abnegation by anyone in India could have done more for Gandhi's cause. Immediately, everywhere, orthodox Hindu women followed Swaruprani Nehru's example. In large religious gatherings, Hindus signed the Yeravda Pact. "No man shall be regarded as an Untouchable by reason of his birth." There was celebration across the subcontinent, but not at Anand Bhavan. There, suddenly, Swaruprani fell and lay still.

Doctors said she had suffered a stroke, and must be taken to a hospital. She insisted, "I will stay here with my children." She tried to rise and stand. "Though her body was frail," Krishna wrote in tribute, "her heart was as proud and strong as that of a lioness." Still she failed rapidly until, twelve days before expiration of his two-year sentence, Jawaharlal was released to go to her bedside.

He would be at liberty only five months and thirteen days; but his presence prolonged her life. She was taken home. Kamala returned from Calcutta. She said she was much better. Indira returned from Rabindranath Tagore's school at Santiniketan near Calcutta. Again, for a while, the Nehrus were a family.

Krishna Nehru's chosen husband came from Bombay. He was Oxford-educated, a Gujerati from Gandhi's province, Kathiawar. Gandhi knew his family. Marriage between Gujerati and Kashmiri Brahmin required only registration and a brief civil ceremony. All was over, and Krishna, now Krishna Hutheesing, had gone to live in Bombay, before Aunt Bibi Amma realized that even a wedding was no longer what it had been when she was young and lived in the world.

She was not alone in realizing that nothing was as it had been. For the first time in their lives, Jawaharlal, at forty-four, and Vijaya Lakshmi, now thirty-three, found themselves discussing money, need for it, and its lack. This might be incredible, in any other family. It was the case at Anand Bhavan because of Motilal Nehru's early decision that no matter what Jawaharlal did, neither he nor his dependents should ever want for anything. But his income stopped, while spending continued. Levies and losses had eaten away the bulk of the estate he left.

Ranjit Pandit's holdings were subject to control by his elder brother, as head of the Pandit family. In any event, neither Jawaharlal nor Vijaya Lakshmi considered seeking help outside their own clan. Nor would either have touched Congress funds, which in fact their contributions continued to enlarge. She said she could and would manage household expenses more carefully. He went to talk with Kamala.

"We decided to sell off my wife's jewelry, the silver and other similar articles that we possessed, as well as many cartloads of odds and ends. My wife did not like the idea of parting with her jewelry, although she had not worn any of it for years and it had lain in the bank. She had looked forward to handing it to our daughter."

What had to be done was done, and no one outside the Nehru circle knew of it. But Jawaharlal brooded. He was tired, disheartened, unsure that he had the right to forget a man's first obligation: the support and care of those he loved, who loved and relied on him. He felt that Gandhi was increasingly illogical. He had gone on pilgrimage, preaching against Untouchability. Meanwhile Congress fainthearts deserted, and even stalwarts said, "A hundred thousand jailed, and for what gain?"

It was years since she was Little Daughter, and listened in puzzled awe while he read incomprehensible poetry. Now he quoted Swinburne and Vijaya Lakshmi understood.

> These many years since we began to be
> What have the gods done with us? What with me,
> What with my love? They have shown us fates and fears,
> Harsh springs and fountains bitterer than tears,
> Grief a fixed star, and joy a vane that veers,
> These many years . . .

13.

Suddenly one morning, Allahabad trembled. Floors cracked and tiles fell from the roof at Anand Bhavan. The cause was an earthquake in distant Bihar, where disaster covered an area of thirty thousand square miles, with a population of ten million. Introspection ended, for Jawaharlal. While his sister worked with the Allahabad Earthquake Relief Committee, he went to Bihar, and almost immediately courted arrest by denouncing British authorities for their slowness in aiding homeless victims.

"To be called inefficient and wanting in nerve struck at the very root of their self-esteem, and disturbed the messianic delusions of English officials in India," he told his sister. "But it produced results." For himself, he seized a shovel and began to dig, inspiring others whose dignity had held them back from dirtying their hands. Meanwhile he challenged Gandhi's proclamation that the earthquake was India's punishment for the crime of Untouchability. "We may just as well have been punished for submitting to alien domination, or for putting up with an unjust social system. Or the British government might call the calamity a divine punishment for civil disobedience!"

After a month in the Bihar shambles, he returned exhausted, and slept for twelve hours without moving. Awake, and already engrossed in Congress business, he was having tea with Kamala and his sister when police came to arrest him. Kamala went to pack the belongings he would be allowed to take with him. She did not return. The police grew impatient.

He went to find her. She had fainted. Slowly, she revived, and apologized for worrying him. He was hustled away, and on February 16, 1934, began his seventh prison term in a tiny cell in Calcutta's Alipore Central Jail, where prisoners were required to bow in reverence when the British superintendent inspected them.

In Vienna, well-meaning men bombarded workers' flats killing a thousand men, women and children. In India, the number of imprisoned workers for *Swaraj* reached eighty thousand. In Allahabad, small Tara Pandit wrote to the District Magistrate, who had been her grandfather's friend until Jallianwalla Bagh. "Dear Mr. Dixon: Since the English people, of whom you are one, disapprove of Mr. Hitler, I should think they would not adopt Hitler's methods. Sending the police to search our house when we are not at home is Hitler's way of doing things."

The family had been away from home because, at her uncle's request and with her father's full approval, her mother had entered her first political campaign, seeking election to the Allahabad Municipal Board. Elected, she was at once made chairman of the educational committee. Now for the first time, she was addressed, and headlined in newspapers, as Madame Pandit. She told Ranjit Pandit ruefully, "I seem to have gotten myself elected the whole city's mother." He said, "It stood in need of one."

Then and thenceforward, he helped where she was called on to command. He told their daughters, "We want to know what the country thinks of us. All these years we have stood for certain ideals and shouted them from the housetops. Now we shall see if anyone has listened and understood. Do these ideals have any meaning for the people of India? That is what we have to find out." Their mother's way of finding out was greatly disturbing to her colleagues on the Municipal Board. She asked them to appropriate funds to provide milk for hungry schoolchildren. This had never been done before. They said, "Oh, quite irregular, and quite impossible."

She placed boxes along lanes leading to the schools, under signs that read, in Hindi, Urdu and English, *A Pice a Day for Children's Milk*. A pice was India's smallest coin. The parable of the Widow's Mite was reenacted by Hindus and Muslims. The very poor gave to help those even poorer. The children got their milk, and she had learned again how to reach hearts. This happened while, though briefly, her brother wondered if anything they did or tried to do had been worthwhile.

On April 17, 1934, Gandhi issued a statement calling for the immediate end of civil disobedience, and advising Congress leaders to cease the *Swaraj* crusade and devote themselves to "nation-building" activities: removal of Untouchability, propagation of hand-spinning and progress toward communal unity. From prison, Jawaharlal cried that to him this was "an insult to the intelligence and an amazing performance for the leader of a national movement."

They had disagreed before, and would again, but at no time were they as far apart, or as close to parting forever. "Of the many hard lessons that I had learned," Jawaharlal said in his *Autobiography*, "the hardest and most painful now faced me: that it is not possible in any vital matter to rely on anyone. One must journey through life alone; to rely on others is to invite heartbreak."

He was wrong. At Anand Bhavan, his mother and sisters and daughter worked devotedly, believing what he believed. In Alipore Jail, he was suddenly aware of Kamala, frail, in pain, yet animated, full of gallant cheerfulness. She had messages from home, and news. His mother was much better. Indira was well and busy. Vijaya Lakshmi had his letters to Indira ready for the publisher. The prison authorities had just told her he was being transferred to Dehra Dun. She could come and see him oftener. And he must not worry about anyone but himself. Saying this, she was gone.

In August, he was taken from Dehra Dun to Allahabad to see her, and allowed to spend eleven days at Anand Bhavan. His mother came running to him, arms outstretched. "Her face haunted me long." So did Kamala's. They had been married eighteen years. Indira was almost seventeen. *What have the gods done with us? What with me, what with my love?*

He was transferred again, this time to Naini Jail in Allahabad, where the superintendent said he should be grateful for British thoughtfulness. He was told he could visit Kamala twice weekly, but this promise was forgotten. It was hinted that if he would guarantee to take no part in politics, he might be paroled. "Then you can be at home all the time, where a man with a sick wife ought to be."

He was granted a brief visit. His sister watched while he bent over Kamala. She was burning with fever, and in pain, but whispered, "What is this I heard about you giving an assurance to the government? Don't do it!" Vijaya Lakshmi and Indira hid their tears. They took Kamala to a sanitorium at Bhowali. With another show of magnanimity, authorities transferred him to nearby Almora Prison.

Visiting him there, Vijaya Lakshmi found that his cell now was a hall, fifty feet by seventeen, with holes in the roof and a broken stone floor. For the second time, he spent his birthday behind bars. "There was continuous war between me and bed-bugs, mosquitos and flies. There were hundreds of wasps in my cell. Inadvertently, I think, one of them stung me. In my anger I tried to exterminate the lot, but they put up a brave fight in defense of their temporary home, which probably contained their eggs, and I desisted and decided to leave them in peace if they did not interfere with me. For over a year after that, I lived surrounded by these wasps and hornets; they never attacked me, and we respected each other."

Once every three weeks, he was taken under guard to spend an hour with Kamala and Indira. During these visits, he received reports and discussed Congress affairs with his sister and Ranjit Pandit. They had little good news to tell. In England, Winston Churchill warned the government, "Sooner or later you will have to crush Gandhi and the Indian Congress and all they stand for." In India, Congress weakened from within.

Jawaharlal was back in headlines suddenly, but not for Congress accomplishment. "Three or four snakes were found in my cells or near them. News of one of them got out, and there were headlines in the press. As a matter of fact, I welcomed the diversions. Not that I appreciate or welcome snakes, but they do not fill me with fear." His fears were for Kamala and for his mother.

Visiting Krishna Hutheesing in Bombay, Swaruprani Nehru fell and lay unconscious, the victim of a second paralytic stroke. Soon she was up again and resolutely active, but doctors shook their heads forebodingly. Then in May, 1936, they said the last hope for Kamala was treatment in Europe. She left Anand Bhavan reluctantly, sending a message that Vijaya Lakshmi delivered. "Keep the flag flying."

Earthquake in the Quetta district took toll of twenty thousand lives. Congress workers still at liberty were refused permission to help in rescue and relief. The refusal was almost contemptuous, dismissing the Congress as no longer strong enough to matter. On September 4, 1936, five and a half months before his sentence was to expire, Jawaharlal was informed "You are free to go, and if you're wise, you'll leave the country." Threat implied would have been sufficient to alter his plans already made, but his sister and mother would not let him stay.

He spent five hours with them at Anand Bhavan, then flew by any planes available, via Karachi, Baghdad, Cairo, Alexandria, Brindisi and Basle, to reach Kamala at Badenweiler in the Black Forest in Germany. She was failing, and in constant pain. For a month, all else forgotten, he was at her bedside. She seemed to grow stronger. He took Indira with him to London, where he met with his publishers.

Since he had seen England last, eight years before, he had become an enemy of the Empire, almost as dangerous as Gandhi, to English headline-writers and editorialists. He said, "I have loved much that was England, and have hoped to keep the silken bonds of the spirit between India and England. These bonds can exist only in freedom. I want India's freedom for India's sake, but also for England's sake." But England's concern was with the collapse of the League of Nations, Mussolini's invasion of Ethiopia, Hitler and his Brown-Shirts.

Another world war meant, inevitably, another call for India's loyalty. A cable from Vijaya Lakshmi anticipated press reports. He had been elected president of the Congress for 1936 and 1937. He tried to keep this news from Kamala, but failed. He told her he had decided to refuse the election, and remain with her. She said "You must go. There is no question of your resigning."

Taken to a sanitorium near Lausanne, she seemed to grow stronger, and insisted she no longer suffered any pain. "You must go home. They need you there." At last, reluctantly, he yielded, with the understanding that he would rejoin her in April. On the morning of his scheduled departure, February 28, 1936, she smiled up at him, whispered inaudibly, and died.

14.

Leaving Indira in a Swiss school, her father boarded a plane carrying the urn that contained her mother's ashes. In Italy, he was delayed by official insistence that he must meet Benito Mussolini. He said, "We have nothing to discuss." From Baghdad, he cabled his London publishers. The dedication for his *Autobiography,* he directed, should read simply *To Kamala who is no more*. When Vijaya Lakshmi and Ranjit Pandit met him at Allahabad, his penitential grief was locked within him.

From April, 1936, to February, 1937, he traveled thirty-five thousand miles up and down India, by plane and train, bullock-cart, boat and bicycle, often going long distances on foot. His days were twenty hours long. Facing crowds of a hundred thousand, he silenced a chant of *Nehruji ki jai!*, calling instead for *Bharat Mata ki jai!*, Hail to Mother India! Meanwhile his sister and her husband became the first married pair to campaign together in India, for election to a provincial assembly.

Since 1919, British India had been governed under a Constitution granted by Britain's Parliament, establishing a dyarchy that divided the central and provincial administrations. Intended as a palliative to quiet India's unrest, the Constitution was announced as being a means to train Indian leaders "by actual practice in the art of government." It granted limited franchise to three million Indian males, and some female suffrage in certain areas.

Any bill passed by central or provincial legislators that might be construed by British authorities as affecting "the safety or tranquillity of British India or any part thereof" was subject to Viceregal veto. The constitution-creating act provided that within ten years, a Parliamentary mission would be sent to India to determine "the time and the manner of advance" toward further Indian participation in India's government. This had been fulfilled by sending out, in 1928, a mission headed by Sir John Simon.

The Simon Commission report provided for Dominion status, provincial autonomy and equal suffrage for men and women. Also, however, it provided that Muslims and Hindus would no longer vote as separate communities with a system of legislative seats reserved for minorities. Muslims *en masse* rejected this provision, but with whatever reasoning, British historians preferred to blame failure of the Simon Commission proposals on "a powerful body of extremists, the Congress

Party . . . tireless in fomenting anarchy in the name of nationalism."

It remained for Lord Irwin, as Viceroy, to promise what Parliament had not offered: Dominion status as "the natural issue of India's constitutional progress." This was interpreted in India as agreement that Britain would negotiate with representatives of British India and the princely states, with the understanding that Britain's Parliament could no longer "decide on India's fitness or otherwise for self-government." Hence it became vital for Congress to place as many party members as possible in India's legislative assemblies.

This made Vijaya Lakshmi and Ranjit Pandit candidates, for the first time, for elective policy-making office. Her candidacy was in the Kanpur district, that had been a scene of massacre during the rebellion in 1857. She opposed Lady Srivastava, wife of the Minister for Education, until then the only woman ever elected to the United Provinces Assembly. Ranjit Pandit campaigned in Jumna-par, across the river from Allahabad. Each helped the other in mapping strategies and preparing speeches. Both had the eager assistance of their small daughters, home from Poona. Enrolled at Woodstock, an American missionary school, Lekha, Tara and Rita joined the Junior Campfire Girls, and learned and used Americanisms that distressed their grandmother but amused their parents. "Someday," their father promised, "we'll all go to America, where they invented revolutions."

There was little money for campaign expenses, none to pay for transporting voters to polling-places from remote villages. Vijaya Lakshmi reminded villagers they often walked many miles to Hindu and Muslim shrines, and said voting booths were shrines to the future. Her exhortation, "On foot to vote!" became a Congress slogan. When votes were counted, Lekha, Tara and Rita paraded waving Congress flags, and garlanded their parents with flowers. Both had won, by large majorities.

In their mother's case, victory was so impressive that the United Provinces Premier asked her to join his Cabinet as Minister for Health and Local Self-Government. Never before in British India had a Cabinet post been offered to a woman. She hesitated, but her brother joined Ranjit Pandit in saying, "Of course you must accept." So on July 29, 1937, the Honorable Vijaya Lakshmi Pandit, Madame Minister, stood at the first milestone on a road that would lead to heights then unforeseeable.

15.

India had a new Viceroy, Victor Alexander John Hope, eighth Earl of Hopetoun, second Marquis Linlithgow, of whom it was soon to be said not only in India that apart from his inherited titles he was distinguished for aloofness, lack of magnetism, and inflexible conviction that "What is, is right, and what isn't, isn't." His triple chins, billowing paunch and pachydermic dignity delighted caricaturists. There was, however, nothing amusing in his policies. He had headed the Committee on Constitutional Reform which produced, in 1933, a report satisfactory to no one. What had ensued, and what threatened in Europe that must surely affect British India, appeared to mean nothing to Lord Linlithgow.

His arrival was concurrent with the return to prominence of Mohammed Ali Jinnah, almost forgotten since Gandhi and then Motilal and Jawaharlal Nehru came to the fore. Long reported "disgusted and done with the 'so-called *Swaraj* movement,'" Jinnah had suddenly injected himself into the London Round Table Conference. Although not a delegate, he confronted Gandhi, demanding guaranteed parity for Muslims with Hindus in allocation of offices in India's central and provincial governments. He dismissed as irrelevant the fact that there were four times as many Hindus as Muslims in India.

There was power in him, and strange ability to awe the British. Accused of sabotaging the London Conference, he took accusation as a compliment. Reappearing in India, he assumed command of the Muslim League. Publicly, he spoke in terms of history, demography, and most of all, irreconcilable religious differences. Privately, he was heard to complain that "Gandhi worked under me, Nehru worked under me," and to say that when the spotlight veered to them, "I was a disappointed man."

A writer in London's *Economist* averred that "Someone in England told Jinnah that Jawaharlal Nehru, whom he despised and hated, said 'Jinnah is finished.' Outraged, Jinnah packed up at once and sailed back to India, 'just to show up Nehru.'" Jawaharlal told his sister and Ranjit Pandit, "I said to Jinnah: 'There are only two parties in India: the Congress, and the British.' He said: 'No, there is a third, the Muslims.'" As events transpired, he might as well have said, "I am the third."

Reviewing events of the decade after Jinnah's recrudescence

as the voice of Muslim dissidence in India, an English historian summarized: "To Cleopatra's nose as factor in history one should perhaps add Jinnah's pride." However that may be, it happened that as the drama of historic change on the subcontinent moved toward resolution, the future of four hundred million human beings rested more and more on the issue between two utterly dissimilar men, whose sisters were their close confidantes and to a great degree their feminine counterparts.

Miss Fatima Jinnah had her brother's icy fire and blade-sharp handsomeness. Didactic, humorless, puritanical, it was said of her that she did not leave *purdah* to enter politics; she brought *purdah* with her. She would never marry. Her only campaign for elective office, sixteen years after her brother's death, was unsuccessful. Studiedly, from her first public appearance to her last, she avoided the warmth and ease of manner that were natural to Vijaya Lakshmi Pandit. Mohammed Ali Jinnah was as proudly unlike Jawaharlal Nehru.

Thirteen years the elder, rail-thin, in fact tubercular, Jinnah was autocratic, irascible, coldly contemptuous of the mob. As a barrister, he had never admitted error. His sacerdotal style was enhanced by a polished monocle and perfectly groomed grey hair from which a white lock rose like a plume. Hindus said the Jinnahs were Khoja Muslims. The Khojas had been Hindus, who converted to Islam; Hindus alleged they did this in exchange for favors from their Muslim overlords. Jinnah was a Hindu name. Jinnah scorned all Hindus.

He ate pork, drank Scotch, seldom entered a mosque; but Muslim *mullahs* christened him *Quaid-i-Azam,* Savior of His People. He could not speak Urdu, the language Muslim conquerors compounded from Arabic, Persian and Hindi; but millions in India who spoke nothing else believed they understood him. Their copies of the *Quran* were in Arabic, which few could read. They pressed the pages to their foreheads, and were inspired to *jihad,* holy war. His pronouncements in impeccable Oxford English had the same effect, in areas as separate as South India's Hyderabad, where the Muslim Nizam ruled a populace predominantly Hindu, and Kashmir, where a Hindu Maharajah held uneasy sway over quarreling subjects two-thirds of whom were Muslim.

Akbar the Great gave Hindus equal rights; but Akbar was accused of heresy by Muslims when he invited Jesuit priests and Buddhist monks and Hindu *sanyasis* to his court at Agra, and asked them to convince him, if they could, that Mohammed was not God's only prophet. It was the British, under the Cross, who gave the Crescent paramountcy in many Indian states, and who by preference employed Muslims, warriors by ancestry, as police and law-enforcers over the Hindu majority.

They also used Sikhs, whose Guru Nanak attempted to combine elements of Islam and of Hinduism, and Buddha-revering Gurkhas from Nepal. But the backbone of British India's conquest and control of the subcontinent was Muslim; and Mohammed Ali Jinnah held that if the British left, no Muslim would be safe from Hindu vengeance long withheld. He had, in sum, the strongest of all arguments: not faith, but fear.

Against this, Gandhi preached, and Jawaharlal Nehru sought to implement, abandonment of mutual suspicion, acceptance of the right to disagree religiously while working side by side for freedom. Physically fit as Jinnah was not, imperious yet prone to mock himself, not ascetic but temperate in use of alcohol and by choice almost a vegetarian, expecting no such awed reverence from his sister as Fatima Jinnah accorded to the *Quaid-i-Azam,* Jawaharlal declined to believe any creed held a monopoly on God. He promoted Muslims over Hindus in the Congress echelon if this was warranted by their ability and dedication to the common cause. No Muslim who chose Congress in preference to service under him could hope for Jinnah's forgiveness.

Gautama Buddha, preaching in a banyan grove to listeners of all persuasions, proclaimed, "The illusion of separateness is the only heresy." Jawaharlal Nehru, disputing with Jinnah, refused to accept the argument that the names men chose to call their Creator, the dogma and doctrine their race and culture made most comfortable, set them apart from each other when their goal was the same.

How much of Jinnah was convinced zealot, how much was man on the make who used fanaticism to further consuming personal ambition, Vijaya Lakshmi Pandit would not presume to guess. Only Jinnah knew; and quite possibly he had forgotten. One loved, one hated; it came down to that. *And never the twain shall meet.*

16.

From his first day back in India, Jinnah was belligerently divisive. Addressing the Muslim League, he declared, "The majority community have clearly shown their hand: that Hindustan is for the Hindus." Gandhi said this was totally

Jawaharlal Nehru speaking at Madras in 1936

Jawaharlal Nehru and his bride, Kamala, on their wedding day

Mrs. Pandit with U.N. Secretary-General Trygve Lie, 1952

Mrs. Pandit and Dag Hammarskjold, September 1953

untrue. "We are all equally children of India." He wrote to Jinnah: "As I read it, your latest speech is a declaration of war." Jinnah's silence said, "So be it."

Gandhi had chosen Jawaharlal over Subhas Bose. Now Bose, more radical than ever, jeered at apparent failure of Gandhi's doctrine of nonviolence, roused Hindu fanatics by calling for action against Muslim aggression, and went everywhere recruiting support to make himself Jawaharlal's successor as Congress president. Nothing could have done more, to strengthen Jinnah's hand.

Tara Pandit was too young to puzzle out complexities that baffled those much older and presumably wiser. Still what she recalls struck at the heart of what was happening around her. "I often asked my parents, 'When will India be free?' It was a question which worried me a great deal, for until my country was free, my parents would keep on going to jail. I was always given the cheerful and noncommittal reply that India would be free when those who fought for her freedom were worthy of it. My parents did not appear unduly concerned with the fruits of the struggle to which they dedicated themselves. It was infinitely more important in their view that the men and women who strove for *Swaraj* should conduct themselves honorably, courteously and with dignity. Unless the struggle itself was an honorable one, free from the poison of bitterness and hatred, independence, when it came, would be a mockery."

Such high-mindedness was not the rule in all quarters. "What has happened and is happening in India," Jawaharlal Nehru wrote to a friend in England, "affects me continuously. The kind of human material that I see around me, the all-pervading pettiness, the mutual suspicion and back-biting, distress me beyond measure. Everywhere the wrong type of person is pushing himself to the front."

He did not name among these, but others did, Subhas Bose, who went to jail but continued disruptive effort from his cell. Of fourteen Congress leaders at liberty, ten formed a bloc against Jawaharlal and three others. He was warned "Your colleagues will desert you if things get any worse. Your own Congress people may send you to the gallows." It was rumored Gandhi had disowned him, saying "My life work is being ruined by Jawahar's utterances." Gandhi denied this. "Jawahar and I cannot ruin each other, for we believe in the same goal." But Gandhi remained in his *ashram*, working his spinningwheel, giving shelter to outcasts he had rechristened Children of God, leaving political problems to the captain he had chosen.

Jawaharlal met his sister's troubled inquiries with "You have troubles enough of your own." This was true. In India's equivalent to America's smoke-filled backrooms, she was learning that "Politics is the art of hoping against hope. One asks for more than one is likely to receive, is resigned to accepting much less, and often gets nothing whatever. One can only keep pushing and pulling, never quite giving up."

She managed to obtain bare-bones appropriations for medical dispensaries and an antimalarial program. Against *laissez-faire* resistance, she was permitted to set up several demonstration playgrounds, with small libraries attached, and classes for the illiterate. Opposition hardened, however, when she proposed encouraging young Hindu and Muslim women to take up public nursing as a profession.

Learning as she went along, she brought into play an asset

new in India's politics. Tara, her always-perceptive daughter, says, "A career, especially a political career, is said to rob a woman of her femininity. It never had this effect on my mother. She continued to be a genius at whipping up miraculous meals out of nothing, at arranging flowers, at all the things that make a house a home. And she has always continued to be the most feminine woman I ever met, dainty and petite, with the time and inclination to look fresh and lovely, no matter how heavy her work."

Yet when a cholera epidemic flared at Hardwar, where throngs of pilgrims were gathered for the *Kumbh-mela* festival, she went to the pilgrim camps. No Minister of Health before her ever took such risks where scores were dying and contagion spread. Cholera subsided, but malaria set in. She remained in the plague-center, confronting the new destroyer, seeming unaware of the image she created.

Assembly speakers praised her courage eloquently. She said, "I beg to suggest that these gentlemen who are so eloquent here, when they go outside, use some of that eloquence to explain to the poor, ignorant, superstitious villagers how they should help themselves and so prevent epidemics and disease from sucking up the life of the nation."

Congress Party politicos called it bad politics, to reply to compliments with such frankness. Her husband and her brother disagreed; and were proved right. She had told them that during the Kanpur campaign she found women in the villages who could neither read nor write, "yet were more alert to issues and responsive to new ideas" than loftily literate ladies in Allahabad and Lucknow. Now women high and low echoed her challenge, to their menfolk.

"Nagging husbands is never really nice. Few of us really enjoy it. But sometimes it is necessary." With strengthening support, she increased her pressure for appropriations, so effectively that a grim old Muslim legislator, until then unalterably opposed, rose to say, "It gives me great pleasure to observe the ability with which Mrs. Pandit fills her office, and the grace with which she adorns it."

Still she had more learning to do. "One is not after all a machine." Her daughters joined her husband in insisting she must rest a while. Yielding under protest, she went to London on brief leave. Her brother was there, and in the limelight. She expected and sought to be unnoticed. But journalists, learning that British India's first woman Cabinet Minister had come to England, left her brother and besieged her.

She said she had nothing to say about Katherine Mayo's *Mother India*. It struck them as odd, that her brother was often called Pandit Nehru, while her marriage name was Pandit. She explained that *Pandit* is Hindi, from the Sanskrit *Pandita*, meaning "a learned person," and is applied as honorific to respected Brahmins. The feminine form would be *Pandita*. Then should they call her Pandita Pandit? They should not. "My husband is the learned one in our family."

Equality of men and women, she told them, was anything but new in India. "While my husband and I were in our prisons, he translated ancient Sanskrit writings. They show that as long ago as three thousand years, a wife in India was regarded as *ardhangini*, 'half the being, essential to the harmonious whole.'" Interviewers took this as propaganda charmingly delivered. However they granted in their summaries: "If

Mrs. Pandit is truly representative, it would appear that India's women have not found it necessary to copy our *Votes For Women* suffragettes, who don bloomers or short skirts and crop their hair and talk tough, thinking thus to prove their equality with men."

She asked her brother, "What should I have done, to make them listen as they would to a man?" He said, "I think you did very well as it is." In fact, experience taught her how to be a personage for the press, which often dealt with her more kindly than with him.

17.

In London that year, they buried Rudyard Kipling, whose fame was founded on six slim volumes written before he was twenty-four, and published originally in Allahabad. The funeral cortege escorting his ashes to burial in Westminster Abbey was disturbed by a parade of Communists chanting *The Red Flag* while they carried Shapurji Saklatvala, the Indian revolutionist, to his cremation ceremonies.

Vijaya Lakshmi and her brother saw strange irony in this. He did not seem much interested in a searingly critical attack on him, signed *Chanakya,* published in the *Modern Review,* for which Ranjit Pandit had once written the article that introduced him at Anand Bhavan. To Vijaya Lakshmi, the signature had pointed significance. Chanakya was chancellor to Chandragupta Maurya, who crushed Macedonian invaders and united India in the 3rd Century B.C. To scholars, he is India's Machiavelli.

"As Jawaharlal Nehru passed swiftly through the waiting crowd," the masked attacker wrote, "his hands went up, and his pale, hard face was lit up with a smile. The smile passed away and the face became stern and sad. Almost it seemed that the smile and the gesture accompanying it had little reality; they were just tricks of the trade to gain the goodwill of the crowd whose darling he had become. Jawaharlal has learned well to act without the paint and powder of the actor. From the Far North to Cape Comorin he has gone like some triumphant Caesar, leaving a trail of glory and a legend behind him. Is all this just a passing fancy which amuses him, or is it his will to power that is driving him from crowd to crowd and making him whisper to himself, 'I drew these tides of men into my hands and wrote my will across the sky in stars'? What if the fancy turns? Men like Jawaharlal, with all their great capacity for great and good work, are unsafe in a democracy. A little twist and he might turn into a dictator. He is too much an aristocrat for the crudity and vulgarity of fascism, and yet he has all the makings of a dictator in him—vast popularity, a strong will, energy, pride, and with all his love for the crowd, an intolerance of others and a certain contempt for the weak and inefficient. His flashes of temper are well-known. His overwhelming desire to get things done, to sweep away what he dislikes and build anew, will hardly brook for long the slow processes of democracy . . . His conceit is already formidable. It must be checked. We want no Caesars."

Heads wagged and tongues clacked. Many said, "I've been saying the same things myself, but now it's out in the open." More came to declare that scurrilous criticism had crystallized their devotion to its victim. Only Vijaya Lakshmi, Ranjit

Pandit, his motherless daughter and his ailing mother, knew the secret that was kept from outsiders. The author of the attack was Jawaharlal Nehru himself.

In another day, he would confess, "I played a little trick which amused me greatly. I watched with great interest its reaction on my colleagues and others." *Post facto* explanation was not necessarily complete. He had done much soul-searching during his imprisonments, and more since Kamala died in Switzerland. Within the family, he had long made it clear he had no illusions about his colleagues. If any remained about himself, he had now held them up against the sun. His final sentence summarized decision. "Who rides a tiger cannot dismount."

Indira came home to be with him. At nineteen, she was too young for Congress membership, but there was much to do at Anand Bhavan. "I was determined," she says, "that I would never marry. I felt I should devote every minute to the *Swaraj* struggle, and marriage would come in the way."

Vijaya Lakshmi had told Lekha, Tara and Rita, "After women have done what God and nature intended, there's still plenty of time for what they themselves want to do." She offered no such advice to her niece; but when guidance was wanted, she was there.

There was hard work for all the Nehrus in 1937. For Swaruprani Nehru, the strain was finally too great. Never fully recovered from injuries received when she led *Swaraj* marchers and was clubbed and left unconscious in the street, she suffered another paralytic stroke. In her sick-room, resolutely untroubled, she demanded news of Gandhi and Vallabhbhai Patel, and Mohammed Ali Jinnah and Subhas

Bose, and Lord Linlithgow. Smiling up at her son, her daughters, their husbands and her granddaughters, she said, "I sleep better when we are all together."

Vijaya Lakshmi bent to kiss her forehead. She was already asleep; and never waked. A few hours later, alone in her shadowed corner, Aunt Bibi Amma followed her sister in death. There could be no funeral rites for her. Orthodoxy decreed that her life ended when her husband died; and she would not have wanted it any other way. But thousands followed Swaruprani Nehru's cortege, to the riverbank where Motilal Nehru lay in state seven years before. Their son lighted her funeral pyre. Returning from the river, those she had loved and served passed what had been her sheltered separate domain, when Anand Bhavan was the Home of Joy. The women's quarters were dark and silent now.

18.

In the summer of 1938, Adolf Hitler decided to seek an ally against England in India. "The *Führer*," Berlin announced, "has invited Jawaharlal Nehru to come to Germany as an honored guest." His sister and his daughter knew, before he told them, that he would refuse the invitation. Instead, he went to Czechoslovakia and Spain. Hitler's troops were massed on the Czech border. In Spain, Hitler's planes and Mussolini's armor reinforced Franco's legions.

In London, he found Anthony Eden, Clement Attlee, others in and out of power, united in minimizing the Nazi-Fascist threat. In the visitors' gallery in the House of Commons, he heard cheers when Neville Chamberlain announced he had been summoned to Munich. He watched Chamberlain go, and return clutching his umbrella and promising "Peace in our time." He told the Manchester *Guardian* "India resents British foreign policy and will be no party to it, and we shall endeavor with all our strength to sever the bond that unites us to this pillar of reaction."

Returning to India, he found Subhas Bose in control as Congress president. Bose saw no evil that need trouble India, in Nazi Germany, Fascist Italy or Japan. At last, Bose believed, he had triumphed over Gandhi's choice. But Nehru *mystique* was stronger than Bose guessed. Villagers, and then their Congress delegates, shouted *Nehruji ki jai!* Suddenly, Bose was fighting for his political life. He scrambled to reelection as Congress president, but immediately was pushed out of the party by the Congress working committee. Before long Bose left India. Jawaharlal went to China, meeting Chiang Kai-shek in Chungking, intending to go north and meet the Eighth Route Army led by Mao Tse-tung. He had been in China fifteen days, when on September 1, 1939, Hitler invaded Poland and war in Europe began.

Vijaya Lakshmi, Ranjit Pandit and Indira told him when his plane touched down at New Delhi that on September 3, concurrently with Great Britain's declaration of war on Germany, and without consulting anyone in India, Lord Linlithgow, as Viceroy, had proclaimed that India was at war on Britain's side "in the fight for freedom." Jawaharlal asked, "Whose freedom?"

"If war is to defend the *status quo,* imperialist possessions, vested interest and privilege," the Congress notified Lord Linlithgow, "then India can have nothing to do with it. If

Great Britain fights for the maintenance and extension of democracy, then she must necessarily end imperialism in her own possessions, establish full democracy in India, and the Indian people must have the right of self-determination by framing their own constitution through a constituent assembly without any external interference, and must guide their own policy."

The gage was down, and Lord Linlithgow took it up. His Majesty's Government, he declared, would consider discussing India's future only with representatives of India who had proved their loyalty to the Crown, when the war was won and over, not before.

The Nehrus had loved much that was English. They did not, and never would, hate England. They loathed fascism, by whatever name. But India, not England, owned their loyalty. The Congress called on all its members serving in the central and provincial legislatures to resign within a month. Vijaya Lakshmi and Ranjit Pandit resigned immediately. There was nothing more for them to do in Lucknow. Returning to Allahabad, they prepared for arrest and imprisonment sure to come.

Gandhi, once again in action, was refused and turned away when he sought an audience with Lord Linlithgow. He announced a new civil disobedience campaign, and chose its leaders. The first of these was Jawaharlal. The next was a new figure in the forefront, Vinayak Narahari Bhave, of a prosperous West Indian Brahmin family. He had left home to escape being sent to school in Germany, and lived as a pauper at Banaras, the Hindu holy city. In 1916 he entered Gandhi's *ashram* at Sabarmati, where he earned his bread by cooking and scavenging.

He told Gandhi he had only one ambition in life: to kill an Englishman. "Gandhi," he said, "taught me how to control the volcano of anger and passion that was ever alive in me." Still he made India miserable for many Englishmen. At twenty, he joined the *Swaraj* underground in Calcutta, and was arrested and jailed. In 1924 Gandhi chose him to lead a demonstration in Kerala, against the Brahmin ban on Untouchables entering Hindu temples. Again, he was imprisoned. In 1940 Gandhi's newspaper named him as India's first individual *Satyagrahi,* or complete self-giver.

The others who organized civil disobedience were as diverse in background and personality as Jawaharlal and the self-giver Harijans called Vinobaji. At Allahabad, Vijaya Lakshmi and Ranjit Pandit awaited Jawaharlal's return from a meeting with Gandhi. Then they heard he had been taken from a train, tried in Gorakhpur Jail, and sentenced to four years in prison. Severity of the sentence was protested even in England. But it set the pattern for what followed.

Lekha Pandit, now fifteen, was ready to enter college. Arrangements were made to enroll her at Isabella Thoburn College, operated in Lucknow by the Methodist Church of the United States. It seemed best for her sisters to remain at home. "You will do your bit," their mother told them, "by keeping the flag flying at Anand Bhavan. This is a big job and you will be helping in the fight just as much as we are." Police came to arrest their father. He left them smiling. They smiled, too, and kept watch for the police coming to arrest their mother.

Strangely, this was put off for seven months. One reason may have been that she was elected president of the All-India Women's Conference. The Raj had begun to deal more warily with organized women. The 1941 conference would be held at Coconada in South India, where she was known of but had not been seen and heard. Great preparations were made for her reception.

She was leaving for Coconada, when Mohammed Ali Jinnah sounded an ultimatum that would drench the subcontinent with blood. Muslims, he said, must have a separate Islamic nation, all their own, in which there would be no room for Hindus. It would be called *Pakistan,* a name coined by a Muslim visionary, Rahmat Ali. "*P* for Punjab, *A* for Afghans, *K* for Kashmir, *S* for Sind, and *Stan* for 'country,' " Jinnah's adherents explained, adding that *Pak* in Persian-Urdu could be translated to mean "pure."

Pakistan, Jinnah declared, would indeed be a Land of the Pure. Where would its people come from? The answer was in the *Quran.* "Whosoever flieth from his country for the sake of God's true religion, shall find in the earth many forced to do the same, and plenty of provisions." So said the Prophet Mohammed; so said Jinnah, the prophet of Pakistan. He set December 22, 1940, as a Muslim Day of Deliverance. Tara and Rita asked their mother, "Why isn't Jinnah arrested?" She said, "The British find him useful."

On December 21, she faced her first audience entirely of women. She told them it had been possible to work for India even in prison. She had persuaded her guards to let her use a storeroom as a nursery for children of women convicts, previously put in cells with their mothers. One political prisoner voluntecred to paint pictures on the nursery walls; another modeled clay toys. Women with long criminal records, women imprisoned only because they marched for *Swaraj,* learned to read and write by teaching each other. Occasionally, she had been able to persuade prison authorities to let friends outside provide milk for children of the prisoners. Many had never drunk milk before.

How could women endure imprisonment? She said it required a special moral courage. But those who really understood and practiced Gandhi's philosophy of self-giving found they could carry on, even develop and mature intellectually and spiritually; prison could be an uplifting, enlightening experience. As she stood saying this, already past the age that for many of India's women meant decrepitude and despair, twice as old as Jhansi-ki-Rani had been when she died fighting for freedom, she appeared no older than when she was married twenty years before.

Prison had refined her beauty. Small, she stood tall. She paced while she spoke, eight paces one way, eight the other, as she had within her cell. Women envied her, but without jealousy. She gave them a model; they told their husbands this, and British agents said the same, in their reports to the Raj. She could not be left at liberty much longer.

19.

Eleven members of the Congress Working Committee, one hundred and seventy-six members of the All-India Congress Committee, twenty-nine former Provincial Ministers, and more than four hundred Congress members who had resigned from legislatures, were in prison. Everywhere, women took up the duties they could no longer perform. "Though unused to public activity, they threw themselves into the heart of the struggle," Jawaharlal Nehru wrote. "Often, they became 'Congress dictators,' who would put up with no weakening, and shamed men by their courage and sacrifice."

Then shock came from an unexpected source. Those who could read newspapers told those who could not, "Nehruji's daughter is getting married. She is marrying outside the Hindu community." At nineteen, Indira had been sure she would never marry. At twenty-four, "I just didn't think things out any more. I just wanted to get married. The whole nation was against it. I got hundreds of letters every day, abusing, threatening. My father never said anything one way or the other, but he was not very happy."

Her chosen husband was Pheroze Gandhi. Wholly unrelated to the Mahatma, in fact he was Parsi, descended from Persian disciples of Zoroaster who fled Muslim persecution in Persia and established a colony in Kathiawar in A.D. 706. Twelve centuries later, there were no more than a hundred thousand Parsis in India, most of them living in Gujerat, largely in Bombay. They were famed for business acumen, honesty and charity. There were no Parsi castes.

A Parsi who made loans to impecunious young English officers was nicknamed Ready-Money. He kept the nickname when he founded a bank, and was knighted as Sir Ready-Money Jeejeebhoy. Many Hindus and Muslims believed the Parsis were more British than Indian. Others pointed out that the first successful revolt against the Raj was initiated by

Parsis, when in 1887 a Parsi priest, Jamshedji Tata, broke British monopolies by opening the first India-owned cotton mill. By 1942, the Tata Trust was Asia's wealthiest non-European enterprise. Its owners were not the only Parsis who gave financial support to Gandhi and the Congress.

Still the masses disapproved of marriage between a Kashmiri Brahmin Nehru and a Parsi Gandhi. That there was precedent for Nehru marriages outside creed and race was little known. In fact, two of Indira's cousins had married Muslims, and another close relation, B. K. Nehru, had married a European girl he met at school in England.

"When he wrote about his plans, his parents were much alarmed. His father couldn't leave India just then, so his mother was sent to England to break off the romance. But Fori, the girl in question, was very sweet. Her future mother-in-law melted. Her future father-in-law was furious. 'Here I spent all that money to settle things, and all my wife can write is that the young lady is a very sweet girl!'" It was finally decided that "Fori must come to India and live in Indian style for a year, to see if she would be a proper wife for my cousin. And she lived with his grandparents, who were very orthodox, and bore herself so beautifully that she was held up to all us modern, rebellious young Indians as an example!"

The marriage took place. B. K. Nehru's career was helped, not harmed. Since then, he has served India with honor as a member of his country's United Nations delegations, as executive director of the International Bank for Reconstruction and Development and as Ambassador at Washington under Jawaharlal Nehru, Lal Bahadur Shastri and Mrs. Indira

Gandhi. But in 1942, orthodoxy clamored against Indira's decision to marry outside her faith, and fanatics made it a political issue.

"We had thought," Mrs. Gandhi says, "we would have a
very quiet wedding and not invite anybody. But Mahatma
Gandhi pointed out that with a wedding as controversial as
this, people might think my father didn't want to do anything
for my husband and me, and this wouldn't be fair to my father. So though we didn't want a wedding in the grand manner, nevertheless a lot of people turned up from all over India."

Astrologers selected a day in March. Krishna Hutheesing
came from Bombay, with her small sons, Harsha and Ajit.
Ranjit Pandit, released from prison, told his daughters how he
and their mother took the Seven Steps together, where their
cousin and Pheroze Gandhi would take theirs. Kasturbai
Gandhi had spun *khadi* for the wedding *sari* their mother
wore. Indira's shell-pink *sari* was made from yarn her father
spun in prison. Whatever his first thoughts had been regarding Indira's marriage, he was completely the proud father during rites so important in India that often a childless man
adopts a daughter so he can be honored by the sacrificial privilege of giving her in marriage. There was an empty place for
Indira's mother.

Watching from nearby, Indira's aunt could see the bleak
shell of what had been the Home of Joy, in which she met her
bridegroom twenty-one years before. She had long since worn
out or given away the one hundred and one *saris* that were her
trousseau. So much had been lost, and how much gained? But
she was smiling when she kissed the bride. Suddenly, Indira
held her close. Married, still and always they were Nehrus

first. They embraced as they would when, widowed, they stood side by side while Indira assumed the burdens her father carried while he lived. Their next reunion would be in a prison cell.

20.

Hong Kong fell to the Japanese. Singapore surrendered. Subhas Bose, financed from Tokyo, began attempts to recruit an Indian National Liberation Army, with a Jhansi-ki-Rani Regiment commanded by a woman, Lakshmi Swaminathan, whose father had tried cases with Motilal Nehru, and left a million-rupee legacy to a woman's college in Madras. From London, Winston Churchill proclaimed that he had not become Prime Minister "to preside over the liquidation of the British Empire."

His fiat was cheered in the Chamber of Princes in India. Said the powerful Maharajah of Bikanir: "Only a federation ruled for Britain by the princes will ever be able to govern India if the Raj withdraws." Said the Prince of Kolhapur: "The gift of democratic government may be made or withheld by Parliament; but no such gift will ever cause the growth of democracy in India."

Said a greatly respected British authority, Major General J. F. C. Fuller: "Until India is de-theocratized, democracy is no more than a will-o'-the-wisp that must land in a slough of despond." Said the British press and its affiliates in India, by consensus: "Any form of democracy in India automatically involves Hindu domination. Muslims will not be ruled by Hindus or Sikhs; Sikhs will not be ruled by Muslims; Hindus will not be ruled by Muslims; the princes will not be overruled by politicians of British India. Yet any offer to get Britain out of India must contemplate these impossibilities."

Chiang Kai-shek came from Chungking to New Delhi, and appealed to the British to grant political participation to the Indians and to Indians to collaborate with the British in the war effort, "for only in a free world can the Chinese and Indian peoples obtain their freedom." His appeal to the Raj was dismissed as presumptuous interference in what did not concern him, and by *Swaraj* leaders as beside the point. Then the situation changed. Japan attacked Pearl Harbor. The United States was in the war. Americans began to be seen in Bombay and Calcutta.

On August 9, 1942, Gandhi was arrested. So were Jawaharlal, his sister Krishna, and her husband. On August 11, police fired into a student procession in Allahabad. Vijaya Lakshmi had written to Gandhi that because her daughters needed her, she doubted if she should leave them to take part in the civil disobedience demonstrations then going on. But this resolve was only momentary. "I could not forget the faces of wounded young students I helped carry to the hospitals."

Lekha, home from college, was in the thick of marches and meetings. Ranjit Pandit was away on a Congress mission. In the middle of the night, Bindu, the porter, wakened Vijaya Lakshmi. The police had come, and insisted on seeing her at once. Looking from a balcony, she recognized the city magistrate and the deputy superintendent of police. They had once been Motilal Nehru's friends. She had worked with them while she was Minister for Health and Local Self-Government. Now they brought constables and plainclothesmen to surround her home.

She dressed unhurriedly. As she went down the stairs, she looked at her watch. It was exactly 2 A. M. She asked the magistrate, "Why is it necessary for so many armed men to come at this amazing hour to arrest one lone, unarmed woman?" The only answer was, "This house must be searched." She flung the door open wide. "Go ahead. Search wherever you wish. We have nothing to hide." She went to wake Indira, who had returned to Anand Bhavan a few hours earlier.

Indira listened to her instructions, then dressed, while Vijaya Lakshmi waked her daughters. They asked no needless questions, and helped gather and pack what she would be allowed to take with her. Rita, only twelve, looked so small that her mother's heart ached. But Rita said, "How wonderful, Mummie, to live in these days. I wish I could go to jail, too." Tara whispered, "Let's say 'Goodbye' on the veranda. I want the police to see how we take these partings."

They went out together. Lekha said "Don't worry, Mummie. I'll look after the girls." Tara said, loud and clear: "'Bye, Mummie darling! We shall keep the flag flying!" They walked with their mother to the gate, where heavily-armed police appeared from the darkness, surrounded her, and took her to a prison van. None spoke. She knew the road to prison. She had gone over it often, to visit her father, her brother, her husband.

The prison matron appeared, puffing and panting "as she always did when new prisoners came in." There was no cot in the cell. Vijaya Lakshmi spread her bedding on the stone floor. Her head ached and sleep refused to come. "I thought of things Lekha had said recently. 'We can't think in terms of normal life any more. There is no going back for us. We must go on to the end, whatever that may be.'" She found it hard to keep bitterness and doubt from creeping into her mind and heart. But it should not happen to the very young.

She slept at last. Waking at dawn, she lay on her pallet until a sweeping-woman, a prison trusty, ordered her out of the way. Her head still ached. There were no sanitary arrangements. In the prison yard, she washed her face at the bathing-tap, then walked up and down until, at seven, the matron appeared and promised to send rations and tea at ten. When these appeared, she gathered twigs, made a little fire and brewed her tea with lukewarm water, "which was already brownish-hued."

She read and napped, and then decided to start a diary. Her brother had written two books, in bits and pieces, during his imprisonments. "I am not prepared to say that the many years I have spent in jail have been the sweetest of my life," he said, "but I must say that reading and writing have helped wonderfully to get through them." The placebo was less soothing to his sister.

At dusk, just when the air began to cool, she was locked in her windowless cell. Then the matron came puffing. The cell would be left open after all. If she wished, she could sleep outside in the prison yard. A bed of sorts, of rope webbing in a wooden frame, was provided. She dragged it out and lay looking up at the stars. At midnight, rain came down in sheets. She dragged her bed back into her cell.

In the morning, there was no tea. She demanded an explanation. Again the matron came puffing, with some tea and a food ration. This was rice, mixed with grit, dirt and tiny pebbles, which she picked out and saved to show to the prison doctor when he made his rounds. She had worked beside him during the cholera epidemic at Hardwar. He avoided looking at her, while he recited news in staccato bursts, as if he gave a radio report.

There were rumors the Japanese were about to launch an invasion of Eastern India through the Manipur Hills. Rommel had won another victory in North Africa. The Nazis were driving toward Stalingrad. Prime Minister Churchill and President Roosevelt had signed something called the Atlantic Charter. The All-India Congress Committee was responsible for *Quit India!* scrawled on walls and sidewalks. Mahadev Desai, Gandhi's secretary, had died in prison.

It was Mahadev Desai who gave her the copy of the *Modern Review* containing the article that introduced Ranjit Pandit to her. She had no idea where her husband was now, or how he fared. She had no news of her brother. But she refused to weep. She found it hard to read, because of prison noises. There were loud complaints, quarrels, fistfights. She heard the cries of young boys being flogged in another section of the prison. Rather than keep them in the overcrowded jails, they were whipped and then sent home. Sternly, she taught herself to ignore the sounds of their punishment.

Sunset was her homesick hour. Sometimes, she said in her diary, she fretted about petty things, and lost her temper. She had found it helped to explode now and then; and never got over the habit, which she shared with her brother. When the superintendent asked if the stick with a leather strap at its tip, which he sent when she asked for a flyswatter, was useful, she said, "At least it helps me to release my feelings." When he asked, "Are conditions satisfactory?", she snapped, "Would I be here if they were?"

She learned jail skills, especially how to be there first when someone was released, in order to appropriate anything useful left behind. Thus she got a rickety table, on which she dined and wrote. She put her cot beside an iron grating, so she could look out at a patch of green in the prison yard, and at the stars by night. Then one day the grating was boarded up.

A young friend of her daughters, Purnima, was arrested and put in the cell with her. Then one morning as she sipped her tea, Purnima cried out unbelievingly. She looked up. There stood the matron, and behind her, beaming, Lekha. Proudly, Lekha announced that at last she had managed to make the police take notice of her.

Her mother asked, "Why were you arrested?" She laughed. "They said I removed some plates from a railroad track, to wreck a train. I wouldn't know how to begin to wreck a train, and I couldn't lift a rail-plate anyhow, but of course I didn't deny anything. They might not have arrested me if I had." The police had come the night before. "They searched the house and found nothing worth taking and went away, but they came back this morning while we were having breakfast. I ate an extra piece of toast to make them wait. I wanted them to know that being arrested is nothing for a Nehru to worry about."

Her mother says now, "The trouble with the young generation in those days was that young men and women who should have been thinking about themselves and their own futures were marching in processions and picketing foreign shops and deliberately getting arrested. It robbed them of so much." But in 1942, "It was easier to laugh than to cry. And although being locked up together in jail isn't what I would recommend as the ideal way for a mother and a daughter to get better acquainted, I must say it was probably good for both of us."

21.

For seven months, mother and daughter were prison cellmates. Both did their best to show their guards that nothing could upset a Nehru. Vijaya Lakshmi taught Lekha how to cook their rations on a tiny oil stove. "It wasn't a very balanced diet," Lekha says, "and I lost ten pounds, besides breaking out in boils. But there were compensations. One of the prisoners, serving a murder sentence, had an infant with her, and I used to bathe the baby and take care of it."

One night a bat fell on Lekha while she slept. "I'm ashamed to say I screamed. Luckily, I wasn't afraid of rats and mice. We had a lot of them." She read the *Ramayana* with her mother. They evolved elaborate plots to improve their menus. When they asked for fresh fruit, they waited ten days, then were given some half-rotted bananas. They asked for coffee, and were told prison regulations allowed for nothing but tea. Then the Superintendent came surreptitiously with a tin of coffee, confiding that he broke the rules because they were Nehrus. They dumped the coffee at his feet. Next day, they were informed coffee could be purchased.

They celebrated this victory, and soon had cause for greater celebration. Framed in the doorway was Indira. She said she and Pheroze Gandhi had been arrested, at the start of a massive *Quit India!* demonstration proclaimed by the Mahatma, with the motto *Karenge ya marenge!*—We will do or die! Sarojini Naidu, Indira said, had been arrested for circulating Gandhi's instructions: "Let every nonviolent soldier of freedom write out the slogan *Do or Die* on a piece of paper or cloth, and pin it to his clothes, so that in case he dies in the course of offering *Satyagraha*, he may be distinguished by that sign from other elements who do not subscribe to nonviolence."

Indira wore *Do or Die* on a slip pinned to her *sari*. She had no idea where her husband was imprisoned, and no news of Ranjit Pandit. Failure of the Cripps Mission had been followed by Winston Churchill's ukase: "What we have we hold!" The Congress had resolved that "The proposal of withdrawal of British power from India was never intended to mean the physical withdrawal of all Britishers from India, and certainly not of those who would make India their home and live there as citizens and equals of others." Churchill was not mollified.

The Mahatma had counseled appeal to the heads of governments allied with Britain against the Axis. "We must look the world in the face with calm and clear eyes though the world's eyes are bloodshot." Then at dawn on August 9, as Gandhi began his morning prayers, he and Kasturbai Gandhi were arrested. Simultaneously, all Congress leaders were taken into custody. Indira said, "My father was staying with the Hutheesing in Bombay and was in his room, asleep, when the police came for him." All the prisoners were taken in a heavily guarded special train to a way station near Poona, a hundred-odd miles southeast of Bombay. There they were separated. Indira's father and all the others but Gandhi and his wife were transported to Ahmadnagar, and imprisoned in a jail that had been a Moghul fortress. Gandhi and Kasturbai were confined, under close arrest, in a palace belonging to the Aga Khan.

The Aga Khan had no use for his palaces in India. He had been president of the All-India Muslim League, and held his Ismailiah Muslim sect in allegiance to the Raj so effectively that the British added to titles already conferred on him the rank and status of a first-class chief of the Bombay Presidency, with a salute of eleven guns. However, he lived mostly in Europe, where his pensions and income from the British were prudently invested, and where he married a Frenchwoman.

He interested feature writers much more than the prisoner in his palace. They did not, however, delve very deeply into fact about him. It was easier to embroider the tale that each year his subjects piled gold and jewels upon a mammoth scale, until the weight in wealth balanced his corpulence, than to state the fact that the Ismailiah, although fiercely orthodox, earned the riches in which he shared as moneylenders extorting usury, in calm rejection of Mohammed's law forbidding this.

In truth, he was His Highness only by courtesy of the British. The first of his line was a Persian, Hasan Ali Shah, who claimed descent from Fatima, Mohammed's daughter, and from the most ancient Persian dynasty, and further, from Beni-Fatemite caliphs who ruled in Egypt at the time of the Crusades. The Persian Emperor, Fateh Ali Shah, scoffed at these claims, and Hasan Ali Shah fled into British India, where he earned the favor of the Raj for services rendered in the First Afghan War, and subsequently during British seizure of Sind and the North West Frontier, where the Ismailiah were numerous. His reward was British support in asserting his rights as spiritual leader of the Ismailiah. Their acceptance of him was rewarded with official protection of their money-lending operations. Aga Sultan, Sir Mohammed Shah, third Aga Khan, was a generous contributor of funds expended by Mohammed Ali Jinnah and the Muslim League. He was not beloved by India's Hindus. Choice of one of his palaces as Gandhi's prison was read by Gandhi's followers as a declaration by the Raj of where British sympathies lay. Nor was it thought to be coincidence, that Jawaharlal Nehru in the Moghul fortress was guarded by Muslim jailers.

Indira found it hard, at first, to adjust to life behind walls and bars. "The magistrate had marked a cross on my card, and apparently the authorities took this to mean I was to have no privileges whatever. I couldn't reply to my father's letters. Very few reached me, anyhow. I thought if everybody was chattering all the time, it would be just too much to bear. I made a rule that nobody could speak to me before 5 P. M. But finally I realized I was living only at a surface level."

Her aunt had done nothing, said nothing, implying criticism of her standoffishness. Example had been enough. Indira joined her aunt and her cousin in doing what could be done for the women convicts with whom they were confined. She made a particular friend of a young mother whose baby had been born in her cell. "I wanted to adopt the baby legally, but this wasn't allowed." Most of the women convicts were illiterate, and suspicious of the Great Ladies thrust among them. "But they had a child-like eagerness to learn," Indira recalls. "They liked to hear stories, especially about women who had made something of their lives." Her father's imprisonment at Ahmadnagar suggested telling the women about a woman warrior of whom Muslims spoke with the veneration Hindus accorded to Jhansi-ki-Rani. She was Chand Bibi, *Bibi Sultana.* Even Mountstuart Elphinstone's *History of India* gave space to Bibi Sultana. She was regent for her nephew, Bahadur Nizam Shah, when Akbar the Great sent his armies to add the Deccan to his Empire of Hindustan. Veiled but wearing armor and wielding a naked sword, she commanded Ahmadnagar's defense.

When ammunition for her cannon was exhausted, she loaded them with coins from the royal treasury, first copper, then silver, then gold. When these were gone, she stuffed a cannon with her jewels and with her own hand fired them at the enemy. The Nehru women had no swords or jewels, but fought in their own way.

Lekha and Indira hoarded their rations for a party to celebrate progress toward *Swaraj,* and debated whether the menu should be written in French or Hindi; "certainly not in English." They polished and repolished their silver, which consisted of three bent forks and a single dull knife. Bits of the ceiling fell on their plates. Ants, gnats and mosquitos harassed them. Bats flew in at night. Once a snake crawled through their only window. "We sat very still. Finally it went away."

Word reached them that Ranjit Pandit was in Naini Jail, not far away. Somehow, he managed to send them cuttings from the garden Jawaharlal helped him plant when they were cellmates. Unexpectedly, they were allowed to visit him, though for only a few minutes. As always, he was gay; but his wife and daughter were not deceived. Confinement had aged him; he was frighteningly thin.

On her brother's fifty-third birthday, November 14, 1942, Vijaya Lashmi wrote in her diary that it was heartbreaking that her husband and her brother were unable to be of service to India when they were so desperately needed. Regarding herself, she wrote that of the many good things life had given her, the best was the love of those she loved.

22.

In England, Winston Churchill told the House of Commons, "The disturbances in India have been crushed with all the weight of the government. Large reinforcements have reached India and the number of white troops in that country is larger than at any time in the British connection." Actually, what was in truth a national uprising continued on into 1943, and "white troops in that country" included increasing numbers of Americans, who asked increasingly why British soldiers were set to shooting at the local populace instead of at the Japanese.

Between August and the end of December, 1942, police and soldiers killed nine hundred and forty *Swaraj* demonstrators and wounded two thousand. Sixty thousand were arrested. British fighter-planes, pulled back from patrol in Burma and Malaya, strafed Congress gatherings in the United Provinces. Whole villages were sentenced to mass punishments. The Banaras Hindu University was closed, then occupied by British soldiers. In Bengal, government forces burned one hundred and ninety-three Congress buildings and camps. Collective fines imposed on villagers totaled nine million rupees. Some who could not pay were flogged. Some died.

Violence was not all on one side. Mobs destroyed six hundred post offices, cut telegraph and telephone wires at thirty-five hundred places, burned seventy police stations, damaged or wrecked other government buildings. Meanwhile Britain's highest award for valor, the Victoria Cross, was awarded to thirty-one Indian soldiers fighting overseas. Indian casualties abroad reached one hundred and eighty thousand. This record had no effect on British policy in India.

"We Americans," said an American news-magazine circulated *sub rosa* in India, "may have some disagreement among ourselves as to what we are fighting for, but one thing we are sure we are not fighting for is to hold the British Empire together." Ambassador William Phillips, in India as President Roosevelt's personal envoy, reported his conviction that Winston Churchill "would prefer not to transfer any power to an Indian government during or after the war." Suggesting American pressure to force matters into the open, he said, "The Indians have no confidence in British promises. The impasse . . . if allowed to continue . . . may affect our conduct of the war in this part of the world, and our future relations with colored races. It is not right for the British to say this is none of our business."

In fact, American pressures were already being applied, by the presence of Americans in uniform. "You like honesty," a veteran of *Swaraj* days said to me in New Delhi on India's tenth Republic Day, "I'll give you some." He was Kashmiri,

Brahmin-born, but so wholly Westernized that bar-boys called him *Sahib.* "You Americans come to India saying 'We're not like those other fellows.' But you speak the same language, you drink the same whiskey, you look the same outside, as the people we spent two hundred years getting rid of. So don't expect us to love you at first sight." Then he grinned. "But you're different when we get to know you."

Few American soldiers in India, he said, were saints, and a good many drank too much and caused commotions. "But they were common citizens of the West, not bumptious bullies who treated us as if we were born to be kicked; slightly nervous, and almost without exception, friendly. They had no illusions of prestige to maintain. *For Europeans Only* signs at swimming pools and hotels and clubs annoyed them as much as they insulted us. We found out, by comparing them with Americans, that our British bosses and their whining *mem-sahibs* were anachronisms; and more and more, we felt we had taken orders from them long enough."

No Americans came to Anand Bhavan, where Lekha, Tara, Rita and their mother took turns working the cyclostyle machine that printed Congress leaflets, and in keeping watch when Congress workers hunted by the police took refuge in their home. "One of them, in his haste to dispose of certain incriminating documents, tried to flush them down the toilet. It refused to swallow them. Mummie wailed in exasperation: 'What a time for the plumbing to go wrong!'" In fact, she welcomed petty troubles, to take her mind from larger ones.

There was no indication that Ranjit Pandit might be released, and she knew his health was failing. Her own parole might end at any hour. Lekha, now eighteen, might be arrested again any time she left the house. Tara and Rita were recklessly eager to defy the enemy on all occasions. Life in the midst of turmoil confused and troubled them.

"I don't know when nonviolence has ever done any good," Tara wrote to her father. "It certainly won't if Germany and Japan get into India. Then we will either have to fight or slave for them. I think we jolly well ought to fight like Patrick Henry, 'Give me liberty or give me death.' P. S. Will you please explain to me what 'communism' means? I asked Lekha, but she says you would explain it thoroughly."

Replying, Ranjit Pandit wrote, "Nonviolence is good. When we are at war we do many violent and vile acts, but when war is over the warring nations sit around a table to discuss peace. It would be much better if human beings were to discuss all matters on which they disagree in a quiet and peaceful manner instead of slaughtering one another . . . If, however, our country is invaded . . . force must be resisted with force. But we must use only as much force as is necessary for defense; otherwise there is the danger of being ourselves brutal and cruel."

Answering Tara's postscript, he said, "Communism means working together in common and sharing benefits in common, with equal justice for all. But between theory and practice there is a world of difference. You know the Sermon on the Mount, and what a Christian should be like. Now watch what the Christian English, French, Germans and others are doing . . . And so it is with the Communists. The Nazi and Communist governments are tearing up the body of sorely stricken Poland bravely fighting against overwhelming odds . . . You must be calm, darling. We shall need strength, physical and mental, for a long time, so that we can help others."

There were many letters. There was not what there should be: a husband and father at home with his family. No wife and mother could face this lack without wondering sometimes if the sacrifice must go on and on. On the last night of 1942, she wrote in her diary "Must the New Year hold more sorrow and suffering for India, or will India at long last come within sight of the Promised Land?"

On New Year's Day, 1943, she wrote "The world has shrunk into two groups: Those who suffer for an ideal, and those who inflict that suffering." Her resolution was that the future, however unpromising, must be faced with dignity and courage. These would be called for, in abounding measure.

Unable in any other way to convince Lord Linlithgow that no amount of repression could halt the *Swaraj* crusade, Gandhi announced that on February 9, he would begin a twenty-one day fast. The Viceroy dismissed this as "political blackmail." Then on February 8, the Raj offered to release Gandhi for the duration of his fast. He refused the offer. The fast began, while Vijaya Lakshmi, Lekha and Indira had their fortnightly visit with Ranjit Pandit.

He said he and his fellow prisoners would fast for twenty-four hours in sympathy with Gandhi. They, too, fasted, while they prayed for Gandhi. He was seventy-three, already in poor health. British as well as Indians feared his fast would kill him. But the Viceroy would not yield; and incredibly, Gandhi survived his ordeal. Mothers whose sons and daughters were marching in tribute to Gandhi came asking for reassurance. Were their children really helping? Was *Swaraj* any nearer?

Prime Minister Nehru and Mrs. Indira Gandhi at the coronation of Queen Elizabeth

Mrs. Pandit, former President Harry Truman, and Dag Hammarskjold at United Nations Headquarters, September 1953

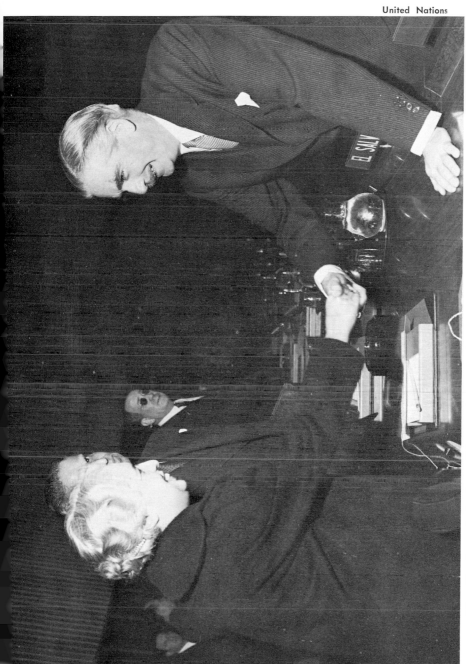

Mrs. Pandit and Anthony Eden at the Seventh Session of the United Nations General Assembly, November 1952

Mrs. Eleanor Roosevelt presents Madame Pandit with a gavel

A messenger brought word that two marching groups had been fired on. This was followed by reports that Lekha, Tara and Rita had been in one of the groups, and then that one of them was wounded. Their mother started out of the house. Bringers of the rumor cried, "You are going in the wrong direction. Your daughters were in the other procession." She said "The others are my children, too."

Then Lekha, Tara and Rita appeared, unhurt, proud of having refused to retreat when police rushed swinging *lathis* and firing into the crowd. She could not bring herself to scold them; but when she was allowed a few minutes with their father in his cell, she confessed her fear for them, not of possible arrest and imprisonment, but of what was happening to their minds and hearts.

The habit of challenging the police, of defiance inviting brutal retaliation, could blind the best along with the worst, to anything beyond the moment. "Convinced of the rightness of protest, the rank-and-file may think no further; busy fighting for freedom, they forget to plan how it will be used. Independence, to too many, is coming to mean not merely the end of British rule; it means solution of every problem. Belief that the British are to blame for everything that is wrong stops thinking where it should begin."

Once more, she learned how Ranjit Pandit's mind was attuned with hers. Already, he had given much thought to the problem she had hesitated to impose on him. He said what she held back from saying. It would be best for them, if Lekha and Tara were sent away from India, to a free country, where they could learn what could not be learned, not yet, in India. Father and mother, facing another sacrifice, strengthened each other. She went to tell Lekha and Tara what had been decided. "We are going to send you to school in the United States."

They wept. "You need us here, to keep the flag flying!" Her firmness weakened. She went to Gandhi, and told him her doubts and fears. "Let them go," he said, "trusting in the upbringing you have given them. If they have learned anything in all these years, it will protect them wherever they are. And above all, they will always have with them the memory of your love, and their father's. That is an armor which no future can pierce."

The memory Tara took with her, as she recorded it ten years later in her book, *Prison and Chocolate Cake,* was of what her mother had said when she was only ten. "Wherever in the wide world there goes an Indian, there goes a piece of India with him, and he may not forget this fact or ignore it. It lies within his power, to some extent, to bring credit or discredit on his country, honor or dishonor." Brave words; but she confesses that as time for their departure neared, she could only think "But they're so young, so terribly young."

Someone sent a book, *The Flowering of New England;* written on the flyleaf was "This will give you a better understanding of the part of the United States to which your daughters are going." Someone else sent a volume of statistical surveys, with markings on pages dealing with crime, divorce and venereal disease, and a note of warning against sending girls to a foreign land unchaperoned.

Even papers filled out in applying for their visas made the impending journey seem "as if they were going into outer space." Resolutely, she joined their laughter over such questions as *Are you a moron or an idiot?* and *Do you plan to over-throw the Government of the United States?* Her cable asking if they could be admitted as students at Wellesley College in Massachusetts brought an immediate reply from its president, Miss Mildred McAfee; Wellesley would be "proud and happy" to welcome them. So finally, there was no drawing back.

Rita could not go with her sisters. She told them "I'll take care of Mummie," and helped their mother by imagining aloud that soon they would all be reunited in America. In fact, all knew that parole from prison might be terminated at any moment; and all hurried their preparations. There was a final half-hour with Ranjit Pandit in his cell. He made farewell a gay affair, giving no advice to Lekha and Tara but "Do what you feel is right, and have a wonderful time doing it. Buy up Fifth Avenue!" They never saw him again.

23.

As their train pulled out from Allahabad station, they called to their mother and Rita, "We'll keep the flag flying, wherever we are." A few hours later, she was back in prison. A month passed before she had any news of them. Then it came in a weekly newspaper, smuggled into the prison, which carried an item datelined Melbourne, Australia. The Army transport on which they were passengers had touched at Melbourne, then headed out across the Pacific. That was all.

They had never been on a ship before. Now they were the only Indian passengers on a converted Italian liner, surrounded by American soldiers and seven hundred Polish refugees who had escaped through Russia to India, and were on their way to Mexico. The ship was blacked out. Japanese submarines prowled, but Lekha and Tara refused to be afraid. "We remembered what Mummie said. 'Do you know what the authorities say about us? They say "If we could just break those damned Nehrus, it would be easy to deal with the rest!" ' " On the day on which their mother's ten-month prison sentence ended, they reached California, ten thousand miles away. Security regulations were so strict that weeks passed before they could let her know "We are in New England where they invented revolution against the British Empire." She could not, nor did she want to, let them know their father had been transferred to Bareilly Central Jail, which was less a prison than an open grave.

Her brother had been in Bareilly Jail. The quality of its staff was capsuled in one of his letters. "A baby monkey managed to come down into our enclosure, and could not mount up again. The warder and some overseers trapped him. The parents (presumably) of the little one saw all this from the top of the high wall. Suddenly one of them, a huge monkey, jumped down and charged right into the crowd tormenting the baby. It was an extraordinarily brave thing to do, for the warder and C. O.s had sticks which they were brandishing about. Reckless courage triumphed. The crowd of humans fled, leaving their sticks behind them!"

Bareilly was overcrowded, surrounded by factories whose chimneys belched choking smoke, with only primitive sanitation, and the barest medical facilities. Ranjit Pandit's Nehru connection earned him especially rigorous treatment. He fainted in his cell, but kept this from Vijaya Lakshmi and

Rita. Hot, dusty days dissolved into torrential monsoon rains. His condition worsened. Finally, authorities decided it would be best to release him, "on grounds of health."

No one at Anand Bhavan was notified. Arriving there, he found that Vijaya Lakshmi was away in Calcutta, where she had gone to work as a volunteer in the midst of the Bengal famine that took three and one-half million lives during a few months in 1943. Her brother had cried out in horror, from prison at Ahmadnagar, "Corpses cannot be overlooked!" But the Raj, having done nothing to avert the famine, was strangely slow in organizing relief for its victims.

Imports of rice from Burma had made the difference between bare subsistence and starvation in Bengal. Japanese invasion cut off this source of supply. There was, however, a rice crop surplus in other parts of India. For whatever reason, officials took no steps to ship the surplus into Bengal, or to curb hoarding and black-market extortion, until Calcutta was overrun by throngs of starving refugees.

Lord Linlithgow, retiring after seven years as Viceroy, and in haste to leave for England, found no time to visit the famine area. His successor, Field Marshal Sir Archibald Percival Wavell, first Viscount Wavell, was of a different breed. He had known India since he came from Sandhurst to begin his military career on the North West Frontier, when Vijaya Lakshmi was a child. Since 1942 he had served as commander-in-chief in India and Burma. A professional soldier had never before been Viceroy, and some observers saw his appointment as a showing of the iron hand; but he went to Bengal immediately, and as rapidly as possible, made up for lackadaisical civilian action.

"You must not think of coming home while you are needed in Calcutta," Ranjit Pandit wrote to Vijaya Lakshmi from Allahabad. In Bareilly Jail, he had dreamed of going to the Nehru mountain cottage at Khali, "to sense the abiding peace and beauty of the forests which are unaware of the agonies and convulsions of a continent." He went there now, but stayed only a few days, then reported for Congress duty in Lucknow. Foreboding brought Vijaya Lakshmi there to meet him.

He joked and spun fancies about the adventures of Lekha and Tara in America, but she saw the truth. "He loved India with a deep and passionate devotion, but prison had been more than his body could bear." He consented to enter the hospital "only so you will stop worrying." At five in the morning on January 14, 1944, a nurse called her from sleepless vigil in the corridor. He smiled up at her, touched her hand, and closed his eyes. An hour later, he was dead.

24.

It was impossible for Lekha and Tara to return to India. They cabled from Wellesley "Be brave, Mother. He can never die. He lives in us." Gandhi, refused parole to attend the rites at Anand Bhavan, wrote from his prison "People will come to console you, but I shall not sorrow for you. How dare I pity you? One does not sorrow for the daughter of a courageous father, the sister of a courageous brother, the wife of a courageous husband. You will find your courage in yourself."

His full meaning came to her slowly. For twenty-three years, Ranjit Pandit had been her constant comrade. Now he was gone. So were her father and mother. Her brother was in solitary confinement. Her sister and her niece had their own family responsibilities. Lekha and Tara could not come to her; she could not go to them. But for Rita, not yet fifteen, she was alone as she had never been.

She had never had to think about money. It was always there. Now there was none. In 1857, Jhansi-ki-Rani was ordered out of her dead husband's palace, because she had not given him a son as heir. The rule was the same in 1944, and would be until 1956. Under Hindu law, ratified by the British, Ranjit Pandit's estate, in its entirety, went to the next in the male line, his brother.

She would be provided for, but only as a dependent, and only if pursuant to orthodox Hindu tradition, she renounced the world, stopped working for *Swaraj*, making speeches, and being arrested, and retired into lifelong seclusion, as Aunt Bibi Amma had done when she was widowed. The British had outlawed *sati*, which they misspelled *suttee*, in 1829. But the Laws of Manu, ancient when Britons painted themselves blue and were accused of practicing human sacrifice, still had validity to Ranjit Pandit's elder brother, and the other members of his family.

Sati actually means "a virtuous woman." Manu decreed "Nowhere is a second husband permitted to respectable women." Where widows had no inheritance, and there was no career for women but marriage, they must be protected against themselves. They could no longer cast themselves into the flames, voluntarily joining their departed mates in death, as Ranjit Pandit's grandmother had done. But her descendants held to belief that Vijaya Lakshmi should willingly and gladly do as her Aunt Bibi Amma had done. They came to take her away with them, and in justice she could not be angry.

Like her father, she respected the faith into which she was born, however she might disagree with custom and tradition grown up around it. In any event, who and what she was obliged her to weigh decision thoughtfully. Indira's marriage outside the Hindu community had raised a storm. When Indira married Pheroze Gandhi, her father's calm acceptance of her right to choose silenced fanatics and enviers. But with the Congress rent by religious faction, the *Swaraj* crusade at seeming stalemate, had Jawaharlal Nehru's widowed sister the right to give enemies and opportunists excuse to question Nehru's right to Hindu support?

Should she, in any case, reject what thousands of widows in India would welcome? She was nearing forty-four, and worn down by work, strain and loss. *I have fought a good fight, I have run my course, I have kept the faith.* She could say that with honesty and honor. In retirement, she could think, read, perhaps write, and above all, rest. Her daughters would be provided for until they married. There would be no more anger and ugliness to endure, no more self-serving politicians to oppose, no more contention with corruptionists. No police would come in the night with warrants. Ranjit Pandit longed for peace. So did she. But so had her mother.

Swaruprani Nehru was as orthodox as Aunt Bibi Amma. But when she was widowed, instead of renouncing the world she went out into it, broke bread with Untouchables, marched amidst strangers of all castes and creeds, was struck down and left unconscious in the street, but rose to march again. *Loving hands have been stretched out to help me.* Memory of her mother brought Vijaya Lakshmi Pandit to a decision from which there could be no turning back.

Thirteen days after Ranjit Pandit found peace at last, she took Rita back to her school, then returned to Calcutta to join the fight against famine. She organized the Save Our Indian Children Fund, and asked all India to contribute. She was distributing rice and milk to starving waifs in Calcutta's refugee slums, when word reached her that Kasturbai Gandhi, who spun her wedding *sari,* had died as quietly as she lived, in the Aga Khan's palace at Poona.

Married for sixty-four years to India's *Bapu,* Kasturbai died on February 22, when American soldiers in India were parading in observance of the birth-anniversary of George Washington, Father of His Country. Engrossed in India's woes and needs, the Mahatma, India's *Bapu,* had never found time to teach his wife how to read and write. For the rest of his life, he spent the twenty-second day of each month in silent recollection of his debt to her.

In 1944 rumor spread that Gandhi himself was dying. Fainthearts said "When the Mahatma goes, the Congress will die with him, and so will *Swaraj.* All the British need to do is wait, while the Americans finish winning the war for them." Vijaya Lakshmi Pandit never joined in unjust slurs on Britain's contribution to Free World victory. But British words and actions lessened hope already tenuous, that victory over Germany or Japan would bring freedom nearer for India.

From Washington, President Roosevelt called on the twenty-two United Nations to prepare for war against hunger, poverty, illiteracy, disease and deprivation, "when the war for human rights is won." But Winston Churchill told the House of Commons that although the Atlantic Charter bound Britain equally with the United States to "respect the right of all peoples to choose the form of government under which they will live," and to "see sovereign rights and self-government restored to those who have been forcibly deprived of them," this applied only in Europe, not at all in the far-flung British Empire.

Lord Wavell, ordering Gandhi's release "on medical grounds," concurrently rejected Gandhi's request for a meeting at which he would offer full war support in return for immediate independence. "I feel that a meeting between us at present could have no value and could only raise hopes which would be disappointed."

Her brother, still in prison, as he would be until June 15, 1945, wrote, "It matters little who is Viceroy. The virus lies in the system. Even the British Labour Party has stressed the resolve of the British people to keep the Empire together, exactly as it was *ante bellum*." At Dumbarton Oaks in the United States, representatives of the Allies against the Axis reported "large areas of agreement on postwar plans." Nothing was said about plans for India.

In Bombay, Gandhi and Mohammed Ali Jinnah met for eighteen consecutive days, but arrived at no agreement. Opinion was widely expressed that in asking "How can we 'Quit India' until Hindus and Muslims settle their differences?" defenders of *status quo* confessed their hope that settlement would prove impossible, "and the British can remain, righteously proclaiming that they do so only because it is clear the Indians are incapable of governing themselves, and the British cannot in conscience depart leaving anarchy behind them."

Vijaya Lakshmi Pandit is not known to have echoed this accusation, but there is no doubt that as the dark year wore on, she reached a point of doubt that would have reduced a lesser woman to despair. All that could be done about famine in Bengal had been done. There was no other work for her. She had no income. She had the Nehru pride. Fear of charity, however cloaked, more than the sin of self-pity she prefers to blame, made her refuse the help friends tried to give.

Then, warning them, "you'll wish you hadn't invited me," she went to dine with the consul for Nationalist China in Calcutta and his American wife. If their kind conspiracy seated her next to General Stratemeyer, she was unaware. "I'm not sure, the mood I was in, I would have behaved any better anyhow." When their meeting produced a way of escape, she hesitated. "One does not desert a sinking ship." But Gandhi said the ship was only becalmed, and would soon move again.

Dumbarton Oaks had produced "Proposals for the Establishment of a General International Organization." Roosevelt, Churchill and Stalin had agreed on a United Nations conference at San Francisco in April, 1945. Even Gandhi cannot have envisioned what would eventuate; but he had strange prescience, and a faculty for discerning potentials their possessors found in themselves only in the course of events.

As he advised, she made her peace with Ranjit Pandit's family. Then, wondering what lay ahead, she boarded the American plane that took her half-way around the globe. There was no one to meet her when she set foot on American soil for the first time. She found a telephone, and after delay that seemed interminable, heard Lekha's voice, now Wellesley-mannered.

"Mummie, where on earth are you calling from?" She steadied before she answered. "Why, from New York, U. S. A." There was brief silence. Then mother and daughter shared the luxury of tears.

IV ❁

"There have been many voices raised in praise."

On the first anniversary of their father's death, Lekha and Tara Pandit joined their mother in New York. They came prepared to take charge. She must not, they informed her, concern herself about how the family would manage. Lekha had the offer of a job in a New York publishing house. Tara was studying shorthand and typing, and beginning to send manuscripts to magazines. Their planning was interrupted by an urgent message. Would Madame Pandit consent to head an Indian delegation to the conference of the Institute of Pacific Relations, about to convene at Hot Springs, Virginia? She would; indeed she would.

It has been testified that the Agent-General for British India in the United States was under instructions to present Gandhi to Americans as a dangerously eccentric and erratic trouble-maker, Jawaharlal Nehru as "the Hamlet of India, a high-minded but ineffective aristocrat dabbling in politics," and the quarrel between Congress and the Muslim League as so insoluble that Britain could do no else than cry *A plague o' both your houses!* There had been no propagandist for the other side.

Now there was one. Press releases described her as "one of the world's most important women, notable for her great ideals and personal sacrifices." Reporters and photographers found her charming. Overnight, her public career on the world stage began. A lecture bureau proposed a speaking tour. She accepted, and spoke on *Why India Wants Independence,* and on *What Kind of a Postwar World?*

Her audiences grew. So did her fees. Jhansi-ki-Rani raised a flashing sword. Her weapon was herself. "Her realization that she could sway American crowds, and influence American editorialists and officials, restored her energy and confidence." Suddenly a Page One figure, she was still able to "stand ten feet off and look at myself and laugh a little." But her new crusade was deadly serious.

"Her life, like her brother's, was initially an escape from snobbism. Wealth and background could have made them the type-products of their time, caste-snobs. Educational advantages could have made them, as these made others who surrounded them, intellectual snobs. Imprisonments and family tragedies could have made them anti-British snobs. The brother first, the sister as first follower, escaped these pitfalls because they knew so well that they were there; which is to say, because they knew themselves." Her brother, under a pseudonym, called himself an actor who had no need for artificial aids. She became an actress, but only so her honesty would reach her audiences.

"She really does her homework!" an interviewer said. She had startled him with statistics. From an acre of land, a farmer in India produced ninety-six pounds of cotton, or a thousand one hundred pounds of rice, or six hundred and forty-one pounds of wheat; from an acre, an American farmer produced three times as much cotton, twice as much rice, or eight hundred and eighty-two pounds of wheat. Of a population estimated in 1941 to be three hundred and ninety millions, no more than twenty million lived comfortably, a hundred and thirty million existed under tolerable conditions, two hundred and forty million endured dire poverty. There was little probability that hunger and misery could be alleviated, while India was enchained by the *status quo.*

Would self-rule work a miracle? She said, "It did, for the United States." But was that a fair comparison? "Perhaps not. But love of liberty is a very powerful force in India today, as it was in America in 1776." What was her brother really like? If, that is, a sister could be objective? She could be; and was. She carried a clipping from a British-owned newspaper in India, in which an Indian journalist appraised him.

"Jawaharlal," the summary said, "is a bundle of contradictions in himself, a personality of divergent and conflicting forces. He has faith, but he doubts; he has dogged determination, and yet is indecisive; he is against compromise, and has had to compromise all his life; he has an innate humility, and still has pride. People like him despite his little foibles and weaknesses, are fond of him, indeed, because of them; for he is no party 'boss,' no idol aloof from the common man, mechanical in behavior and dealings with others, divine in his claims. He is of the earth, earthy. He laughs, and loses his temper, and jostles with the crowds and pats somebody on the back. He is one of us, like many of us, although very much higher up in stature and in quality. We salute him with pride and affection." Miss Fatima Jinnah was never known to admit mere mortal flaws in her brother. Vijaya Lakshmi Pandit's smiling frankness made Jawaharlal Nehru familiar to Americans, while Mohammed Ali Jinnah was hardly heard of.

Tara Pandit studied her mother thoughtfully. "She had a flair for human relationships and attracted people like a magnet. She lived with a robustness of response and a generosity of gesture." The psychologist may see in this why Miss Fatima Jinnah schooled herself so differently. "Humility, high in the Indian hierarchy of virtues, was no part of her. Modesty, considered so characteristic a trait of the Indian woman, was suspect in her eyes since it was so often donned for an occasion and just as easily discarded."

She fascinated Americans, while she often bewildered her daughters. "The lightning speed with which she made decisions and altered programs sometimes left us dazed. We asked her why she didn't look before she leaped. 'My children,' she told an American friend with an air of resignation no one was supposed to take too seriously, 'are a great disappointment to me. They have no sense of adventure.'"

Everything in America was an adventure for her. She was away in California, lecturing, when Lekha received her diploma at Wellesley. She made up for unavoidable absence by giving a grand dinner-dance at the Waldorf, to celebrate Lekha's twenty-first birthday. "That party did wonders for me, after years of prison guards and locked doors. I was happier than I had been for years!"

Rita, arriving by boat from India, was welcomed in a new

Home of Joy: a walkup apartment just off Park Avenue, above a wineshop and across the street from a Gay Nineties saloon. "Don't forget," Tara told her, "we don't live over an ordinary liquor store. The proprietor is a belted British Earl!" Soon the three daughters formed a committee to assist their mother in preparing to twist the tail of the British lion.

"Her most characteristic feature is her delight in a challenge," Tara wrote in her *My Mother, Vijaya Lakshmi Pandit,* "and she is not the person ever to refuse one. 'But it's never been done before!' has been a familiar refrain in her life. Invariably her answer has been, whether in actions or words, 'Oh, hasn't it? Well, it must be done now.' And she has calmly proceeded to do it, whether it has been some formidable official task or the minor miracle of cooking a meal for twenty people at short notice. My mother happens to have inherited a dogged determination from her remarkable father, in whose face circumstance had been known to tremble and give way. Because of this she has been able serenely to achieve a good deal that no woman before her had ever done, and very few have done since."

2.

No woman before or since has equaled the smiling skill with which she stirred up and then rode the crest of a storm at the United Nations conference in San Francisco. Fifty countries, great and small, came together to implement what the United States, Britain, Soviet Russia and Nationalist China had proposed in October, 1944: an organization empowered to use armed force to maintain world peace. Turkey, Egypt, Syria, Argentina and others had declared war on the Axis solely so they could qualify for seats at the planning-board. President Truman called on all concerned to "rise above personal interests." But it was well understood the question of British India was not on the agenda.

Vijaya Lakshmi Pandit put it there. She could not attend the conference, even as an observer, unless she represented some officially recognized organization. She found cosponsors: the Committee for Indian Freedom and the India League. Arriving at San Francisco, she was greeted by Indian nationals living there, most of them young students. They garlanded her with flowers. Pictures of her pushed those of distinguished statesmen from newspaper front pages.

How she managed matters from this beginning fascinated K. P. S. Menon, today his country's most respected diplomat-in-retirement, in 1945 a senior careerist in the Indian Civil Service and chief advisor to the British India delegation—regarding whom it should perhaps be repeated that he is in no sense related to a sharer of his name much better-known to Americans, the intransigent Krishna Menon. K. P. S. Menon recalls that "Pursuant to established policy, the British India delegation was carefully balanced between Hindus, Muslims, and the princes, and between Indians and Englishmen."

Headed by Sir Ramaswamy Mudaliar, "a government servant who had risen high both because of his ability and his anti-Congress outlook," the delegation included Sir Firoze Khan Noon, "who had been thrown up by Muslim communal politics," and would later be a Prime Minister of Pakistan and Pakistan's fiery spokesman against India in Kashmir debates before the United Nations; Sir V. T. Krishnamachari, "who had a long record of service in British as well as Princely India"; Sir John Bartley and Major General Cawthorne. None of these favored Indian independence.

In London, they had been briefed by Prime Minister Churchill, "who described the conception of China as a Great Power as 'the great American illusion,' pooh-poohed the principle of 'sovereign equality of states proposed in the Atlantic Charter,' and when he learned Liberia expected United Nations membership, said 'Liberia? A hundred thousand diseased Negroes!' " The delegates had known her father. They wanted nothing to do with Vijaya Lakshmi Pandit.

"Ramaswamy Mudaliar thought it best to keep her at arm's length. He would not ask her to the receptions he gave at our hotel." There was no room at any inn for her. "Are you a delegate?" Not officially. "We're sorry. All our rooms are reserved for delegates." She had slept on a wooden cot, in the pouring rain, in prison yards, and on a pallet on stone in prison cells. She was wholly aware of cameras focusing on her as she settled down to spend the night in a chair in a hotel lobby. Nor were British observers oblivious to awakened American sympathy for unprivileged India, resulting from her inwardly amused performance.

Hotel managers, reading the papers, suddenly remembered accommodations they had overlooked. English correspondents labeled her "a nuisance," but American delegates came to call, in the suite she accepted. Among them was Harold Stassen, then considered a promising candidate for President. He was puzzled by discovery that other delegates had their own definitions for words Americans thought the whole world understood to have the meaning given to them in the American Plan. One of these was *democracy*. She said she accepted her brother's definition.

"Democracy, as he understands it, 'means something more than a certain form of government and a body of egalitarian laws. It is essentially a scheme of values and moral standards in life. Whether you are democratic or not depends on how you act and think as an individual or as a group. Democracy demands discipline, tolerance and mutual respect. In a democracy, changes are made by mutual discussions and persuasions and not by violent means. Democracy means equality; not merely the equality of possessing a vote, but economic and social equality.'"

Harold Stassen was impressed. Interviewed, he spoke of her highly. This did no harm, when she called a press conference. So many reporters and photographers turned up that it had to be held in the Scottish Rite Auditorium. She faced them, small, elegant, wearing a pastel-hued *sari* and no jewels, and in her unaccented English read the memorandum she had sent that morning to the Secretary General of the conference.

"I speak here for my country because its voice has been stilled by British duress. But I speak also for those countries, which like India, cannot speak for themselves. The voice of six hundred million of the enslaved people of Asia may not be officially heard at this conference . . . but there will be no real peace on earth as long as they are denied justice." Her statement was given more space than that of Sir Ramaswamy Mudaliar, which K. P. S. Menon described as "like his politics, a Victorian hotchpotch." One reason was that an attempt was made to keep her from being heard.

"Mrs. Pandit eclipsed the official Indian delegation in the

public eye because of the conduct of a stenographer for Sir Firoze Khan Noon, who, without the knowledge of any of us except Noon, invaded her press conference and tried to heckle her. He was thrown out by American reporters, and next day we read that the British had planted a member of their delegation with orders to raise a disturbance. This was not really accurate, but from the British view, the damage had been done."

More damage was to come. The California Legislature invited her to speak at Sacramento. She spoke with passion and dramatic eloquence, and was given a standing ovation. Five thousand welcomed her in the Sikh Temple built at Stockton by emigrants from India's Punjab, now American citizens. She paid tribute to sons of India "who have died for the Free World on every battlefront," and asked "Where is that freedom?"

News reports described her as "dainty and deft, with the velocity of the wind, that rides roughshod over all obstacles," and as "A daring robin that dashes in and steals the tidbit right from under the beak of some bigger, more ferocious bird." She says, "I had great fun! One can, when one has no responsibility. I had none, except to India. I was aware I was stealing the show from the British Indian delegates, and loved doing it. In fact I deliberately went out to do so whenever possible." But not for herself; for India.

3.

Growing skill in dealing with the press saved her from recourse to "All I know is what I read in the papers," but in fact she was completely out of touch otherwise, with happenings in

India. Her first news that her brother had been freed at last, after a thousand and forty-one days in prison, was buried beneath a San Francisco headline: *Native Chieftains Summoned to Simla.* He was listed among the "native chieftains."

Much later, she learned that he went on pilgrimage in memory of Ranjit Pandit, before he joined Gandhi at a summit conference convened by Lord Wavell in British India's summer capital. This began on the day on which, at San Francisco, United Nations organizing delegates adopted a resolution "designed to insure lasting peace." She could not sign. She could only pray for peace in India.

End of war in Europe had been followed by a breakup of Winston Churchill's coalition Cabinet. A pilot who did not propose to be dropped while safe harbor was still not reached, he called a general election. His Labour opposition cried, "Never mind about the Battle of Britain; that's over and done with. What about the mess in India?" Lord Wavell, recalled to England, was sent back to offer a peace plan under which all members of the governing Executive Council, but the Viceroy and the commander-in-chief, would be Indians.

"This," Lord Wavell said at Simla, "is the utmost progress possible under the present Constitution." It could, however, be a step toward Muslim-Hindu unity. With this in mind, Gandhi and Jawaharlal nominated two Muslims for Executive Council membership. Within three years, one of these, Maulana Azad, at this time the Congress president, would be India's first Minister of Education; the other, Asaf Ali, first Indian Ambassador to the United States. To Mohammed Ali Jinnah, they were renegades; that they collaborated with Hindus made them so.

Lord Wavell's ground rules, made clear in advance, specified that "No party to the conference will be permitted to obstruct a settlement out of willfulness." However, Jinnah declared that unless he and he alone named the Muslim representatives, the Muslim League would boycott the proceedings and whatever might ensue from them. American headlines read *India Peace Effort Fails*.

Vijaya Lakshmi Pandit kept what she thought of Jinnah to herself, and continued to impress American reporters and lecture crowds with her calm confidence that, in spite of setbacks, the march to freedom would continue. Great change in Britain made this credible. By overwhelming majority, British voters retired Winston Churchill from the post he had filled heroically since 1940. On July 26, 1945, Clement Attlee succeeded him as Prime Minister.

Convinced by victory that the British people were weary not only of blood, sweat and tears, but of dominion over palm and pine, the Attlee government immediately began the obsequies of Empire, ordering elections in India for the central and provincial legislatures at the earliest possible date. Those elected would be called on to form a constitution-making body, "in order to give India complete self-rule." The entire process must be completed not later than June of 1948.

Two hundred years before, Clive of India began British capture of the subcontinent with transactions described by a Muslim historian as "done and finished in less time than would have been taken up in the purchase of a camel." Now in Little Englands scattered over India, bearers of the White Man's Burden complained that with equal haste, politicians at home had sold them out. But June of 1948 was still a long way off.

On August 6, 1945, the first atom bomb was dropped on Hiroshima in Japan, destroying sixty percent of that city. On August 9, the second atom bomb fell on Nagasaki. One-third of Nagasaki was erased. The two bombs killed more than one hundred thousand, injured nearly eighty thousand; fifteen thousand were listed as "missing." On August 15, Japan surrendered. Then it was learned that in the last years of the war, Subhas Bose had died in a mysterious air crash on Formosa.

His Indian National Liberation Army, recruited from among Indian officers and soldiers captured by the Japanese in Burma and Malaya, had been little larger or more effective than the Irish Legion enlisted by Sir Roger Casement during the First World War. Its rally cry was *Chalo Delhi!* On to Delhi! The shout was never heard in combat. But now the Raj made *Chalo Delhi!* a call to arms in India.

Suddenly, it was announced that three officers who served under Subhas Bose would be tried for high treason. With what may or may not have been bureaucratic ineptness, someone somewhere in the labyrinthine structure of the Raj selected as archetypes of treason a Hindu, a Muslim and a Sikh, thus in effect placing India's three majority religious communities on trial.

Compounding error, if error it was, the trial was ordered held in the Moghul Red Fort in Old Delhi, itself a symbol of once-united India. Subhas Bose had been almost forgotten. Now he was metamorphosed into a national hero. The Hindu and Muslim and Sikh, who took Japanese pay through him, were transfigured into martyrs. No matter what the Attlee government had ordered, decision at Delhi could ignite such violence that British withdrawal would be impossible.

It was not Vijaya Lakshmi Pandit's place or right to attempt explaining to Americans the possibility of deliberate sabotage behind a case in which, in any event, they were not greatly interested. Nor did she need to be. She could stay on in America, where she was happily settled with her daughters, had made a new life for herself, was surrounded by voices raised in praise. So could she and Ranjit Pandit have stayed on in London, when they went there for their second honeymoon.

If they had, there need have been no separations, no imprisonments, no early death for him and lonely widowhood for her. They reached decision together. She made hers now. Arranging for Lekha to return to India by ship, leaving Tara at Wellesley and Rita at Putney in Vermont, she said "Goodbye" to American friends with no expectation that they would ever meet again, and left on the first available plane, to join her brother in Delhi.

He showed no surprise when they met. For the first time in twenty-five years, he wore a barrister's robe and wig. He had volunteered, together with Bhulabhai Desai, India's most brilliant courtroom pleader now that Motilal Nehru was gone, and Asaf Ali, next to Mohammed Ali Jinnah the most highly regarded Muslim lawyer, to defend the Hindu, Muslim and Sikh on trial for their lives at the Red Fort.

He had disagreed with Subhas Bose, and with the thinking that led Indians to serve the Japanese, but he said, "This has become a trial of strength between the people of India, all the people, and those who have held power over them." Contrarily, Vijaya Lakshmi learned, Jinnah had refused to appear for the defense, or to have anything to do with the case.

By letter of the law, the three defendants were guilty as charged. But impassioned presentation of their reason for disloyalty to Britain, their loyalty to India, however wrongly shown, supervened the technicality. Convicted, they were immediately granted full pardon by General Sir Claude Auchinleck, the British commander-in-chief. "The end of an era is brought closer," a British commentator summarized, "by those who thought it could be indefinitely prolonged. A deadly blow has been dealt to the remnants of British prestige, and by the British themselves. Bluster has faded to an apologetic whine."

News of victory at the Red Fort went before her, in the Kanpur villages to which Vijaya Lakshmi Pandit returned, campaigning for reelection to the United Provinces legislative assembly. At Allahabad, she walked in the old city, and at Anand Bhavan told her brother "It's dirty and the people are inefficient and everything seems to have stood still while the rest of the world races ahead, but I'm glad I came home!"

Setting out to seek votes, she vowed "If I'm elected, it's going to be a busy day for everybody, cleaning up this corner of the country!" A month before, she trimmed a Christmas tree, in the walkup flat over the wine shop just off Park Avenue in Manhattan. Now in her homeland she renewed acquaintance with men and women not one of whom would ever enjoy what was ordinary to Americans. "But what I had heard some Americans call a bother and a waste of time was wonderful to them. They had a voice; they could vote. I stopped making speeches, and just told them about the neighbors they hadn't known they had."

She did her best to explain the United Nations, the United

States and Americans: "not always the wisest or most diplomatic, but I truly believe, the most instinctively generous and friendly people, happy to help and hoping to be liked, of any people I have known." Voters for the Great Lady, who won friends for India so far from them, elected her by majority that again led to her appointment as Minister for Health and Local Self-Government.

Now she campaigned among Congress members, in her brother's behalf. He was one of three nominees for Congress president, a post that had never been as important as it was now. Mohammed Ali Jinnah confidently expected appointment as interim Prime Minister. Jinnah at the head of negotiations could dominate, delay, perhaps destroy. Brought to realize this danger, Congress closed ranks.

Jawaharlal Nehru, not Jinnah, would be the one invited to serve as Prime Minister. Jinnah ordered all Muslims elected to legislatures to boycott constitution-making proceedings. Congress planners went ahead, with the Constitution of the United States for a model, "because it is based on a series of agreements as well as a series of compromises." Jinnah's strategy of obstruction was aided suddenly, by impatient Indian sailors in the Royal Indian Navy.

They had always been paid less, fed and treated less well than their shipmates who happened to have white skins. On February 19, 1946, at Bombay, three thousand of them demonstrated, demanding equal pay and treatment. Brawls broke out. British officers and men were driven ashore. Disorder spread, until lorries loaded with rebellious Indian seamen, flying Congress, Muslim League and hammer-and-sickle red flags, cruised streets in Bombay, Karachi, Calcutta and

Madras. A thousand Indians in the Royal Indian Air Force joined the rebels.

Military police opened fire. The rebels retaliated with hand grenades. By February 22, Indian sailors were in full control of twenty Royal Navy vessels, including the British Vice-Admiral's flagship. Finally, Mohammed Ali Jinnah joined Vallabhbhai Patel in appealing to the rebels to surrender, under guarantees that their grievances would be arbitrated, and none would be punished.

Civilians, however, went on rioting. Police fired indiscriminately on Hindus, Muslims and Sikhs. Two hundred were killed, and a thousand injured. Jinnah was occupied elsewhere, while Gandhi and Jawaharlal risked themselves recklessly to reason with the rioters, warning misled mobs that fratricide imperiled the freedom for which they thought they fought. Briefly, rioters appeared to welcome armistice.

Then a British Cabinet Mission, dubbed the Three Wise Men, having parleyed exhaustively with spokesmen for Congress and the Muslim League, issued a White Paper, which rejected Jinnah's demand for a separate Pakistan, and proposed a six-point plan for a constitution making India a united nation. Gandhi urged acceptance of this "seed to convert this land of sorrow into one without sorrow and suffering." But on July 29, 1946, Jinnah proclaimed: "This day we bid goodbye to constitutional methods. We will either have a divided India or a destroyed India."

His adjutant, Sardar Abdur Rab Nishtar, told foreign correspondents "Pakistan can only be achieved by shedding blood, and we Muslims are no believers in nonviolence." Jinnah set **August 16** as Direct Action Day. On that day, Muslims rioted in Calcutta and at Sylhet in Assam, launching what newspapers described as *The Great Killing*. Hindus and Sikhs fought back. In Bombay, aloof from the bloodshed, Jinnah trumpeted, "India stands on the brink of ruinous civil war." His sister was proud beside him.

4.

Vijaya Lakshmi Pandit could not be beside her brother. She was back in the United States, heading India's first delegation to the United Nations General Assembly, convening at Lake Success in a building left over from New York's 1939 World's Fair. Lord Wavell had appointed her. Her brother said she must accept. "India," he said, "cannot play a secondary part in the world. She will either count for a great deal or not count at all." So while nightmare ran its course at home, she was sent to convince representatives of fifty-three nations, if she could, that India, though not yet free, belonged in their company.

No other woman has borne such responsibility. No precursor had charted guide lines. Before her, only Sarojini Naidu went abroad to speak for India. Since India had only an interim government, her appointment had to be confirmed by the King-Emperor. Mounting crisis in India could cancel her credentials at any time. In San Francisco she was free to improvise, teasing and troubling British Indian delegates. At the United Nations, she spoke officially; and one careless answer to a baited question could end her usefulness.

Reporters and photographers pursued her, and kept her on newspaper front pages. There was no such hesitance as there had been in San Francisco, to provide her with hotel accommodations. Noted statesmen accorded courtesies to her that they would have extended to no other newcomer entering their lofty sphere. She had only to smile and charm, preside graciously over her colleagues, play the role of gentle princess grateful for deference from giants and the forebearance of ogres; and more than ever, voices would be raised in praise. Safe courses, however, never attracted her. She came to get things done; and she set about this with matter-of-fact immediacy.

The witness to what ensued was K. P. S. Menon, the only member of the San Francisco delegation reappointed to serve with her. Also in the delegation at Lake Success was V. K. Krishna Menon, who lacked the other Menon's respect for voices other than his own. "I found him insufferable," K. P. S. Menon says. "He looked so superior. It was as if he, and he alone, knew all about international affairs, and the other members of our delegation were but playboys, with one playgirl."

Krishna Menon's own biographer, T. J. S. George, says, "He was simply too big to be confined to one diplomatic mission where there was too little diplomacy and too much administration. The United Nations, on the contrary, suited his own genius." Whether Krishna Menon authorized this conclusion, deponent sayeth not. The record shows he had volunteered many directives, on how India's new constitution should read, in lengthy correspondence from London. His basic concept, that India should be a socialist welfare state, was firmly rejected.

Commissioned to offer suggestions for organization of India's Foreign Service, he conferred at length with the Soviet Foreign Minister, Vyacheslav Molotov. Harold Laski, regarding whom Americans had conflicting opinions, was not alone in the opinion that Menon had done more for India than any other man. Vincent Sheean wrote that "He has never been personally mistreated by a government or an official. He has never been imprisoned, nor has a *lathi* ever fallen across his shoulders. But . . . the kind of work he was doing and the way he did it amounted to self-immolation."

Thus introduced to Americans, he was immediately the target for cameras that dramatized his saturnine countenance, while his manner during interviews prompted New York's *Herald Tribune* to call him "one of the most militant champions of colonial people." To his admiring biographer, his first appearance in the United States was "the beginning of the roving Ambassador, the representative of Nehru, the negotiator, the militant voice at the United Nations."

Militant was also the word for him as second to Vijaya Lakshmi Pandit in the Indian delegation. They had had little contact since casual meeting in London in 1926. In 1939 she had written from India introducing Ranjit Pandit's nephew and niece, who were on their way to Cambridge, and asking him to "be a dear and keep an eye on these kids while they are in England." He obliged; but at Lake Success in 1947, he was not obliging. "When he opened his mouth," K. P. S. Menon says, "barbs of satire came out."

The woman who stood above him was to speak on a resolution to admit Ireland, Portugal and Mongolia to United Nations membership. K. P. S. Menon drafted her speech. "Krishna Menon started picking holes in it. I argued my point of view and showed that his criticisms had no substance in them. This only made him more cantankerous. Finally I told Mrs. Pandit that if a single comma in my draft was altered, I would have nothing more to do with it. She could not, or would not, choose between us."

He thinks this may have been because "She found a little feminine pleasure in the spectacle of two men squabbling." The odds are that this was not the answer. Often, when she was still Little Daughter, her father roared, her brother stiffened stubbornly, and while she judged between them, she let neither guess which one she thought was wrong. At Lake Success, she gave K. P. S. Menon's speech as written.

Krishna Menon's biographer dates their estrangement from this first crossing of swords. "It . . . became a favorite topic of gossip in the United Nations. 'They are so good at finding solutions for world problems. Why don't they find a solution to the problem of their own mutual relations?' " On the evidence, if there was bitterness, it was all on one side. Vijaya Lakshmi Pandit holds with Gautama Buddha, who said "If I refuse to accept my enemy's anger, he is left with it, and he, not I, must live with it."

5.

On her desk at Lake Success was Lord Elton's *Imperial Commonwealth,* just published. "The road of the reformers of 1919," according to Lord Elton, at the end of 1945 had "reached the destined goal, deadlock within politically conscious India, deadlock therefore among the unconscious masses, deadlock, let us say, between the one hundred and eighty millions for whom Congress spoke, eighty million who would welcome 'Pakistan,' eighty million subjects of the native states, fifty million members of the Depressed Classes."

She disagreed with Lord Elton. So did the Attlee government, which advanced India's Independence Day from June of 1948, to August 15, 1947. With freedom still in the future, she told the United Nations, "Two commitments are the keynote of Indian policy: First, to end racial discrimination; second, to help free the countries of Asia from political and social bondage." She was fully aware that this set a murmur going among varied groups of delegates.

She continued forthrightly. "Having herself suffered from all the evils of colonialism and imperialist domination, India is inevitably committed to this course. There is no feeling of hatred or antagonism for foreign powers, but simply the conviction that colonialism is contrary to the principles of the United Nations and endangers the purposes of the Charter itself. Both issues contain the seeds of future wars."

She surprised interviewers by taking a text not from Mahatma Gandhi, but from America's Great Emancipator. "Abraham Lincoln's words are too much forgotten. 'What constitutes the bulwark of our own liberties? It is not our frowning battlements, out bristling seacoasts, our army and our navy. These are not our reliance against tyranny. Our reliance is the love of liberty which God has planted in us. Our defense is in the spirit which prizes liberty as the heritage of all men, in all lands everywhere.' "

The press might persist in picturing her with adjectives usually applied to film stars. Krishna Menon might resent her as a playgirl intruding where only he should tread. She was

India personified when on October 25, 1946, Paul-Henri Spaak of Belgium, president of the General Assembly, announced "I now call on Mrs. Vijaya Lakshmi Pandit," and for the first time in history, a woman spoke as equal of men who ruled the world.

She went to the dais as calmly as she had gone to improvised rostrums in the Kanpur villages. "I stand before this great Assembly, unique in the annals of human affairs, where representatives of freedom-loving countries of the world are gathered together," she began, "to proclaim not only the adherence of my country to the principles and purposes of the United Nations as embodied in the Charter, but the determination of our people to help make it a reality."

She spoke of "our Prime Minister," not of "my brother." This was her rule on all occasions. She was, she said, instructed to inform the United Nations that India, although not yet at the end of the long climb to freedom, was ready to participate fully in United Nations activities. "Our country stands for the independence of all colonial and dependent peoples, and their full right to self-determination."

She claimed for India a place on the Security and Trusteeship Councils. "Let us recognize that human emotions and needs of the world will not wait for an indefinite period. To this end let us direct our energies, and, reminding ourselves that in our unity of purpose alone lies the hope of the world, let us march on."

The press reported: "She was poised, dignified, and beautiful. She spoke eloquently and forcefully. She said Indian women were now taking part in all nation-building work, that India believes responsibility must be shared jointly by men and women in order to create a better and more balanced world. Applause for her was loud and long." *Many voices have been raised in praise*. But now she was required to do battle against a warrior few men had challenged without regretting the encounter.

The first controversial issue raised by India was being talked to death in the joint political and legal committees. Technically, debate was on a resolution affirming that South Africa's racist policies, against which Gandhi crusaded for twenty years, endangered future relations between that country and her own. In effect, the United Nations was asked to establish precedent condemning racism anywhere.

There was strong desire among delegates to bypass delicate subjects. Members of her delegation doubted that the resolution, however watered down, would be allowed to reach the General Assembly floor. What Krishna Menon thought is not recorded; he appears to have been absent, while she carried the flag. Her antagonist was Field Marshal Jan Christiaan Smuts, who headed the South African delegation.

A hero against the British in the Boer War, then commander of British forces in Africa during the First World War, a member of Britain's Imperial War Cabinet, a principal architect of the Union of South Africa and twice its Prime Minister, at seventy-six he was prepared to fight and die in defense of white supremacy. His stand was curt and clear: South Africa's way of treating Coloureds was none of India's business, and no affair of the United Nations.

He and Gandhi had liked each other, man to man, and he was personally fond of Vijaya Lakshmi Pandit, but he sat silent while a member of his delegation, Heaton Nicholls, shouted at her. India, Nicholls inveighed, was guilty of "treating her own Untouchables worse than any Indian is treated in my country." South Africa was "upholding Christian civilization in a dark continent inhabited by primitive natives and polygamous races." So saying, he gave her weapons she used with a woman's skill.

Addressing brownskinned Muslim delegates from the Middle East, she said she believed the Prophet Mohammed had sanctioned plural marriage. As for Christian civilization, she said to American and European delegates, under South Africa's racist laws if Jesus Christ were to appear in that country, "He would be listed as a 'prohibited immigrant.' " With a touch of awe, K. P. S. Menon records "The resolution passed." He adds, however, that "Whether it would secure the necessary two-thirds majority in the plenary session of the General Assembly was uncertain."

He had more to learn about her. "Many people thought that Mrs. Pandit, whilst delivering her final plea, was in tears. Whether this affected the voting or not, I do not know; but to our great joy, the resolution was carried, by a majority of one." Accompanied by her daughter, Tara, now nineteen, the one responsible went immediately to Field Marshal Smuts.

"My instructions from Gandhiji before I left India," she told him, "were that I should shake your hand and ask for your blessing. I hope I have not said anything to hurt you." He said to Tara, "You think I'm a terrible old man, don't you?" He patted her mother's hand. "She is like a daughter to me. Can you understand that? It grieves me to have to fight her." Tara asked, "Then why do you?"

The question went unanswered. He told her mother "Well,

my child, you have won. But it will be a hollow victory." K. P. S. Menon thinks he was wrong. "The resolution adopted in 1946 was the beginning of the stirring of conscience in United Nations members which in 1962 led to a unanimous resolution against South Africa and Portugal."

In what she believed was her last appearance at the United Nations, she said "I want to express the gratitude not only of the people of India and the Indians of South Africa, but of the millions in every country whose hearts have been warmed and whose minds are eased by this impressive expression of world opinion in defense of justice and fundamental human rights." Her mission was accomplished. For the first time, India had emerged, and been accepted, as a force in international relations. Now there was other work to be done.

She said another farewell to Tara and Rita, leaving them in the United States while she returned to resume her place in the United Provinces Legislative Assembly at Lucknow. There the presiding officer said, "I take this opportunity of offering our heartiest congratulations to the Honorable Member, Mrs. Vijaya Lakshmi Pandit, for the great work she has done for India in America." She hardly heard. What mattered, all that mattered, was what was happening at home.

6.

In advancing the date on which Britain would quit India to August 15, 1947, Prime Minister Clement Attlee conditioned this on establishment by then of "a government which, resting on the sure support of the people, will be capable of maintaining peace and administering India with justice and efficiency." Toward this end, he announced that Queen Victoria's great-grandson, Admiral Lord Louis Mountbatten, would succeed Lord Wavell, as British India's twentieth and last Viceroy, "entrusted with the task of transferring the responsibility for government to Indian hands, in a manner which will best insure the future happiness and prosperity of India."

There would be no constitution, the British would not withdraw from India, unless Mohammed Ali Jinnah got his way. "Terrific disasters await India," he warned, "unless there is a separate Pakistan." As if on signal, violence raged in Bengal, where Gandhi preached Hindu-Muslim brotherhood, and in the Punjab, where the Muslim Premier resigned in repudiation of Jinnah's separatism.

The Buddhist Emperor Asoka, uniting India as a secular nation in which all faiths were honored equally, had no Muslims to contend with; they did not exist in India until nine centuries later, and the first Muslim conqueror, Mahmud of Ghazni, did not appear, gaining converts to Islam with fire and sword, until shortly before the Norman Conquest of the British Isles. Even now, Pathans on the North West Frontier were allied with the Congress, not with the Muslim League, and their Muslim leader, Dr. Khan Sahib, declined to take orders from Jinnah.

"The Pakistan idea," in the opinion of Sir Olaf Caroe, who governed the North West Frontier Province at this time, "appealed at first, mainly to the Muslim population down-country, where Muslims, though culturally well-established and proud of a long history, were numerically swamped by Hindus. Jinnah, though born in Karachi, had made his home in Bombay, and Liaquat Ali Khan, his deputy, came from the heart of Hindustan, a district close to Delhi. On the Frontier, where Muslims formed ninety-four percent of the population, the two-nation theory was in the balance, and its acceptance still uncertain."

If the Frontier could be held, unity might still be won. "Jawaharlal Nehru came up to Peshawar to rally his supporters. It was a brave effort, but ill-conceived and bound to fail; it was also fatal to those who thought in terms of a united India. The majority of Pathans thought they were witnessing the impossible about to happen: Afghan submission to direction and homily by a Brahmin. The flags of Islam were unfurled, and Jinnah had his way."

The Raj had mobilized all its strength, military and civilian, against attackers of the *status quo*. That fight was lost; but the losers still clung to last hope. "Few British officials had their hearts in the job of maintaining law and order. In the minds of some of them at least the prospect of civil chaos on the eve of independence was not without its allurement." Nor could this be wondered at.

Death of the Empire was the end of the only world they knew for thousands of *Sahibs* and *Memsahibs* in a hundred Little Englands dotting the subcontinent. Eight generations of bearers of the White Man's Burden had called England "home," while they lived and died in India. Sons and daughters, sent to England for their education, returned to marry in the Army or the Indian Civil Service, and their sons and daughters did the same. Young Sandhurst graduates joined the regiments in which their fathers and grandfathers had commanded. They shared the article of faith that Rudyard

Kipling propounded when Victoria Regina reigned: that brown soldiers would fight only if Englishmen led them. *Always the English watch nearby, to prop them when they fall!*

Lancers and Gurkhas and Guides were their families. The British Cantonments, always set apart from India's cities, were green and clean and guarded. Each had its burial ground, with gravestones honoring the fallen in Kipling's Thin Red Line of Heroes. Each had its polo field, and silver trophies polished daily by *abdars* in the Officers' Mess. Each had its proud traditions and its whispered scandals. "Polo playing, pig-sticking, horse racing, shooting big game, played a constant part in our affairs," Winston Churchill wrote in 1897, when he came to India planning a lifelong career in the Cavalry, "with a brief interlude now and then for putting the lesser breeds back in their proper place. If you liked to be waited on, India was perfection."

Now all that was over, or about to be. "Our troops are housed in cool, colonnaded barracks. Splendid roads, endless double avenues of shady trees, abundant supplies of pure water, imposing offices, hospitals, and other institutions, and ample lawns and gardens, characterize these centers of the separate life of white communities isolated in India." Now all this must be surrendered. Or could it still be saved?

If it could not, then a whole ruling class would be left with nowhere to go. Home regiments had no room for officers from the Army in India. They had no other career. Some, swallowing pride, asked to be kept on, as advisors to brown inferiors now moving up in rank. Some were needed; but none were wanted. Retirement on half-pay meant genteel poverty, no servants for their wives, no *amahs* for their children. Many were deep in debt to Parsi and Ismailiah moneylenders. Loans allowed to run on for years, at two percent per month, must now be settled in full, through forced auction of belongings accumulated during a century.

The Bengal Lancers, electing to go with Pakistan, erased "Bengal" from their standard with its hundred-odd battle-ribbons. For a hundred and thirty years, the Gurkhas, terrible little fighters from Nepal, had served the Raj. Now four Gurkha regiments transferred allegiance to the British Army and were sent out of India. The rest chose to remain in the new Indian Army, for the first time serving under officers of their own race and faith. Again, in the slow march of British soldiers leaving cantonments laid out by Lord Cornwallis, bag-pipes skirled *The World Turned Up-Side Down*. None inter-vened between Hindus, Muslims and Sikhs, who killed each other just outside the gates.

Jawaharlal Nehru went to Rawalpindi, into the midst of frenzied slaying. "I have seen ghastly sights," he told his sis-ter, "and I have heard of behavior by human beings that would degrade brutes." On the eve of Lord Mountbatten's arrival, the Punjab death toll passed two thousand. In Assam, Hindus rose savagely against Jinnah's insistence that their homeland must be part of his Islamic Pakistan. Gandhi pleaded with wild mobs in Bihar, charging Hindus with "hav-ing forgotten in a fit of insanity the brotherhood of man under the Fatherhood of God." Fanatics threatened him. "I would forfeit my claim of being a Hindu," he replied, "if I bolstered the wrongdoings of fellow Hindus."

It is difficult, and in fact almost impossible, to induce Vijaya Lakshmi Pandit to discuss the horror that swirled around her in those times; but sometimes memories darken her lambent eyes. She was present, when Mountbatten, a regal figure in white naval uniform, took the Viceregal salute at New Delhi; she saw, from not far off, his first meeting with Jinnah. "My God, he was cold!" Mountbatten told his adjutant.

Mountbatten offered to send a plane to bring Gandhi from Bihar, for truce talks with Jinnah. Gandhi chose to come by train, so he could continue pleading along the way for an end to violence. At each stop, he raised funds for relief of Muslims and Hindus alike. Then from March 31 through April 12, Gandhi, Jinnah and Mountbatten met and met again.

"Those two weeks and the two months that followed," Louis Fischer wrote, "were the most fateful in Indian history." According to Mountbatten: "Personally I was convinced that the right solution would be to keep India united. But Jinnah made it clear from the first moment that as long as he lived, he would never accept anything but partition." Mountbatten had his orders, and was too much the military strategist to settle for less than his assigned objective. How much help he had from others who wore English uniform, no one could say. He had none from Jinnah.

7.

Muslims lived everywhere on the subcontinent, from the Khyber Pass to Cape Comorin, from the Bay of Bengal to the Indian Ocean. Millions of them had nothing in common beyond belief in Allah. Most Muslims in thickly settled Bengal descended from Hindu converts. Their social and economic structure was still stratified by Hindu caste tradition. Jinnah took no account of this, nor of millions of Hindus settled for generations in areas he now claimed for Islam.

Geographically, his Pakistan was a nonesuch: "two patches on the map with India between them." Even to many Muslims, it was "an artificial creation born of tense emotions and British manipulations." More than half of its proposed population lived a thousand miles from the rest, and farther away than that in heritage and culture. The two groups spoke completely different languages. Those in the West Wing cherished a militant history; those in the East Wing, often conquered, had never been conquerors. The majority in both Wings were poor and illiterate. Hindus were the business people, the industrialists, the money-makers.

To outsiders, it seemed logical to sum up: "Pakistan is not a country, and never can be." They prophesied early disintegration, return at least of Bengal to the Indian Federal Union. But Jinnah's single-mindedness made the difference. The emaciated, dying Quaid-i-Azam towered over his people like another Gulliver. Pakistan he would have, or there would be no freedom, for Hindus or for Muslims.

Suddenly, surprising almost everyone and Jinnah most of all, Gandhi proposed, "Mr. Nehru will resign. Mr. Jinnah can then take his place as interim Prime Minister." He told the startled Mountbatten, "I am absolutely serious and sincere. I can see no other way to end the communal bloodshed." Notably, neither Jawaharlal Nehru nor his sister protested Gandhi's seeming surrender. And slowly it dawned on watchers of the duel, that Gandhi had in fact trapped Jinnah in dilemma. He wanted to be Prime Minister. But if he accepted now, acceptance could be construed as admission of culpability.

He said "No," and joined with Gandhi in a published appeal to all communities "not only to refrain from all acts of violence and disorder, but also to avoid in speech and in writing, any words which might be taken as an incitement to such acts." He did not, however, withdraw or temper the demand that incited the rioting of which, publicly, he washed his hands.

Vijaya Lakshmi Pandit knew her brother's convictions were as strong as Gandhi's. He had worked almost as long for a united secular India. He was sure, and so was she, that partition into two nations, on no basis but religious separatism, set them almost inevitably on collision course. She watched him, silently, while he fought out within himself decision between death at the door, and surgery that could not cure but might not kill. Loyalty, she knew, was the virtue he esteemed above all others. He had disagreed with Gandhi, on occasion flatly opposed him, but where Gandhi was adamant, he had deferred to the older, wiser man he had followed for so long.

Gandhi had said as early as 1942, "Jawaharlal will be my successor. He says he does not understand my language, and that he speaks a language foreign to me. This may or may not be true. But language is no bar to a union of hearts. And I know this, that when I am gone, he will speak my language." But Gandhi was not gone. His chosen heir must appear to usurp authority, if he went contrary to Gandhi's insistence that partition "will bring thirty-two years of struggle to an inglorious end."

"I have not convinced India," Gandhi had told Louis Fischer two years before. Now it was impossible to convince him. Her brother had only to say "As always, Gandhiji, you are right," and whatever ensued, the blame would not be his. But she knew him too well to expect he would shirk responsibility he felt was rightly his.

"The alternatives," he said finally, "are Pakistan, or continued British rule, and independence never." Grimly, Vallabhbhai Patel concurred. "We have reached a stage where otherwise we must lose all." He told Maulana Azad, "I am convinced Pakistan is not viable and will not last. I think acceptance of Pakistan will teach the Muslim League a bitter lesson. Pakistan will collapse in a short time and the provinces that secede from India will have to face untold difficulty and hardship. They will ask us to let them come back."

If he believed this, and was not merely attempting to justify decision after the fact, he had company. Gandhi told a prayer-meeting, "Jawaharlal is our king, but we should not be impressed by everything the king does or does not do," but he also said, "We Muslims and Hindus are interdependent on each other; we cannot get along without each other. The Muslim League will ask to come back. They will ask Jawaharlal, and he will take them back." Jawaharlal himself said, "One day, integration will come. If it will be in four, five, ten years, I don't know." Wearily, finally, he told Jinnah in Mountbatten's presence: "Well, if you insist on Pakistan, have it."

And Jinnah, having won all he asked for, asked for more. All negotiations had been with the understanding that until British withdrawal was complete, Mountbatten would continue as governor-general of both India and Pakistan. Now

Jinnah suddenly produced his own version of the Prophet Mohammed's *La Sharik Allah:* God has no partner! He would share rule of his Pakistan with no one. He, not Mountbatten, must be its governor-general.

Englishmen as well as Congress leaders saw in this intent to wreck the Pakistan-India settlement by raising an issue of no real importance. Mountbatten's titular governor-generalship would be only temporary; it made transfer of authority easier for all concerned. "Jinnah doesn't want a settlement. He wants Hindu defiance, loosing Muslim *jihad,* ending in total conquest!" However that might be, Mountbatten told Jinnah, "Mr. Nehru says he has no objection, nor have I."

Mountbatten was in London, reporting "We have a settlement finally," when Jinnah announced all commitments would be canceled, unless Pakistan was given a corridor across India, linking the Islamic Republic's West and East Wings. This meant surrender of Kashmir, the Nehru homeland, and the Himalayan bastion facing Soviet Russia and China. It called for repudiation of the formula for partition to which Jinnah and his chosen Prime Minister, Liaquat Ali Khan, had agreed, on which in fact they had insisted: that rulers of native states not legally a part of British India, including the Hindu Maharajah of Kashmir, were free to decide whether to join Pakistan or India. It struck at Jawaharlal Nehru's very heart.

His love for Kashmir was lyrical and mystical. After visiting Kashmir in 1940, he wrote, "It seemed to me dreamlike and unreal, like the hopes and desires that fill us and so seldom find fulfillment. It was like the face of the beloved that one sees in a dream and that fades away upon awakening." Twelve years later, he told India's Parliament, "I am called a Kashmiri in the sense that ten generations ago, my people came down from Kashmir to India. That is not the bond I have in mind when I think of Kashmir, but other bonds which have tied us much closer."

What those bonds were was not revealed when, in 1947, he rejected Jinnah's demand for Kashmir as "fantastic and absurd." His sister knew part of the story, if not all. There had been a movement in Kashmir since 1932, for a democratic state with equal rights for Hindus, Muslims and Sikhs. In 1946 the National Conference declared for freedom from autocratic rule, and Sheikh Abdullah, a Muslim, was arrested as a rebel.

Kashmiri leaders invited her brother to come and advise them in their crusade. At the Kashmir border, he was halted by the Raj, arrested and taken back to prison. He continued, however, to be in touch with Kashmiri leaders, both Muslim and Hindu. Now it became known that Jinnah had sent his military secretary to Hari Singh, the Kashmiri Maharajah, with letters urging him to accede to Pakistan.

The Maharajah's Prime Minister, M. C. Mahajan, recorded in his diary, "The Pakistan representative compelled me to see him. He had accession draft in one hand, sword in the other. This is Pakistan speaking!" But the Maharajah's *rajguru,* his private soothsayer, Sant Dev, opposed the Pakistan demand, not in favor of India, but with wild prophecy.

Allan Campbell Johnson, Lord Mountbatten's secretary, transmitted the report of a Kashmiri historian, G. L. Kaul, that "Sant Dev convinced Hari Singh he need only wait a bit, play India against Pakistan and vice versa, and their quarreling over Kashmir would leave him an independent monarch.

Hindus and Muslims would fight each other after independence. He would march to Lahore with his army and capture the throne once held by Ranjit Singh, the hero of the Sikhs."

None of this came out, nor is there confirming evidence. If there were, the Kashmir controversy before the United Nations might have gone differently. As matters stood in 1947, Jinnah's demand for Kashmir was suddenly withdrawn. Another move was in the making, soon to be revealed. Jinnah, though he was now in the terminal stages of tuberculosis, was sure he could afford to wait. Sourly, he said "Better a moth-eaten Pakistan than none." Progress toward India's first Independence Day resumed.

Very soon, what seemed unthinkable to Motilal Nehru and was only a child's dream-fantasy to his Little Daughter, when she play-acted Jhansi-ki-Rani, riding across the lawns at the Home of Joy, raising a flashing sword to waken India, would be a fact of history. Vijaya Lakshmi Pandit, risen to fame in her own right, could stand beside her brother as witness when the future dawned, and feel "I helped. I did my part, as best I could."

8.

Rabindranath Tagore's *Morning Song of India* was adopted as Free India's national anthem. The national emblem was evolved from the Lion Capital of Asoka, who united India three centuries before Christ: Four Indian lions back to back, with a frieze depicting an elephant, a galloping horse, the Harappa bull, symbol of the vanished Indus River civilization, and another lion. The inscription read *Satyameya jayate:*

Truth alone triumphs. Free India's flag would be the Congress flag; saffron, white, dark green, with the *chakra,* Gautama Buddha's Wheel of the Law, in the center.

Buddhism, born in India, spread over Asia. Two thousand five hundred years after the death of the historical personage who began his ministry by preaching a sermon called *Setting in Motion the Wheel of the Law,* in a deer-park near Banaras, India's holiest city, five hundred million human beings believe they walk Buddha's Eight-Fold Path. Yet like Christianity, Buddhism has almost vanished from the land of its birth.

Still Gandhi, crusading against caste, preaching universal brotherhood, quoted Buddha's *The illusion of separateness is the great heresy,* as he quoted Jesus Christ's *Love one another.* Now the man in whom many in India thought they saw a Buddha avatar was about to set in motion new laws that revoked the Laws of Manu, sacrosanct since unrecorded time.

Outlawing caste discrimination and Untouchability, the Constitution of the Republic of India guaranteed "Justice, social, economic, political; liberty of thought, faith, belief and worship; equality of status and opportunity." Constitutions in themselves accomplish very few miracles. But liberation was begun for victims of a system imposed by the conquering race from which the Nehrus descended.

Vijaya Lakshmi Pandit was as aware as her brother that the end of colonial rule meant immediate need for administrators and civil servants to fill the vacuum. "Leaders must quickly learn new roles and themselves become the scapegoats, in case of failure, instead of the rulers now departing. They must either risk elections which might well throw them out before they had a chance to prove themselves, or—a much more tempting choice to some—govern by fiat, which is dictator-ship's progenitor. And this must be done amidst civil strife and the paying off of old scores between religions, communi-ties, even neighboring villages."

British careerists had held all senior posts. Now they were stepping down. There were not enough experienced Indian diplomats to replace their former superiors. Legend attributes to Queen Victoria's statesman for all seasons, Benjamin Dis-raeli, the definition: "A diplomat is an honest man sent abroad to lie for his country." This was not what Jawaharlal Nehru wanted. He told his sister his Cabinet Ministers agreed that she should go to Soviet Russia as India's first Am-bassador.

Completely surprised, she argued that she knew absolutely nothing about Russia or the Russians. He said "Nobody in India does." He had abiding respect and affection, so had she, for many Congress leaders. The fact remained, as her daugh-ter Tara summarized it in her novel, *This Time of Morning:* "There were men among them of little education, little imagi-nation, men with the limitations of a narrow, peasant upbring-ing, men who had spent years in prison and lost touch with the world outside, men who had never set foot outside of India."

Her brother said, "You have proved you are good at making friends of strangers." She still resisted. "I suppose behind all my protestations, there was selfishness. You can't hope and wait for half a lifetime, without wanting to be there when what you prayed for happens." What her daughter saw in her cast the balance. *Her most characteristic feature is her delight in a challenge.* Friends said, "You'll simply disappear without trace in that frozen wilderness." Orthodox Hindus and Muslims found one point of agreement. "Ambassador is no job for a woman." She told her brother "All right. I'll go. I'll do the best I can."

Her decision was headlined. A Bombay newspaper editor wrote "If ever one woman could hold the scene in Russia, it will be this little lady. Napoleon and Hitler got lost on the steppes, but she is not going as an invader, and so she may conquer, as she did in the United States." Other comments were less sanguine. "I still half-wished I could back out." But on August 5, 1947, ten days before Independence Day, she boarded a plane at New Delhi bound for Moscow.

Lekha, who had studied journalism at Wellesley, was assigned to accompany her mother as press attaché, "a title she wore with much dignity." The flight took three days. Theirs was the first foreign plane, but for one belonging to the American Ambassador, allowed to land on Soviet soil. "I looked at the Kremlin towers, and shivered." A week later, she presented her credentials at the Kremlin. "I hoped, of course, to be received by Stalin. He never appeared."

Since the Republic of India did not yet exist, her letter of credence was signed by King George VI. It stated "special trust and confidence in the discretion and faithfulness of our Trusty and Well-Beloved the Honorable Madame Vijaya Lakshmi Pandit, a person of approved Wisdom, Loyalty, Diligence and Circumspection," and authorized her to "represent Us in the character of Our Ambassador Extraordinary and Plenipotentiary, with the special object of representing the interests of India." It was countersigned *By His Majesty's Command: Jawaharlal Nehru.*

No other brother had sent his sister on such an errand as hers. No sister had more pride in her brother than she felt, when on the night of August 14, 1947, she sat beside her daughter, as isolated in Stalin's Russia as they had been in a British prison cell not quite five years before, and they heard a familiar voice, "at first low and metallic, then suddenly buoyant and vibrant." It was nearly midnight in India. Delhi Radio brought him close.

"Long years ago," he said, "we made a tryst with destiny, and now the time comes when we shall redeem our pledge, not wholly or in full measure, but very substantially. At the stroke of the midnight hour, when the world sleeps, India will wake to life and freedom. A moment comes, which comes but rarely in history, when we step out from the old into the new, when an age ends, when the soul of a nation, long suppressed, finds utterance."

Now his voice was solemn and sad. "The ambition of the greatest man of our generation has been to wipe every tear from every eye. That may be beyond us, but as long as there are tears and suffering, so long our work will not be over." Not her brother's; and not hers. Silently, his sister and his niece echoed the vow he spoke.

"At this solemn moment, when the people of India, through suffering and sacrifice, have achieved freedom, I . . . do dedicate myself in all humility to the service of India and her people, to the end that this ancient land may attain her rightful place in the world, and make her full and willing contribution to the promotion of world peace and the welfare of mankind." As he spoke, India's darkest hour began.

9.

Eleven and one-half million Muslims, Hindus and Sikhs, uprooted from their homes, as Pakistan had been ripped out of India, were on the move in opposite directions across an area thirty thousand miles square. At least forty million Muslims chose to stay in India, but eight and a half million set out for Pakistan, in belief it was their sacred duty to join the Islamic Republic, or in sudden blind dread of Hindu and Sikh neighbors with whom they had lived peaceably until then. Meanwhile millions of Hindus and Sikhs were on the move, in the opposite direction.

Refugees in columns sixty miles long straggled through the Punjab plains, the Rann of Cutch, and East Bengal's swamps and jungles. Meeting head-on, they went mad. Fanatics desecrated temples, mosques and Sikh *gurudwaras*. Whole sections of Amritsar, Lahore, Karachi, Delhi and Calcutta were set aflame. Pillage, rape and slaughter spread; atrocities multiplied. Trains crossing the still-disputed new frontier reached destinations carrying only corpses. Mountain tribesmen swarmed into Kashmir, crying *jihad*. Augmenting the horror, floods drowned uncounted thousands.

How many died, no one wants to be sure. A generally accepted estimate is twenty in every thousand. Some say a million would be closer to the mark. Twenty years after, in Pakistan as often as in India, survivors of history's most tragic mass exodus say, "It might have been better in the long run if we had fought a civil war and settled it, as you did in the United

States." The American South still shows its scars; but in Pakistan and India, open wounds still bleed.

When what Jawaharlal Nehru and his sister foresaw in 1947 as inevitable, sooner or later, came to pass in 1965, and Pakistan and India fought across the United Nations cease-fire she had helped to establish in Kashmir, officers and rank-and-file on both sides went berserk, killing to avenge their families exterminated during the two-way migration eighteen years before.

In Moscow in 1947, she heard her brother speaking over Delhi Radio. "This morning, Mahatma Gandhi came to Delhi, and I sat by his side and wondered how low we have fallen from the great ideas he placed before us." Diplomatic-pouch reports said he drove or walked alone into holocaust, protecting intended Hindu victims from Muslims, and Muslims from Hindus, telling all, "You will have to kill me before you kill one of these, your brothers." At any time, she might hear he had been killed.

She must stay at her post in Russia. No one read Stalin's mind successfully; but everyone knew his expertise at planting Communism where chaos plowed the field. Communism had flowered in India since it was brought there, not from Soviet Russia but from London, by English radicals who tried, and failed, to seize control of the *Swaraj* crusade. India's Communist Party had no difficulty in finding money to finance agitprop activities; and it did not come from dues paid in by members.

Whatever part the Kremlin had in this, her brother's stated policy was clear. Only six days after he formed India's interim government, he had notified both the Soviet and the United

States that "We propose, as far as possible, to keep away from the politics of power groups, aligned against one another, which have led in the past to world wars and which may again lead to disasters on a much greater scale."

Soviet sensitivity was offended even by the fact that Russia came second, when he said, "We send our greetings to the people of the United States to whom destiny has given a major role in international affairs. To that other great nation of the modern world, the Soviet Union, which also carries a vast responsibility for shaping world events, we send greeting." Small wonder, if his name seldom appeared in *Pravda* or *Izvestia,* and none of his statements were published.

Testing her footsteps, she mentioned casually her surprise at finding, in her studies of Russian history, that the *Great Soviet Encyclopedia* described Mahatma Gandhi as "a reactionary . . . who betrayed the people and helped the imperialists against them, pretending in a demagogic way to be a supporter of Indian independence and an enemy of the British . . . and has widely exploited religious prejudice." She was answered by silence. The *Encyclopedia* bore Stalin's *imprimatur.* There was no more to be said.

She asked for permission to visit the Central Asian Soviet republics. She was told "Hotel accommodations there are not yet nice enough for a lady." The following day, two Indian Communists arrived in Moscow, and were at once provided with a special plane and given permission to travel anywhere they pleased.

She asked repeatedly for a meeting with Stalin. It never came. "Our foreign policy," her brother's directive summarized, "will eventually be governed by our internal policy. That policy is far from being Communistic and is certainly opposed to the Communist Party. We cannot afford to antagonize the Soviet Union. At the same time, there is much goodwill in India toward the United States. We do not wish to, and we must not, antagonize the Americans."

This placed her on a tightrope, which she walked gracefully. A foreign observer called her "A highly interesting person in a highly interesting position, who may well be a pilot light toward understanding between East and West." With Lekha, she studied Russian, read Russian history, went regularly to the Ballet and Opera. Her *sari*-clad figure became familiar on the children's playground across the street from the Indian Embassy. She went there every day to talk with youngsters bundled in snowsuits. She was, however, never invited to visit a Russian home.

She organized the first exhibition of Indian art in Moscow. It was well-received, but though Russians were voluble regarding India's past, when the present or future was mentioned they looked nervously over their shoulders, and changed the subject.

Her brother, instructing India's first Ambassadors to "function as Indians and not as imitation Englishmen," said, "They will represent a great country and it is right that they should impress this on those with whom they deal. But they also represent a poor country where millions live on the verge of starvation. They cannot forget this nor should they do anything which seems in conflict with it."

V. K. Krishna Menon had been named as India's first High Commissioner to the United Kingdom, though both Clement Attlee and Sir Stafford Cripps said anyone else would be preferable. He bought a fleet of limousines including a Rolls-Royce for himself, purchased an official residence in Kensington Palace Gardens, personally selected hangings, crockery and furnishings for India House in Aldwych, and in four months increased his staff to fifteen hundred, making India's the largest foreign mission in England.

In Moscow, the American Embassy had a staff of four hundred, including a doctor, a dentist and a crew of full-time carpenters. The British Embassy employed almost as many. Vijaya Lakshmi Pandit made do with a staff of seventeen, including Lekha. When Ranjit Pandit walked beside her, she flinched from the mysteries of budget-paring. By now, she was an expert. The residence allotted to her by the Kremlin was old, ill-heated, gloomily furnished with battered odds and ends left over from the Revolution. She proceeded to make it warmly home-like.

Things cost too much in proletarian Moscow. Thriftily, she bought furniture in Stockholm, where capitalistic free-enterprise competition produced bargain sales. She had asked in Delhi, "When I entertain officially, am I to leave the men to their coffee and cigars after dinner and retire to the drawing-room with the ladies, or should we all stay in the dining-room?" The Manual of Protocol gave no precedents. She created her own. Often, she did the cooking for her dinner parties, which were small, informal, and so successful that Kremlin dignitaries welcomed invitations.

In Delhi, Indian Civil Service veterans briefed her. One of them said, "We Indians usually talk too much, which is a failing diplomats must not have." Clearly, he expected her to be a chatterbox. But while she talked without apparent reserve, she interspersed truths about India, not reported in *Pravda*. If, as everyone in the foreign colony averred, all Embassy servants were Laventri Beria's spies, some of what she said may have reached Stalin in the Kremlin.

Much ado was made in the Soviet press about invasion of Kashmir by Muslim tribesmen pouring out of Pakistan. She stated the Kashmir case as she understood it. Kashmir's Hindu Maharajah, ruling over a populace predominantly Muslim, had temporized while other princes acceded to India or to Pakistan. A mysterious "General Tariq" commanded raiders in Kashmir. They were armed and equipped with modern weapons: "General Tariq" was identified as being actually a General Akbar Khan, subsequently chief-of-staff of Pakistan's Army. Kashmir's Maharajah, finally frightened into decision, acceded to India, begging for Indian troops to halt killing that took eleven thousand lives in a few weeks.

India had gone in, but not, as Pakistani claimed and a section of the Soviet press maintained, in imperialist aggression. Invasion had been stopped, just short of Srinagar, Kashmir's capital. Now India was taking the Kashmir issue to the United Nations Security Council. It seemed to her, she said mildly but tellingly, that Russian sympathies ought to be on India's side, in the Kashmir controversy. As it turned out, the Soviet eventually supported India against Pakistan.

She granted that much was wrong in her country; but on the other hand, much was going well. Her brother and Vallabhbhai Patel drove straight ahead with their nation-building program. Within less than twelve months, forty-eight percent of the subcontinent's area had progressed from authoritarian to democratic government. Dr. B. R. Ambedkar, born an Untouchable, now by Gandhi's grace a *Harijan,* Child of God, was the chosen pilot moving India's Constitution toward its final form.

"For thousands of years, such sayings as *Janata janardana,* 'The people are God,' and *Panchamukhi Parameshwara,* 'The voice of the people is the voice of God,' have been meaningless in India, where once they were true. Now they are true again." She told of the end of the reign of the Maharajahs. Five hundred and sixty-two Indian princes, great and small, had been removed from place and power the British perpetuated. Only one, the Muslim Nizam of predominantly Hindu Hyderabad, held out against the change and soon gave in. None had been arrested; not one had faced a firing squad.

Invidious comparison was not her style; but her guests and other listeners knew how Czarist Russia's ruling class was erased in 1917. That her calm reports were verified by their own must have given pause to any strategists who based their planning on Indian Communist Party claims that the Nehru regime would collapse, and Communism take over.

She found ways, too, to tell those who would tell others that in India refugee rehabilitation was under way, with Hindus helping Muslims, Muslims aiding Hindus; that Maulana Azad and other Muslims held high office in the secular government; that Gandhi, backed by her brother, had convinced India's Cabinet that Pakistan should receive nearly eight hundred million rupees as a fair share of tax moneys surrendered by the Raj; and that finalization of the Constitution would enfranchise nearly one hundred and eighty million Indians, nearly half of them women, millions of them Muslims.

She admits, "I often felt frustrated." But an English correspondent wrote, "She has made a strong mark in Moscow. She leaves now for a while, to again head India's delegation to the United Nations, but will no doubt return armed with more facts to make the Russians more respectful to her young country."

10.

Lekha went with her, and there was a reunion with Tara and Rita. At Lake Success, she voted on Pakistan's application for United Nations membership. Her vote was "Yes." This began what led to establishment of the United Nations cease-fire line in Kashmir on January 1, 1949. She arranged for Tara, whose college work was finished, to go to India and live with her uncle and Indira and Indira's two small children, in the Prime Minister's house in New Delhi. Before returning to her corner in Moscow, she allowed herself a few days in India, and called on Gandhi.

It was Monday, his day of silence. It would be two hours before his rule allowed him to speak. "Our relationship could well bear the strain of silence. All I needed was his soothing presence and the strength that emanated from him." He sat leaning against a large white bolster. His seventy-eighth year had been the cruelest of his life. The day before, he had visited a Muslim refugee camp. "I hung my head in shame when I saw them." Now he planned a fast unto death. He took up the pad that was always near his hand, and wrote, "Will you be happy to leave Russia?"

She had not complained. Her term of duty at Moscow was not over, nor had she been told of any other assignment planned for her. Gandhi never asked questions casually. She framed her answer, wondering, and a vagrant thought intruded. There was a legend that after one of his long imprisonments, some well-meaning person decided relaxation was his need. He had never seen a motion picture. A showing was arranged.

The film was *Mission to Moscow,* a Hollywood version of history that purported to tell how Ambassador Joseph Davies grappled with Stalin in Russia in 1936. Gandhi watched without expression, and said nothing when it was over. Asked "Didn't you like it?", he said "No." Was he annoyed by the politics in the picture? He said he had not noticed any politics. What he disliked was the only scene he remembered: one of dancing-girls.

Of her own mission to Moscow, Vijaya Lakshmi Pandit said, *"Bapu,* I have very mixed feelings. There's something in Moscow that is indefinable. Nearly every day there's a problem to be solved, and there are innumerable petty annoyances. But I'd like to stay there and see if I can't find some way to make being there worthwhile."

He wrote, "What India is trying to say to the world is the essence of our creed, and fundamental to an understanding of our way of life as well as our political stand. The end is not important, unless the means we follow to achieve it are right. The countries of the Western world would do well to try to understand this. It is what you must explain, to the Russians and to the Americans."

He leaned back and closed his eyes. Her heart ached for him. She told her brother her concern; and as she spoke, saw that he, too, as much as Gandhi in his way, was sick with

shame and grief. There was harsh truth in an American journalist's report that he was borne down by "the wordiness all
around him, and the fussiness, and the ineffectuality, and the
begging and the prevarication," with which he must contend;
most of all, by bloodshed he had not been able to prevent,
could still not bring to an end, that threatened to grow worse.

With Lekha, she returned to their lonely outpost. From
Moscow, she wrote mock-seriously, hoping to help him smile,
at least for a moment. "It's bad enough me being small, but
everyone around me is always small, too." She suggested that
to make a proper showing for India, he ought to recruit "some
really tall men" for the Indian Foreign Service. His reply was
in a postscript to his letter of good wishes, which reached her
on her forty-eighth birthday, three days after India's second
Independence Day. Her sisterly joke had succeeded.

Gravely, he reminded her that "diplomats are not chosen for
stature or muscle power," and that "nearly all the world's
great men have been short." Mother and daughter chuckled
together, envisioning him standing on his head in front of a
mirror. He, too, was short; and he could still laugh at himself.
Then they heard that Gandhi had begun his fast unto death,
and he was fasting in sympathy.

Gandhi asked him not to do this, in a painfully scribbled
note that ended "May you long remain Jawahar, the
Jewel of India." Gandhi's own sacrifice had the effect he
prayed for. Promises were given that Muslims would be let
alone, and Hindus and Sikhs would evacuate mosques they
had seized and fortified. He broke his fast; but while he gave
thanks for return to sanity, at his evening prayer meeting, a
crude bomb exploded near him.

A Hindu youth, a refugee from the part of the Punjab absorbed by Pakistan, was arrested. A hand grenade was found in his pocket. Gandhi came to his defense. "It is not his fault if he has been led to think I am an enemy of Hinduism." Coded Foreign Service messages revealed that many made this accusation. Her brother and Vallabhbhai Patel insisted he should be protected by bodyguards. He refused protection. "If I am to die by the bullet of a madman," he told Princess Amrit Kaur, Vijaya Lakshmi Pandit's longtime friend and co-worker in the Congress, now India's first Health Minister, "I must do so smiling. There must be no anger within me. God must be in my heart and on my lips." That was on January 28, 1948.

On January 30, he went to hold his evening prayer meeting on the lawn surrounding a mansion owned by G. D. Birla, an industrialist who had joined his following. He had promised to have a long talk with Tara Pandit, about her hopes and plans. Actually, she wanted to get married, but hesitated to trouble her mother with family affairs when India was in such turmoil. To Tara and her cousin, Indira, he said, "The next time you see me will be in a crowd."

He was always in a crowd. Tara and Indira, having tea in the Prime Minister's House, asked each other why he had spoken so strangely. Meanwhile Gandhi walked slowly across the grounds at the Birla Mansion. He was to meet later with Tara's uncle and Maulana Azad. But Nathuram Vinayak Godse stood in the way. He bent as if to touch Gandhi's feet, then fired three shots into his body.

At India's Embassy in Moscow, Vijaya Lakshmi Pandit chatted with Lekha and the staff, while a secretary turned the radio dial. It was time for the Delhi broadcast. This began. Suddenly: "We interrupt to announce . . . We regret . . ." There was a drowning rattle of static, then long silence. Then "Mahatma Gandhi, while on his way to evening prayers, was shot. He died a few minutes later."

The light has gone out of our lives, and there is darkness everywhere. So her brother said. But then he went on: "I was wrong. The light that has illumined this country for these many, many years will illuminate this country for many more years, and a thousand years later that light will still be seen in this country and the world will see it and it will give solace to innumerable hearts." The night was black in Moscow.

Next morning, she listened while Delhi Radio's professionals pictured the funeral rites at Rajghat on the banks of the Jumna, where seven hundred thousand of her people paid tribute to her country's *Bapu,* "the greatest man India has known since Buddha." The great throng chanted *Amar hogeye:* He is rendered immortal. Two days later, she heard her brother's voice again.

"He would chide us if we merely mourn. That is a poor way of doing homage to him. The only way is to express our determination, to pledge ourselves anew, to dedicate ourselves to the great task which he undertook and accomplished to such a large extent. So we have to work, we have to labor, we have to sacrifice, and thus prove to some extent at least worthy followers of his."

She was already committed to further service that would call for all she could give. But first, she was allowed to be a mother, two of whose three fatherless daughters were in love.

Mrs. Indira Gandhi with her aunt, Mrs. Pandit, in New Delhi, 1966

Madame Pandit, Indira Gandhi and Jawaharlal Nehru.

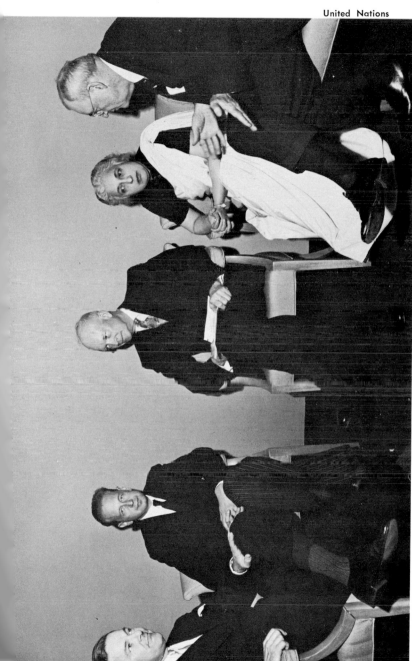

President Eisenhower's visit to the United Nations. (l. to r.) Mr. Henry Cabot Lodge, Jr., Mr. Dag Hammarskjold, President Eisenhower, Madame Pandit, Mr. John Foster Dulles.

Mrs. Pandit, President of U.N. General Assembly, with Dag Hammarskjold and Lester B. Pearson.

II.

"Preparations for my wedding when it was finally scheduled were hasty," Tara says, "because her leave from foreign duty was brief. If it is difficult to make hurried arrangements for a proper wedding with all the trimmings in the West, it is doubly so in India. I know of no occasion involving more hectic, long-term preparation and paraphernalia than an orthodox Hindu marriage. Yet in the space of two weeks, Mummie brought back to life our long-closed home in Allahabad and supervised its painting and repair. She found time to shop for my trousseau, and the wedding took place in the traditional Hindu manner with no detail left incomplete." Immediately afterward, she flew back to her Moscow post. Soon she was traveling again. In March, 1949, it was announced she would succeed Sir Benegal Narsing Rau as India's Ambassador to the United States. But before going to Washington, she took charge of another wedding.

In the Prime Minister's House in New Delhi, Lekha was married to Ashok Mehta of the Indian Foreign Service. "If Rita had been in a marrying mood, I don't know how I could have managed it, there was such a rush to get me off to America." There was barely time for brief sisterly scolding of her brother.

India had begun to call him "the beloved slave-driver." He had faced armed rebellion in Hyderabad, and been driven to order use of force. Then Jinnah's death in Pakistan was followed significantly by surrender of Muslim troublemakers who had threatened to carve a state as large as France out of

India's heartland. Against strong opposition, he had kept India within the framework of the British Commonwealth. He had crystallized support for *Panchshila,* his Five Tenets: nonaggression, noninterference, recognition of other national sovereignties, mutual help and peaceful coexistence. He was nearing sixty, and when offguard seemed older.

"Look at Churchill," his sister commanded. "Look at any man who lives a grueling life given over to the public. In Europe and America such people are protected by an avalanche of secretaries and protocol, apart from wives who see to their comfort and privacy. The busiest man takes a week off, or at least a Sunday in the country, to collect his thoughts and relax. You listen to the radio even when you eat. Would the world stop turning if you relaxed one day a week?"

No one but his sister could scold Jawaharlal Nehru. With her, he was fondly sardonic. "You're getting old. That's your trouble." She said "I certainly am. And I wish some other people would realize they're not getting any younger, and live sensibly." He asked, "What is 'sensibly'?" She said "Like a human being, not a driven animal." Ruefully, he conceded, "It would be pleasant to do all the reading one wants, and I haven't been inside a restaurant or a shop for years."

She urged, "Then do it!" He shook his head. "There isn't time. We're here to work, until we're thrown on the rubbish heap." She drew herself up. "I'd like to see anyone throw me on the rubbish heap!" He chuckled. So did she. Then brother and sister went their separate ways, to go on with work that never ended.

On May 5, 1949, dignitaries, reporters and photographers

awaited her plane landing at New York, where five years before no one met her and she wondered where to go and how to manage. Now she was escorted to Washington, to the White House, where President Truman waited to welcome her. Then she faced her first Washington press conference. Her brother's *Panchshila* doctrine and insistence on India's nonalignment ran contrary to the stand taken by John Foster Dulles, then American Ambassador-at-Large, that "He who is not with us is against us." She expected, and was prepared for, sharp-edged questioning.

Instead, a woman columnist, whose colleagues said she typed with claws, purred, "Tell me, Mrs. Pandit, how does it feel to be World Feminist Number One?" She said "I am not a 'feminist.' As far as I can see, the question of being male or female has nothing to do with the duty of both sexes to take their part in world affairs." To her questioner "Mrs. Pandit sidestepped gracefully."

A noted correspondent devoted his report to explaining that her unaccented English was the product of British education, now unavailable in her country. A commentator complimented her. "Wisely, she eschews the affectations and mannerisms that might be expected from the handsome sister of her country's present idol, herself a nominee for the title, 'Woman of the Century.' "

In London years ago, after her first encounter with molders of world opinion, she asked her brother "What should I have done, to make them listen as they would to a man?" Since then, she had learned much. In Russia, in the shadow of the Kremlin, she found ways to work against undeclared but palpable resistance to hearing truths not passed for publication in *Pravda*. In the United States, her mission's purpose was impeded by her singular celebrity.

She made her first speech as Madame Ambassador, and read reports of this with wry surprise. " 'Her hair caused many of those present to sigh with a tinge of envy . . . silvery and cut short, but not too short, curls soft around her well-shaped head . . . a type of coiffure most women dream of but seldom achieve . . .' This was not the Hairdressers' Convention. This was the Women's National Press Club. I gave a serious talk. I wonder if anyone was listening." Speaking engagements took her back and forth across the continent. She went on wondering who listened.

When she spoke for India unofficially, in San Francisco in 1945, her own countrymen had tried to silence her. Now San Francisco's Mayor gave her the key to the city. It did not appear to open ears. Addressing the California League of Women Voters, she said Gandhi brought a new motivating force into the lives of India's women. "They do not use femininity or depend on dress or makeup to emphasize their feminine qualities. They take their political work seriously, and their success in it with humility." Reporters continued to write about her enviable coiffure, her pastel *saris,* her Great Lady elegance, "as if I were a visitor from Hollywood."

Indian students attending American colleges came to pay their respects. Newspaper stories made it appear she granted them *darshan:* the privilege of looking from a distance at a superior being. In fact, she invited them in, sat on the floor and talked with them in Hindi and Urdu, and came to grips with a problem that would not be openly discussed by American educators for a decade. Many young men and women, brought from India under a well-intended program of specialized higher education, wanted to remain in the United States, where life was easier and tangible reward much greater. She convinced some, though not all, that they owed it to themselves to go home when their studies were completed, and help where help was needed. This was not what American editors called "Madame Pandit copy."

Cameras surrounded her, when at Howard University she received her first honorary degree, that of Doctor of Laws. Feature-writers noted happily her dialogue with a distinguished collector of academic honors, who asked what graduate degrees she held. She said she held none. "In India, 'So and So was in prison with me' is another way of saying 'We were at Oxford together.'" Columns were spun from such quotable remarks. Her underlying seriousness went undetected.

A somewhat pompous pedagogue told her India's first Five-Year Plan put the cart before the horse. "Progress is impossible until you eradicate illiteracy." She said, "It is very difficult for a human being who may starve to death tomorrow to center his thinking on ABC's." A crusader for family planning lectured her on India's dire need for birth control, "even if it is resisted by people who know no better."

Mildly, she said that contrary to popular legend, there was no such opposition to birth control in India as she heard there was in Europe and America. "The problem is lack of methods sufficiently simple, harmless and inexpensive, to be of use to people cursed by poverty and lack of personal privacy." Triumphantly, the crusader displayed a patented device. "You see, Mrs. Pandit, it's very simple. It is conveniently placed on the bedside table . . ." Gently, she said, "Good lady, our villagers have neither bed nor table." Her audiences grew. Still she wondered if her message was heard and understood.

As Madame Ambassador, it was her duty to preside when two baby elephants, Shanti and Ashok, arrived at Washington's National Zoological Park, as a gift from India's children to children in America. This gave the press and its photographers another Page One package. Wherever she went, she was applauded, pictured, praised. Many women might have asked what more a woman could want. But this was not what she came for.

At India's Embassy, she employed two cooks. One was Ram, a Kashmiri from Allahabad, who spoke only Hindi. The other, Etienne, was *Cordon Bleu,* from Paris, and spoke only French. She interpreted between them, kept them from stabbing each other, and taught recipes to both. Often, they stood aside while with an apron over her *sari,* she prepared the main dish for an official dinner with her own hands.

"Even in this modern age," her daughter Tara says, "when it is no longer regarded as a phenomenon for a woman to combine homemaking with a career, those who have watched my mother ably conduct a political gathering have been charmed by her effortless transformation into a gracious hostess, presiding over a table as perfect in its every detail as though she had devoted a lifetime to mastering the household arts. Nothing of the sort is true. She never studied how to cook, sew, plan a menu or perform any useful domestic task, any more than she took lessons in public speaking. She just did what needed to be done."

12.

What needed doing most urgently had to be done most carefully. There was a climate of preference for Pakistan, that chilled her brother's reception during his first visit to the United States, a few months before her appointment as Ambassador. He had attempted to clarify India's policies in an address to Congressmen in Washington by comparing the pattern of India's history to that of the United States at a comparable period following independence. "Our foreign policy, like yours, is motivated primarily by enlightened self-interest."

In private conversations, he asked Americans, "How well do you know George Washington's Farewell Address?" Response was courteous and cautious; behind it, unspoken, was "Who are you to ask that of Americans?" His *Glimpses of World History* had been on American bookshelves since 1942, but his credentials as historian were little-known to most of the Americans he or his sister met.

He said, "As I understand the advice your first President gave when your country was young as India is now, which guided your foreign policies until 1914, he urged avoidance of 'entangling foreign alliances' until you should be strong enough to be a partner, not a subject. We are following that advice in India."

Americans in general saw it differently. Twenty years after it first appeared, Katherine Mayo's *Mother India* was still a textbook for many. Its sweeping denigration of Hindus en masse may have had something to do with general attitudes *pro* the Islamic Republic of Pakistan, *contra* the Hindu-majority Republic of India. In any event, questioners in her audiences began to rise, asking questions based on what they read; and Vijaya Lakshmi Pandit saw how her mission could be fulfilled.

Campaigning in Kanpur villages, she laid aside the speeches she prepared, and talked about neighbors in America. Now she talked to Americans about their neighbors in India. One hundred and eighty million of them, men and women, would cast ballots in a national election in her country. She had heard of no plans for a national election in Pakistan. But, a questioner objected, there was law and order in Pakistan, while there seemed to be nothing but trouble in India.

The authority he quoted seemed unimpeachable to him. The *Encyclopaedia Britannica,* in its Book of the Year reviewing events of 1950, said "Pakistan's strength lay in the fact that unlike India, it was untroubled by internal dissensions. Communism was nonexistent, and the only political party was the Muslim League." She said she would not presume to quarrel with the *Encyclopaedia Britannica.* However, it was her impression that there had been dissensions within the Muslim League. In India, by last report she had received, seventy-seven political organizations had put up seventeen thousand candidates for less than four thousand elective posts. Among contestants was the Communist Party of India, legally constituted under a Constitutional provision very similar to that which permitted the Communist Party to appear on ballots in the United States.

"We believe in India as you do here, in the right to disagree, even the right to be wrong." She quoted Gandhi: "The truest test of democracy is in the ability of anyone to act as he likes, as long as he does not injure the life or property of anyone else. It means complete freedom of opinion and action without interference with another's right to equal freedom of opinion and action."

From what her questioner quoted, this definition did not appear to be accepted in Pakistan. Parenthetically, the author of *Britannica*'s summary was an Englishman, whose tenure as a college president in India ended with the British withdrawal. She would not call him a prejudiced witness. But she took leave to think all Americans were prejudiced, in favor of inalienable rights which were denied when, for example, *Trains ran on time in Mussolini's Italy.*

Men and women were listening now. "Americans are instinctively polite, especially to foreigners from our part of the world. They hesitate to embarrass us by discussing religion, for fear they may sound like missionaries; they feel it would be inhospitable and unfair, to raise subjects that place backward races on the defensive." In her case, the barrier was down. Questions proliferated, as if they were fired from a machine gun. She answered frankly, using no shield of feminine evasion.

"Why won't India let Pakistan have Kashmir?" She said the record showed that Kashmir acceded to India under the same agreement that joined Bahawalpur to Pakistan. "In fact Pakistan was first to insist the agreement allowed for no exceptions." But were not most Kashmiri Muslims? "According to Pakistan, seventy percent of them are Muslim. However India, like the United States, is a secular republic. You cherish separation of church and state. So do we. Fifty million Mus-

lims are citizens of India, by free choice. Should we order them
to leave, because they are not Hindus? Should we hand
Kashmir over to Pakistan, for no better reason than that so
many Kashmiri pray to Allah?"

Perhaps not; but why did India oppose a Kashmir plebiscite? "India, not Pakistan, brought the Kashmir issue to the
United Nations. Pakistan admits armed invasion of Kashmir.
Under the United Nations charter, a plebiscite cannot be held
until the aggressor withdraws. Pakistan refuses to withdraw its
armed forces that seized and continue to hold one-third of
Kashmir and Jammu."

If what she said about India as a true democracy was correct,
"Why is India neutral, between the Free World and Communism?" She said, as her brother had said: "Between good
and evil, there can be no neutrality. Where freedom is men-
aced or justice threatened or where aggression takes place, we
cannot and shall not be neutral." Then why did India urge
admission of Communist China to the United Nations?

"We believe that in the end, between countries as between
people, things must be worked out face to face. We believe it is
important to open the way to talk across a table. As long as
two people, or two nations, can talk openly, there is hope for
understanding, no matter how wide the breach between
them." The way for her to talk to Americans had been
opened. They listened, at last, as they would listen to a man.

She claimed no conversions, but events indicated a rising
tide of friendliness toward her country. In Washington she
asked for a grant of two million tons of wheat from surplus
stored in warehouses, for which India would pay in counterpart funds. "She didn't beg," an administrator said. "She

had done her homework. She had the facts and figures. She stated a case, and it made sense." Congress, however, delayed a vote on the necessary enabling measure. She said, "The crisis is now. The threat of famine and the shadow of death lurk around the corner." Americans sent petitions to Congress, and contributions to her. Among these were dimes from children's piggy banks, "for the hungry people in India." President Truman called for Congressional action. Finally, the grant was authorized. Two months later, the first shipload of American wheat reached Bombay.

13.

Few Ambassadors were busier. Still she managed matters so she could be a mother about to be a grandmother. When Lekha and Tara informed her they were expecting their first babies, she decreed "Every girl should have her first baby in her parents' home." Tara protested. "That was all right when your parents lived in the next town." Her mother said, "The next country is almost the same thing now. And unless we're never going to meet, you'll have to get used to traveling long distances to see me."

Tara and Lekha surrendered, and traveled to America together, arriving just when their mother was elected "Mother of the Year for India." Ambassadorial duties made it impossible for her to attend the international Mother of the Year luncheon in New York. By telephone, she delegated Tara to represent her. "Left holding the telephone and looking at myself in the mirror opposite, plumply pregnant, it was too late to say I would not go. I felt uncomfortably tongue-tied in that roomful of women from all over the world who had distinguished themselves in different fields of endeavor, and it was a relief when the Mother for Pakistan, seated beside me, turned out to be a man with a luxuriant mustache and a friendly smile. He told me he had rashly agreed to represent his wife at the function. We spent a pleasant lunch hour together sporting our badges and accepting the tributes neither of us deserved."

Lekha and Tara made lists of the layettes their babies should have. Their mother took the lists, put them in her handbag, and proceeded to buy whatever caught her eye. " 'Here she goes,' we grumbled, 'wasting money on us for no reason, getting us all kinds of extravagances we don't really need.' Mummie reminded us that not a single thing she was buying was for either of us. 'You must remember I am about to become a grandmother and I have certain privileges. I didn't get you all the way here so that you could buy the bare necessities from your foolish lists.' "

They asked her how it felt to have a baby. "Old and weary and horribly depressed for a while," she said, "and when that stage is over, one feels younger than ever and a woman of the world full of immense confidence and the feeling that one can tackle anything." She loaned them her chauffeur, Big Al. "He was short and thickset. He had a beet-red face, a thick red neck, an unexpectedly soft voice, loved a good cigar, and looked like the popular idea of a Chicago gangster." Like her friends the New York taxi drivers, he lectured her. Her daughters say "He would have died for her."

In February, 1951, having been appointed Ambassador to Mexico as well as to the United States, she visited the republic below the border, and was royally received. Newspapers described her *sari* and her coiffure, but she no longer concerned herself about reporters who viewed her as a celebrity on a personal appearance tour. Her thinking centered on what was about to occur in India.

On October 25, 1951, she announced she was leaving her Ambassadorial posts, to return to India and campaign for election to Lok Sabha, the House of the People in India's Parliament. Diplomats and American friends asked "Why?" Women said, "You've risen above all that. What have you to gain by going back in politics?" She said, "Nothing matters as much as being a part of one's country." After a pause, she added, "I've been away such a long time."

Tara records: "Having been out of India while vital changes were taking place, her need to reacquaint herself with the nation's moods and conditions was urgent." But on reaching New Delhi, she found that Tara's baby daughter, Nonika, was ill. "Picking up the telephone, she quietly canceled her campaign speaking engagements. She moved in with us, and it was she who got up twice every night to give the baby her medicine. She would not think of leaving until Nonika's crisis was past and she was on the way to recovery. It was the sort of thing an understanding mother would do, but I wonder if any other politician whose election hung in the balance would have done it."

Much more than her own election was at stake. The Congress Party, having delivered independence to the country, had given its people the means to vote it out of leadership if they chose. Congress solidarity weakened. Acharya J. B. Kripalani, long the Congress general secretary and once its president, led secession of a party segment, to the Praja Socialists. Conservatives joined Swatantra, "for free enterprise," founded by a former Congress stalwart, C. Rajagopalachari. Jana Sangh demanded "India for Hindus." Communists, financed from unnamed sources, stirred the boiling pot.

India's masses had an ancient saying: *Delhi dur ast!* Delhi is far away! Their only contact with government had been in terms of tax collectors and the police. Now Great Ones came among them, saying "You own India." Under the Republic's Constitution, anyone over twenty-one and of sound mind could vote. There were no restrictions as to sex, caste, race, religion, literacy or property. This opened the polls to more men and women in India than there were human beings in the United States.

Now that Vallabhbhai Patel was dead, her brother carried the campaign load alone. He traveled twenty-five thousand miles up and down the subcontinent, "by plane, by car, by train, in bullock-carts, on elephants, in boats, on foot." It was estimated that he spoke face to face with thirty million newly franchised citizens. Radio played no part; even today, television is unknown in India.

In her own constituency, Vijaya Lakshmi Pandit walked miles for lack of roads or transport, wore her sandals through, stained her *saris* with mud, ate what peasants ate, talked with them as a woman of India, not as Madame Ambassador. Roving everywhere, her brother preached "India will be what we are: our thoughts and actions will shape her. We are little bits of the India of today, and yet we are also the parents of the India of tomorrow."

Gandhi had seen beauty in poverty. Her brother saw only

ugliness in it, and said it could be conquered if its victims threw off ignorance and passive resignation. "He believed what he said; and the belief was communicated. He praised and scolded, allowing himself no rest and others little leisure, galvanizing the people with his own effort and example." Crowds of a hundred thousand surrounded him, shouting *Nehruji ki jai!*

"Occasionally," he wrote in his *Discovery of India,* "I would find a small town almost deserted, all its shops closed. The explanation came to me when I saw that almost the entire population, men, women and even children, had gathered at the meeting place, on the other side of the town, and were waiting patiently for my arrival." He slept in snatches between one stop and the next, and often went hungry for lack of time to eat.

His sister heard, and told her audiences, how he was confronted by marchers waving red flags, and went among them singling out the organizers of the march, denouncing them, demanding, "Why don't you go and live in the country whose flag you are waving?" She wished doubters of India in America could be present, to see the truth about his rejection of Communism. She, too, fought hard against its standard-bearers.

14.

Never anywhere had a democratic election been conducted under similar circumstances. In order not to interfere with local planting and harvesting, it had to be spaced out over several months, with voting at different times in different areas. More than two million ballot boxes were scattered at a quarter of a million polling places. Illiteracy made it necessary to identify the contending parties by symbols: a pair of yoked bullocks for the Congress, a tree for Praja Socialists, an elephant for former Untouchables, a sickle for Communists.

Primitive tribes came out of jungles and deserts, blowing flutes, pounding drums, announcing they came to worship the new god named *Vote*. Asked which party they chose, great numbers replied "We know nothing about these 'parties.' Show us the Nehru box." Ballots overflowing from Nehru boxes gave Congress candidates more than eighty percent of all elective offices. The vote for Vijaya Lakshmi Pandit in her constituency was almost unanimous.

Now a Member of Parliament, she took a house in New Delhi and said, "At last I can settle down." Then news came that an invitation her brother extended two years before in the United States had been accepted. Mrs. Eleanor Roosevelt, with whom she had worked in United Nations committees in efforts to continue and enlarge the Children's Emergency Fund, was coming to India by way of the Middle East and Pakistan.

At the United Nations, a Pakistan delegate had fleered at Mrs. Roosevelt: "All you care about is the children of Europe; they are white. You don't care what happens to the children of Asia; they are colored." At sixty-eight, she had set out across the world to show the scorner he was wrong. Vijaya Lakshmi Pandit, pleased to guide and escort her, hurried to Allahabad to reopen the long-closed Nehru home so Mrs. Roosevelt could be welcomed there.

Widows, grandmothers, linked by warm empathy, they learned from each other. "Mrs. Pandit," Mrs. Roosevelt wrote, "told me she often slept outdoors under the stars at night. She had developed this habit during her long imprisonment. We visited a prison where her father and her brother had been confined. Seeing it, I realized what India's leaders willingly endured, and I felt I had a better understanding of the fire that burns in so many of them."

A picnic, American style, taught her another facet. "Mrs. Pandit had packed a delicious lunch of a variety of sandwiches, fruit and little cakes. We found a government resthouse beside a canal, and stopped there to eat. It was delightful by the running water; everyone was relaxed and happy." Then an untoward incident shocked her hostess, and showed the quality of greatness in the guest.

Mrs. Roosevelt was to receive an honorary degree at the Allahabad University. A student organization sent her a letter containing "many of the usual allegations found in Communist propaganda." She said she liked to talk with young people, and suggested inviting the ten students who signed the letter to come for tea. Their leader was loudly rude.

"Mrs. Pandit said his bad manners to a guest of India made him unwelcome in her home. He left, and reported what she said to the other students. Three thousand of them, with a loudspeaker, gathered outside the gates, and insisted Mrs. Pandit must come out and apologize for having ejected one of their number." Apology was not a Nehru habit; but what she might have said to the shouters was averted. Mrs. Roosevelt said she would like to visit the university campus, and talk to the students there.

"When Mrs. Pandit and I entered the students' hall, it was jammed. They presented me with a list of questions reminiscent of those young people in the United States used to ask during the 1930's. I answered these to the best of my ability, and I think they were convinced I was honest, even if they did not agree with me. They applauded, and we left with a perfectly amiable spirit on both sides."

Vijaya Lakshmi Pandit was relieved that India had not been shamed, and grateful when Mrs. Roosevelt said, "It is not surprising to me that there should be frustration among your young people when there is so much that needs to be done and they are so ill-equipped with the skills to do it. They will surely straighten out, as soon as there are jobs for them to work at and they have the training to fill them."

They parted, not expecting to meet again. Back in the United States, Mrs. Roosevelt championed India's cause. "Prime Minister Nehru feels that the Hindu religion, with its emphasis on nonviolence and truth, is inherently incompatible with Communism, and the Communists will never gain a real foothold in India." In India's Parliament, Vijaya Lakshmi Pandit dueled capably with its few but always vocal Communist spokesmen.

Then word came that she had been chosen for another mission entrusted to no woman before her. Accepting responsibility she had not sought, she left India again, this time at the head of a strangely assorted delegation of observers sent to find out the facts of Communism, as it was practiced in the People's Republic of China.

15.

Her adventure behind the Bamboo Curtain began in April 1952, and continued on through June. Her appointment was not universally acclaimed. The editor of the 114-year-old *Times of India* said of it only that "Mrs. Pandit is decorative and petite. The shampooed sleekness of her white coiffure would distract attention from the burnished gold of many blondes." A Lucknow editor sniffed, "Apparently she is supposed to atone for our cultural deficiencies otherwise."

She led a group of fourteen, who had as many sets of convictions. They included Frank Moraes and Chalapathi Rau, journalists; Durgabai, a woman lawyer, soon to be a member of India's Planning Commission; Bendre, a popular sketch-artist; and Shanta Rao, a dancer, who was mortally airsick during the long flight to Peking, but ready to give her first recital when she stepped from the plane.

Raja Hutheesing, husband of the former Krishna Nehru, accompanied the group as correspondent for an Indian news bureau. Mrs. Roosevelt, when she met him in Bombay, thought he showed "decidedly left-wing sympathies." Later, in her *India and the Awakening East,* she wrote that "I believe what he saw in China changed his mind; for he found glaring discrepancies between the extravagant propaganda claims and the realities."

He knew his sister-in-law too well to dismiss her as a mere charming figurehead. Whether the truth was suspected by men and women who held authoritarian sway in the People's Republic, there is no way of knowing. Clearly, however, India's Ambassador at Peking, K. M. Panikkar, felt she needed his guidance. "It may be," he informed her, "that Mao's China is the biggest fact to emerge from the Second World War. Here in China freedom from want is a primary need. If you accept that, you must accept the system of control that insures it." What she actually accepted, what she rejected, she kept behind her always pleasant smile.

It had been impossible for her to meet Stalin in Moscow. Here she was taken immediately to be received by Chairman Mao Tse-tung. Before the presentation, K. M. Panikkar briefed her. "Chairman Mao is your brother plus ruthless peasant." Frank Moraes saw meaningful contrast between Kashmiri Brahmin Nehru, and farmer's son from Hunan. "His huge, broad frame was magnified by her slight figure. He gave the impression of a cross between a Chinese Buddha and Charles Laughton. She was the princess out of her ordained element."

The Soviet Ambassador strode to shake hands with her. "The medals on both sides of his chest clanked noisily when he bowed like a performing bear." She returned his greeting in Russian. He asked in Russian what she thought of China under Mao. She answered, in English, that she had not yet had time to crystallize her impressions. Fact justified the diplomatic evasion. Throughout her waking hours, she was hurried here and there, to admire this and be awed by that, while her escorts recited statistics, always in the millions. "I soon learned," she said when she was back in India, "that modesty is not a Communist Chinese failing."

There seemed to be Russians everywhere. Casually, she inquired if they learned to speak Chinese, "to make giving orders easier." The gambit drew offguard frankness from her guide. "Have you ever seen one of those Long Noses order a Chinese about?" Then his face went blank. Another guard had overheard. She did not see him again. "Secretly, the Chinese sneered at the Russians. Their inherent dislike for 'foreign devils' was concentrated officially on 'the American imperialist bandits,' but actually it extended even to fellow Asians."

Scientists, teachers, artists and writers were paraded before her. Many had degrees from European or American universities. She asked a woman physicist who had graduated from Columbia in New York, "How did you enjoy your stay in America?" The woman said, "I hated every minute of it." All assured her, as if they read from a copybook, that their country and hers must stand together "against the Americans with their Santa Claus false-faces."

K. M. Panikkar agreed. He said Chairman Mao had told him of seeing airplanes turned out one per minute in the U.S.S.R. "Not until your country and mine can do this can we act decisively. Until then we must move slowly." On May Day she watched half a million men, women and children march past Peking's Gate of Heavenly Peace. They were workers and students, but had a faceless army's in-step discipline. In the reviewing stand, near Chairman Mao and Premier Chou En-lai, was an Indo-Chinese she had seen last in Brussels in 1926, when he called himself Nguyen-Ai-Quoc. K. M. Panikkar said, "That is Ho Chi-minh. If Indochina falls to Ho Chi-minh, it will be difficult to assess Chinese influence in that country."

She was taken to inspect Communist Chinese schools, and saw textbook maps that showed not only Indochina but Formosa, Korea, Burma and Tibet, as Chinese territories that must be reclaimed. At Mukden, Kao Kang, Mao's Viceroy for Manchuria, asked bluntly, "How far do the British really control India's external and internal policies?" Told no British control was exercised or would be tolerated, he snapped, "I do not believe you." Vice-Premier Kuo Mo-jo said cryptically, "We shall pay our ancestors' debts to India." *Straws in the wind;* but a woman of India could be excused for seeing more danger in the women of Communist China.

She visited Madame Sun Yat-sen, who could not or chose not to recall their previous meeting in Brussels, twenty-five years before, when the widow of the Father of the Chinese Revolution was no more confident of change to come in China than Vijaya Lakshmi Pandit, her husband and father and brother, dared to be that *Swaraj* would be achieved in India. Now Madame Sun Yat-sen was the only woman vice-chairman of the Central People's Government, that had overthrown and forcibly driven to Formosa the Kuomintang regime headed by Chiang Kai-shek and his wife, her younger sister.

Large pictures of Stalin, Lenin, Marx, Engels, Chairman Mao and Vice-Premier Chu Teh frowned from her office walls. There was no picture of Sun Yat-sen. She said she was instructed to show the visitor a model school for children of party members who had to be away on nation-building business. The children ran to surround the smiling, *sari*-clad stranger. The oldest was seven. She cuddled a two-year-old in her arms, and was told this was against the rules. A woman director snapped her fingers. The children formed in military order. Vijaya Lakshmi Pandit saw the Red Guard of the future. "They will sing for you." Piping voices rose. "They are singing 'How good is Communism.' "

They were taught the *Five Loves* prescribed by Chairman Mao: For the fatherland, for labor, for the people, for science and for public property. Nothing was said about religion, home or family, the hearthstones of love in India. The People's Republic had a *Common Programme,* not a constitution. Its Article Six abolished "the feudal system which holds women in bondage." She saw women, not men, imposing another system of bondage on the next generation in China.

Frank Moraes unearthed, and told as parable with very present pertinence, a tale of Confucius, who while crossing the Tai Mountains encountered a woman weeping and wailing beside a grave. He asked, "Why do you weep?" The woman said, "My husband's father was killed here by a tiger, and my husband also, and now my son has met the same fate." Confucius asked, "Why do you not leave so fatal a spot?" She said, "There is no oppressive government here"; and Confucius told his disciples: "Remember this, my children, oppressive government is fiercer and more to be feared than a tiger." No one the observers from India were allowed to question admitted that oppression existed in Mao's China. No one mentioned tigers.

Moraes summed up: "To have your body imprisoned behind prison walls is degrading. But to have your mind captive with invisible chains is more degrading. In the democratic spectator such a spectacle creates a pain and nausea difficult to describe or overcome." Vijaya Lakshmi Pandit knew, as New China's women did not, what physical imprisonment was like. It had never chained her mind. But Communist China's female leaders pitied her for bourgeois blindness to the light that shone from Mao.

Madame Li Teh-chuan, the Minister of Health, born to be beautiful, was as studiedly unfeminine as close-cropped hair, flapping trousers, shapeless padded jacket and drillmaster's grating voice could make her. Chou En-lai's wife, known as Ten Ying-chao, an alternate member of the Central Committee, copied her husband's dress and manner. Ting-ling and Trao Ming, whose novels pleased Chairman Mao, were like parrots self-denuded of bright plumage, croaking stilted phrases over and over, their eyes always wary. Only Madame Shih Liang, the Minister of Justice, showed concern for her appearance, wearing tailored white linen suits and using lipstick. She was merciless to revisionists, especially if they were women.

Ho Hsiang-ning, elderly, crippled, curt, was chairman of the Commission for Overseas Chinese. Kung Peng, cautious, competent, emotionless, directed the Information Department of the Ministry for Foreign Affairs. They said matter-of-factly that none of the ten million Chinese living abroad were excused from responsibility to the fatherland, no matter what adopted nationality they claimed. They sorrowed for women in India. "You have prostitution. We have eliminated it. All women here have nation-building tasks. None need to sell themselves."

Other members of the delegation pleaded fatigue or illness, to avoid joining an inspection trip down the Hwai River in Shantung. The boat provided was small, old and dirty. Accommodations were primitive, sanitation facilities were bleakly basic. But "Mrs. Pandit insisted on coming. So did the always cheerful and energetic Durgabai and Lili Gazdar, Mrs. Pandit's secretary. They were the only women in our party." The only other woman aboard was Chien Chen-ying, a hydraulic engineer, deputy chief of the Hwai River Harnessing Committee.

She had learned her profession from her father, who got his training in an American university. She hated the United States; in her thesaurus, "Americans" and "imperialist bandits" were synonymous. Herself "a shambling, awkward Donald Duck of a woman, who waddled rather than walked," she was contemptuous, not envious, of the women from India who managed somehow, even on a work-boat tossed by the turbulent river, to be well-groomed and womanly.

Frank Moraes saw Chien Chen-ying as "The Communist incarnate, the 'sea-green incorruptible,' who, wedded to her own creed, was not interested in individuals as individuals, not even in herself. To her, all things were subordinate to the leadership of the Communist Party. On her face was the dedicated look of a saint or a martyr rapt in her cause; behind it, she was hard and flintlike." Vijaya Lakshmi Pandit never forgot the archetype of Communist womanhood in New China.

16.

What conclusions she stated, what warning she may have uttered when she returned to the Prime Minister's House in New Delhi, I do not presume to guess. Two years later, he was Peking's guest, on a visit of state to a neighbor pledged, as India was, to peaceful coexistence. Returning, he called a press conference. Correspondents from Communist China and Soviet Russia, and for Communist-favoring publications in India, crowded the conference room. For whatever reason, no Delhi-based American correspondents were present.

I watched pens and pencils fly, while Jawaharlal Nehru said

he had gone to the People's Republic "to see for myself." Like his sister before him, he had been shown many proofs of progress. "Many of China's problems are like ours: need for land reform, for industrialization, for increased agricultural production, for education of the illiterate, for liberation from the curse of poverty. In China, these are being conquered to an impressive degree." Then he said, "However . . ." Around me, writing stopped. The word hung in air, until finally he resumed.

"Change," he said, "is being accomplished there by an authoritarian central government. We in India seek the same change, and it must come, and will. But we intend to accomplish it by democratic process. This may take longer, but also, it may last much longer." I saw no one write this down. When clippings from California newspapers came by airmail, I read dispatches datelined New Delhi, headlined *Nehru Praises Red China Successes*. I could find no mention of his declaration of principles, which surely was frowned on at Peking.

At the Alps Bar on Janpath, the street once called Queensway in honor of Victoria Regina, I recognized a veteran newsgatherer, last met in Chicago. I remembered him as notably abstemious. He was drinking *burra pegs,* double Scotches, straight. I asked why I hadn't seen him at the press-conference. He said he had stopped covering them, because in two years, not one report he cabled to his editors in the United States had been printed as he wrote it. *In vino veritas* or otherwise, it is true that beginning in early 1952, annoyed antagonism was implicit in almost everything about India published in America.

I happen to think one angry man was largely responsible for this. On the record, he was never angrier than when it was announced, following her mission in Mao's China, that Vijaya Lakshmi Pandit would again head India's delegation to the United Nations General Assembly, convening for the first time in the Big Glass House in New York, where almost everyone throws stones.

V. K. Krishna Menon's most admiring biographer says, "As one who has made great personal sacrifices for Indian freedom, he is contemptuous of those who demand a share in freedom's fruits merely on the basis of a term in jail or an arrest during the days of the Raj. As a man of exceptional abilities, he is intolerant of those whose only asset is the flair for insinuating themselves into positions of responsibility."

Targets of his intolerance said he had small cause for complaint. Since 1948, as India's High Commissioner to the United Kingdom, he had comported himself as viceregally in England as any Viceroy ever sent to British India. He had come unscathed through what was headlined in India as *The Great Jeep Scandal,* involving alleged overpayments to European firms and delivery of substandard equipment to India's Defense Ministry. But in June, 1952, he was suddenly notified that he was being replaced, by one of the *Swaraj* veterans he called opportunists.

"He wanted to stay on until August 15, but had no alternative but to hand over to his successor, two months before completion of his full term. From June until September, he was in the wilderness." He talked of retiring from public life, to practice law in London. Walking absent-mindedly across

Trafalgar Square, he was struck down by a speeding taxi. In the hospital, he read the news that he had been posted to the United Nations, "as deputy to Mrs. Vijaya Lakshmi Pandit."

"Nehru," his admirer avers, "had told him that after the High Commissionership he would be wanted as leader of the Indian delegation." This is not documented. But pictures on Page One in American newspapers documented the manner in which he seized the spotlight from the woman who held the post he thought belonged to him.

"When he arrived in New York, bruised both in body and in mind, he was so sick that he had to be carried out of the aircraft. Extreme mental depression combined with the accident made him a pathetic figure. Doctors gave him six months to live. Why, asked New York, had India sent this decrepit old invalid to the United Nations? But neither the doctors nor New York knew the caliber of this invalid."

His dramatic arrival was followed by dramatically rapid recovery. "His way of dealing with the personality problem was to forget that it existed. There was no better way of achieving this end than by burying himself in work. The thorniest problem facing the United Nations was Korea. He adopted Korea as his special interest." He could not have found a surer way to interpose his angry image between Vijaya Lakshmi Pandit and Americans who until then, thanks largely to her, had regarded India as a sometimes puzzling but well-intentioned and friendly neighbor.

"The distaste the West developed for Krishna Menon was in reality a distaste for India; Menon merely happened to be in the front line of attack." This interpretation is that of T. J. S. George, a journalist from Menon's home state of Kerala in

India, who hailed him as *The Tremendous Representative.* If the accolade was earned, it was in terms of one man's ability to fasten his personal unpopularity on a nation.

17.

India had voted with the United States, for United Nations condemnation of North Korean aggression across the 38th Parallel. In the autumn of 1950, after General Douglas Mac-Arthur's victory at Inchon, New Delhi informed Washington that India's Ambassador at Peking was warned: "If United Nations forces cross the Parallel into North Korea, the People's Republic will enter the war." The warning was dismissed as "bluster from a paper dragon." General MacArthur drove toward the Yalu. Communist China struck with startling strength. American losses pyramided.

Truce talks begun at Panmunjom in June, 1951, were broken off, resumed, broken off again. In autumn of 1952, deadlock seemed hopeless. Polls showed American weariness of White House policies, and weakening of American faith in the United Nations. Korea was a major issue in the presidential election campaign. Altogether, it was a time when diplomacy, if nothing more, prompted other foreign representatives to curb their tongues. But Krishna Menon "became an institution that compelled attention, grudging on the part of some, no doubt, but attention all the same."

Vijaya Lakshmi Pandit's education in the art of diplomacy had progressed so far that Krishna Menon's opposite, K. P. S. Menon, credited her with being the only woman he knew who fitted the description written eight centuries ago by

Bhavabhuti in his *Malati-Madhav:* "He is a true diplomat who, behaving and conducting himself outwardly in the most pleasing and charming manner, can seal inwardly even the minutest aperture of escape for others very firmly, and thus he accomplishes all his aims and acts of policy by remaining seemingly indifferent and neutral to them, and keeping his mouth shut."

Krishna Menon was said to have read everything of any importance ever written. He may have missed the *Malati-Madhav;* or he may simply have decided it was as out-of-date as Mahatma Gandhi's theory that no end justifies the means by which it is gained, if they are less than admirable. "His gaunt arresting face appeared in all the newspapers, his statements made headlines, and some at the U. N. began to think he was the brains for which Mrs. Pandit's beauty was but a facade."

An American Senator, William Knowland from California, called India support for Communist China's admission to the United Nations "shocking." Krishna Menon "unleashed a fury of words upon the Senator. 'As for being shocked, that is a question of a state of mind and the thing to do is to go to a doctor or a psychiatrist about it!' " An American businessman asked why India did not denounce Soviet aggression in Hungary. "Menon flew into a fit of temper. He brandished his cane at the accusing American, and began shouting at the top of his voice. 'I am not accountable to your country! I'm tired of being bullied by you!' Reporters ran to the spot, but Indian officials put Menon in a car and drove off before the press could get at him."

These incidents are chosen out of chronology; but they

synopsize his course of conduct from the first. Its effect was to convince reporters and newspaper readers, and many delegates gathered in the Big Glass House, that Krishna Menon, not Vijaya Lakshmi Pandit, spoke for India. Still she held her peace.

General Dwight D. Eisenhower was swept into the White House "on a tidal wave of change." He named John Foster Dulles as his Secretary of State. Mr. Dulles frankly liked nothing about Krishna Menon. He was fully apprised of Menon's activities at the United Nations. "Menon would spend hours with the leader of a Communist delegation, and then hours with the leader of a Western delegation." He spent few hours with the leader of his own delegation. "The way in which he was going about his business aroused tremendous curiosity."

Meanwhile, amidst Christmas shopping crowds on Manhattan's Fifth Avenue, a woman urging her five year old away from a store-window Santa Claus was halted by a *sari*-clad stranger. "I'm so sorry to trouble you, but your little boy has such a lovely coat. Could you tell me where you bought it? It's just what I've been looking for, for my grandson." A feature writer's fancy embroidered the anecdote.

"The proud mother named the store and the bargain price. Then suddenly, 'Haven't I seen your picture in the papers? Aren't you Madame Pandit from India? Are you still at the United Nations?' 'Yes,' said the head of India's delegation, 'I'm still at the United Nations.'" She mailed Christmas packages to India, then found time to prepare an Indian dish which she sent as a friendship gift to a group of American college girls on holiday, being entertained in the delegates' dining room. Then in the Big Glass House, she watched Krishna Menon take the center of the stage.

He proposed a seventeen-point Korean Formula, which he said was "not a solution but a way to a solution." It met immediate opposition. "The American press howled that Menon was 'smuggling China into the civilized world.' But the worst cut came from Russia's Vishinsky. Delivering one of his bitterest speeches, he attacked the Indian plan as a 'rotten solution,' and hurled personal abuse at Menon. Vishinsky had suddenly realized that a small newcomer was assuming too much importance in an arena meant primarily for the giants. It served Communist purposes then to hold India up as a stooge for the Americans, and Vishinsky did just that."

The interpretation belongs to T. J. S. George. So does "Vishinsky's stand gave the United States a god-sent opportunity to win the confidence and sympathy of Asia. But John Foster Dulles began bullying and blackguarding India, which made the Soviet Union reexamine its own policy and quickly readjust its attitudes toward India and Asia." This quarrels with the record. Actually, although Dulles disliked the Menon plan and said so loudly, he criticized the man, not the country; and in any event, the Eisenhower Administration did not speak officially for the United States until January 20, 1953.

On December 3, 1952, an amended version of the formula, backed by the American delegation, was adopted by the full Assembly, despite the Soviet bloc's unanimous *"Nyet!"* It is only fair to add that this was the basis for the signing of an armistice at Panmunjom on July 27, 1953, after thirty-seven months of war and twenty-four months and seventeen days

Irene Andrews Photo

Nehru and Walt Disney at Disney-land

Author Robert Hardy Andrews with Nehru in an Indian garden

Mr. and Mrs. Robert Hardy Andrews with Nehru and Los Angeles Mayor Samuel Yorty

India's 13th Anniversary Independence Day, August 15, 1960

B. K. Nehru, Mrs. Pandit's cousin, and India's Ambassador in the United States

Madame Pandit at the opening of the Eighth Session of the U.N. General Assembly

Crown Prince Akihito of Japan visits Mrs. Pandit and Dag Hammarskjold at the United Nations

President Eisenhower addresses the United Nations, December 1953 of fruitless effort to end it; with an important additive that not even Krishna Menon had proposed. India was made chairman of the Neutral Nations Repatriation Commission; General K. S. Thimayya, a longtime friend of the Nehru family, headed prisoner-of-war exchange; and India was established as a Third Force in Asia. But Krishna Menon went on being anathema to Americans.

"It is Krishna Menon's misfortune," T. J. S. George laments, "that the good he does is so often obliterated by the publicity given to the bad." In American consensus, he asked for what he received. He also, however inadvertently, and certainly without love, added his hands to those that helped Vijaya Lakshmi Pandit toward heights to which he could never climb.

18.

No one won the Nobel Peace Prize in 1952. When the General Assembly recessed at year's end, to reconvene in February 1953, confidence in the United Nations' ability to make peace or keep it was at the vanishing point. American casualties in Korea under the United Nations' banner totaled one hundred and twenty-five thousand, including more than twenty thousand killed, in a war of which Americans said, "Nobody can win it, lose it or stop it." A million Communist Chinese troops were reported deployed north of the Yalu. Three hundred and fifty thousand Viet Minh fought the French in Indochina. Belligerents snarled in North Africa and the Middle East. *Apartheid* hardened in South Africa. Peking massed forces in the Himalayan wilderness. No progress was made toward a plebiscite in Kashmir.

Yet Vijaya Lakshmi Pandit, briefly free to be at home again and back in her place in the House of the People, refused to join the chorus of doom-shouters. Invited to contribute to a symposium sponsored by The Ford Foundation, for publication in the United States, she wrote "It is unreasonable to expect unanimity of opinion on momentous issues, but disagreement can be softened by an effort at mutual understanding."

She endeavored, as Krishna Menon had not, to explain India's point of view to Americans. "India has tried to follow in all modesty what she considers the right path, and has tried to understand others' viewpoints. She does not claim infallibility of judgment, nor does she recognize such infallibility of judgment and monopoly of rectitude in any other country. The crisis of the world requires every country to search its conscience and seek the ways of action which lead to the peace which we all desire. We must not sacrifice tomorrow because of the passions of today."

In South India, where he had been a stranger for a quarter of a century, Krishna Menon was named by the Congress Party hierarchy at Madras for membership in Raja Sabha, India's equivalent to Britain's House of Lords. This did not require a vote by the people. It would, in fact, be several years before popular election sent him to Parliament.

"He had," says T. J. S. George, "accumulated many enemies at home. His apparent roughness of behavior had antagonized many who felt insulted or ignored. He was also hated by the business world. The last category of anti-Menonites were merely men who were opposed to Jawaharlal

Nehru, but had not the courage to come out in the open. Nehru was too much of a hero and mass magician to be effectively attacked in public, so they attacked him by proxy; and the proxy was Krishna Menon."

Vijaya Lakshmi Pandit could be forgiven if she doubted that anyone was ever proxy for her brother. He was fully aware who his enemies were, whether they attacked openly or behind a smoke screen. "I have learned," he told his sister, "that a Prime Minister cannot afford to be sensitive." The Nehru temper was not always bottled up; but his explosions were brief and soon forgotten. He asked for no scapegoats.

Even T. J. S. George, after conferring a martyr's crown, continues, "Menon himself perhaps deliberately pushed people into the lobby that was growing against him. He never yields to bullying, and the growth of the lobby in fact increased his obstinacy. The result was that a movement, that might have been at worst a right-left tug-of-war in New Delhi, became an international campaign of revenge and personal vendetta."

Menon might be India to America. In India, the headlined name was that of a man unheard of by Americans, whose emergence from shadows was a proof to Vijaya Lakshmi Pandit that there was truth as well as hope in her brother's "All over India there are now centers of human activity that are like lamps spreading their light more and more in the surrounding darkness. This light must grow and grow until it covers the land."

The man was Vinoba Bhave. With reverent affection, millions in India, including Vijaya Lakshmi Pandit and her brother, called him Vinobaji. In 1940 Gandhi honored him as

"India's first complete self-giver." In 1948, with Gandhi gone, he stepped aside from the rush for victory's awards. No record existed that he attended any Congress conclaves, or sought or was considered for any government appointment. Then in 1951, he reappeared from obscurity, and with two words made himself better known to India's masses than Krishna Menon, the *Tremendous Representative*. The words were *Bhoodan Yagna:* gift of land.

They were first heard in Hyderabad State, where Vinoba Bhave, on a byroad near the village of Pochampalli, encountered starving wanderers who barred his path, but were humbly careful not to step on his shadow. He was Brahmin. They were born Untouchables, and India's Constitution outlawing Untouchability had failed thus far to ease their misery. They asked if it was true that Gandhiji made them Children of God. He said it was true, "and the government has given you equal rights with all men." They asked "What is this 'government'?" He said, "The government is you." They thought the Brahmin mocked them. Seeing this, he knew what he must do.

Entering the village, he went to the communal well, from which Untouchables were not allowed to drink. The *panchayat,* the council of village elders, was gathered there. He broke in on their deliberations, asking, "Is there anyone here who would like to give a portion of his land to these homeless persons, for the love of God?" He recounted what ensued. "The last man from whom I would have expected charity stood up smiling. He said, 'I am glad you came today. I had made up my mind I ought to get rid of half my land. It is too much to cultivate at my age, and I have no sons. I offer a hundred acres to you for these Harijans, if they will care for it properly.' "

Vinoba Bhave asked the wanderers how much land they could farm. They whispered together. Then the eldest said, "Sir, eighty acres is enough for us, two acres for each of our families. Sir, is it permitted for us to suggest that the rest should be given to others whose need is greater?" The donor said, "I agree." Distribution was made immediately. Then Vinoba Bhave walked on to a hill where he sat and meditated.

Next morning just at sunrise, when in another village cooking fires were lighted and men, women and children prepared to begin the day's work in their fields, he appeared, half-singing, half-reciting verses from the *Bhagavad Gita,* the Song of God. Few knew the *Gita* as he did. His rendering in Marathi verse sold a hundred thousand copies in Maharashtra. His translation of this into Hindi has had five large editions. But he was not selling books. A crowd formed. He prayed. Then he preached.

"I do not believe in *Samyavada,* Communism," he told the villagers. "I believe in *Samyayoga,* the practice of equality." Several youthful Communist converts muttered. "I do not hate the Communists," he said. "I pray God to let the feeling of love for them also reside in my heart. And I pray God that He will kindle good faith in their hearts. If they really believe their ideology, let them come in the daytime, not by night. Let them give up class warfare, and work for the good of all. Let them loot the people as I propose to do, with sincerity and compassion."

He chose his action-word deliberately. British soldiers, sent to India to civilize the lesser breeds, borrowed the Hindi *lut,* to take, and made it *loot,* to plunder. Peasant landholders, suspicious of smooth speech, read honesty in Vinobaji's bluntness. They were congenitally devout. He appealed to this in them. "I do not believe God wants humanity to suffer. Thus I am not able to keep quiet while millions are suffering. I ask for land for the love of God."

19.

The very poor gave land to those poorer than themselves. *Bhoodan Yagna* began. Bent, ill, his broken spectacles wired together, the soles of his cheap tennis shoes worn through, clad in a single garment, weighing less than a hundred pounds, Vinobaji walked ten miles each day, remaining in a village only until land was given, or the gift refused. Malnutrition and exhaustion brought on fainting spells, but he refused to accept the automobile offered by a *zamindar.* "The poor must walk. While they must walk, so must I."

At a village called Pukharyan, he found seven landless families. Land given, in his judgment, was sufficient for only two of these. He recited verses that called selfishness the deadliest sin, and said it would shame Pukharyan to have it said in other villages. "Pukharyan is only one-fourth dedicated to God." A wealthy miser made up the deficit, and awaited praise. It was not given. Vinobaji said "If God is grateful, you will hear from Him," and led his *yatridal,* the growing column of disciples that now accompanied him, along the road to another village.

Near Patna, agitators waving red flags assembled a managed mob. A stranger from the city harangued through a loudspeaker not made in India, as the *yatridal* approached. "The people insist that the *Bhoodan* promoters shall stop this cheat of extorting land-gifts from the deluded poor!" Vinobaji told the throng, "When people talk about heaven in New Russia and New China, I want to remind them that it is much too soon to be sure anything good has happened there. And even if violence has actually rendered such benefits as the Communists claim, any sensible person can surely see that non-violence can do much more, while not doing harm, as they cannot deny harm has been done in the Communist countries."

Resting crosslegged in a banyan's shade, having walked a hundred miles and collected pledges of twenty thousand acres in ten days, he told politicians and reporters who came to investigate him, "I believe India's land problem can be solved by the pressure of public opinion, without violence or seizure by the government. Thus I act as an instrument of God's will as I see it, to help in bringing about a peaceful change by which all, rich and poor alike, will benefit."

The Communist press called him a charlatan, stirring up a storm so he could extort bribes from *zamindars;* then alleged he was a hired agent of the Congress Party, "promised a sinecure in Nehru's government if he can delay land-reform a little longer." Tara Pandit says in *From Fear Set Free* that Vinobaji "seemed unconcerned that it was today, not a thousand years ago. He walked on, and village after village greeted him with leafy archways of welcome. If the gift-land was at times not cultivable, if a gift were revoked after he departed, he had still shown what one man with a will could do towards the solution of a problem."

Peasants who received gift-land had to farm it themselves, and were bound not to transfer or sell it for at least ten years. State governments hurriedly passed special legislation to facilitate land transfers. The *Times of India* said, "Vinobaji has begun to waken the slumbering idealism of our thinking people." A Calcutta editor wrote: "Where legislation for land reform has been agonizingly slow, due to the unavoidable delays of democracy, Vinobaji is getting positive results through pure Gandhi-ism, and may save democracy in India."

Jawaharlal Nehru, as Prime Minister, and Dr. Rajendra Prasad, as President, invited him to New Delhi to confer with the Planning Commission. They offered to send a plane, but he chose to walk, a thousand miles, preaching *Bhoodan Yagna* on the way. In New Delhi, he chose to stay in the hut in Rajghat in which Gandhi had been cremated. To Tara, his appearance was that of a *sadhu* of the ancient past. But "He had set in motion a unique, if miniature, agrarian revolution, all the more significant because throughout history land had come to be associated with war and bloodshed." To her mother, he proved the importance of the individual.

In the House of the People, Vijaya Lakshmi Pandit heard vociferous Communist Party members complain that "This Vinoba Bhave is making India ridiculous in the eyes of the modern world, posing as some kind of reincarnated Mahatma, dragging the ignorant back to the Dark Ages of mythology and superstition!" She had seen nothing in their "modern world," in Soviet Russia or Communist China, to equal what was done in India by Vinobaji, who by 1953 had gained more than two million acres of India for men, women and children who owned not one inch of it until he began to walk the roads crying, "Land for the love of God!"

Her brother's name stood first on the long list of India's leaders who supported Vinobaji and *Bhoodan Yagna*. He guaranteed there would be no expropriation of property, on the Soviet-Communist Chinese pattern. Private ownership would be preserved, while land was redistributed equitably, "until no person possesses more than he needs, and every man owns enough to feed himself and his family."

There was more to tell Americans, when she returned to the United Nations. A slogan coined by an American, Dr. Frank Laubach, "Each one teach one," was echoed in the villages, where the literate taught the illiterate. American engineers were in charge at the massive Bhakra-Nangal project in the Punjab, which when completed would end floods, irrigate three and one-half million acres and produce power and light where there had been none of either. On Gandhi's birthday, fifty-five development programs were launched, affecting twenty-five thousand villages and more than sixteen million people. "Not all was good, but much was better."

20.

Word came from K. P. S. Menon, her friend and sometime mentor, now her successor as India's Ambassador at Moscow, that he had been granted a privilege denied to her during her term of service in Russia. He was allowed to see Stalin, at a time when rumor said Stalin was ill, dying or dead. He told correspondents "Stalin looked healthy to me." A dispatch datelined New York, written by a correspondent expelled from Russia the year before, scoffed, "K. P. S. Menon was fooled. The man he saw was not Stalin, but his double, a Bolshoi Theater actor named Krutikov." The fact was that no one outside the Kremlin knew what was happening there.

She was back at the *India* desk in the Big Glass House in Manhattan, when Moscow bulletins reported, on February 28, 1953, that Stalin was ill, and on March 5, that he was dead. Mystery shrouded his passing, and its aftermath. Malenkov, Stalin's man since 1925, took the reins, but it was said they were only loaned to him by Lavrentri Beria, Stalin's bloodhound. Then Beria was reported under arrest, charged with treason. Whoever won the power struggle in Russia, unsteady balance in the cold war would be affected. The United Nations, its fabric already tattered, might rip apart under its new Secretary-General, Dag Hammarskjöld, whose election the Russian delegation had opposed.

To a not unprejudiced analyst, a more important struggle went on between John Foster Dulles and Krishna Menon. "Dulles, obsessed with his own notions of the containment of Communism, was incapable of appreciating any other motivating force in the world. Menon, obsessed with the Indian revolution and the need for a climate of peace in Afro-Asia, was incapable of appreciating anti-Communism as a motivating force at all."

However accurate this *reductio,* there was much discussion of a new Formula Menon: "Since the opposition to French colonialism in Indochina is being led almost exclusively by the Communists, the United States has begun plans to internationalize the war." Menon "went out of his way to be unpleasant toward Western nations and their delegates." But Vijaya Lakshmi Pandit had not come back to the Big Glass House to throw stones.

Assembly adoption of a modified Menon plan for Korea had not ended the Korean War. Chinese Communist attacks intensified, with more use of heavy artillery than at any previous time. United Nations and South Korean forces were pushed back, with mounting casualties. Exchange of sick and wounded prisoners-of-war began, then stopped. Every day's delay in effecting a truce cost more lives.

In the so-called First Committee, she worked long hours, doing her best to progress agreement on a blueprint for repatriation of American, South Korean, North Korean and Communist Chinese prisoners; lacking which, no truce was possible. While Krishna Menon and the press and its cameras seemed inseparable, she was busy behind closed doors. When she could, she hurried from First Committee debates to meetings of the Commission on the Status of Women.

Creation of this body, composed entirely of women, had been regarded dubiously by many delegates, who felt the United Nations had quite enough to contend with, in the field of great affairs, without concerning itself with women's rights and wrongs. But skeptics now began to quote an American advertiser's billboard slogan: *Never underestimate the power of a woman.* Very few underestimated Vijaya Lakshmi Pandit.

"The delegates," a First Committee member said, "are developing great respect for her wisdom and experience, and for her patience and open-mindedness and tact in dealing with those with whom she disagrees. She is very much a woman, but she has a man's grip on her job."

A working program for the Neutral Nations Repatriation Commission was finalized and sent to Panmunjom before the session ended on April 23, and she was free to fly home again, and briefly, be a mother arranging her daughter's wedding. Rita, the youngest, was engaged to marry A. K. Dar, a Kashmiri Brahmin, a career officer in India's Foreign Service. Changing times made such elaborate weddings as there had been at Anand Bhavan no longer right and proper; but every detail of Rita's marriage must be as perfect as her mother could make it.

A great event impended in London. Three hundred and fifty years after Sir John Mendenhall, as emissary of Elizabeth of England, obtained from Akbar the Great the trading rights that began the history of British India, a second Queen Elizabeth was about to be crowned. At the coronation, Jawaharlal Nehru and his daughter, Indira, would represent the independent Republic of India, a partner, not a subject, by free choice continuing within the framework of the British Commonwealth of Nations.

Vijaya Lakshmi Pandit's meeting with the new Queen was put off to another time. She had told her three daughters, more than once: "After you marry, you can stand on your heads, or fly to the moon; but first things first. Girls are only potentials, until they marry. Marriage makes them actual, brings them to full flower, draws out all the hidden best in them." Fondly, they accused her of being greedy for more grandchildren.

Lekha and Tara had already given her five. "These five

mischief-makers," Tara wrote in 1954, "have no idea that 'Nani,' Grandma, is an international celebrity, but they do know she is fun. When she is away, gaily wrapped parcels arrive for them accompanied by urgent requests for their snap-shots, and picture postcards of weeping pussycats and forlorn teddy bears haunt the mail, announcing that 'Nani' is missing her babies. It is all quite incomprehensible to anyone who is not a grandmother." In 1953 not even her daughters guessed what their mother knew: that soon she would face an experi-ence shared with no other grandmother.

On May 29, 1953, two men who were archetypical of two nations, two races, two religions, reached the top of the world together. Edmond Hillary from New Zealand, and Tensing Norkay, born in Nepal but a citizen of India, stood atop Mount Everest, where no man stood before them. They took photographs, and ate mint cake. Tensing, a devout Buddhist, dug a hole in the snow and left food for the gods, before they began their descent. News of their conquest of earth's tallest mountain reached London on the morning of the second Queen Elizabeth's coronation.

Seated side by side, watching the ceremonies, were Indira Gandhi and Winston Churchill, who had been called back as Prime Minister in 1951. "Suddenly he said, 'Isn't it strange that we should be talking as friends when we hated each other such a short while ago?' I said, 'We didn't hate you, Sir Winston.' He said 'I did! I did!' Then he added, 'But I don't now.' "

Indira and her father, homeward bound, visited Moscow, and were greeted by a Russian choir of five hundred voices, singing India's national anthem in Hindi learned phonetically. *Pravda* and *Izvestia* gave columns to the welcomed guest whose statements were never published while Stalin lived. Among functionaries in the background in group photographs was a pudgy personage identified as N. Khrushchev. Vyacheslav Molotov, like Winston Churchill back in power after a period in forced retirement, made first moves as Foreign Minister toward a Soviet-India trade agreement.

The Soviet claimed credit for pushing Communist China and North Korea into resumption of truce talks at Panmunjom. These bore fruit when on July 27, an armistice was signed at last. Exchange of prisoners began, supervised by General K. S. Thimayya and the first soldiers sent overseas by the Republic of India, there not to make war but to serve the United Nations in promoting peace.

Abroad and at home, it was agreed that after only six years of independence, nonaligned India had gone far toward establishing importance in the world community. Vijaya Lakshmi Pandit had done her part, and more than many, in this achievement. But brief official announcement in New Delhi stirred a wondering hum. Except during her two years as Ambassador at Washington, she had headed India's United Nations delegation since she was first appointed by Lord Wavell, Viceroy of still-British India. Now it was announced that India's delegates to the eighth General Assembly session would be led not by her, but by Krishna Menon.

Smilingly unperturbed, she disposed of concerned questioners with "You can't expect the mother of the bride to talk politics at a time like this." On Rita's marriage morning, she cast her "Yes" vote in the House of the People, for a measure to increase employment opportunities for former Untouchables, before rushing home to take charge of Rita's wedding. "It was the most leisurely of the three in our family," Tara says, "but still it had to be hurried. Mummie had to be on the move again."

She was with the Indian delegation, flying to the United States, when United Nations correspondents stumbled on a headline story. First order of General Assembly business would be election of a president to succeed Lester Pearson of Canada. Paul-Henri Spaak of Belgium, Aranha of Brazil, Arce of the Argentine, Evatt of Australia, Romulo of the Philippines, Entezam of Iran and Nervo of Mexico had preceded Pearson. Consensus had settled on Prince Wan of Thailand as his successor. Suddenly it was revealed that India had nominated Vijaya Lakshmi Pandit.

21.

More reporters and cameras surrounded her, when she stepped from her plane, than had greeted any other arriving newsmaker. She had, of course, known she was to be nominated. She has never indicated she knew in advance that Washington had informed her brother the United States would support her candidacy. Asked for comment, she said, "I am honored and grateful," nothing more.

She did no campaigning. A good deal was done in her behalf, however, by Henry Cabot Lodge, Jr., then American Ambassador to the United Nations. As to what ensued, Krishna Menon's biographer has a strange explanation. Assembly members, according to T. J. S. George, decided to solve the personality problem to which he says his hero paid no heed. "They elected Mrs. Pandit president, thus leaving the field clear for Menon." It is doubtful in the extreme, that any favor to Krishna Menon was intended.

Assembly members knew, respected and liked Vijaya Lakshmi Pandit. When Trygve Lie resigned as Secretary-General in November, 1952, there was cloakroom talk of proposing her for the post that went eventually to Dag Hammarskjöld. Now the members were worriedly conscious that United Nations prestige was tarnished by a year of indecision. Admission of more new Afro-Asian nations impended. No one knew yet who would emerge as maker of Soviet policies. Over all, there was the spectacle, in which some saw a specter, of women everywhere on earth coming out to join the march for freedom and equality that was begun by women in India.

The Assembly voted for the prototype and protagonist of those women. Not quite a month after her fifty-third birthday, on September 15, 1953, the Assembly gavel was placed in her hands. Now Motilal Nehru's Little Daughter was Madame President, in the highest elective office any woman ever held.

To the world outside the Big Glass House, it may have seemed she had only to be herself as the press pictured her: a poised and pleasant Great Lady, as above and apart from mundane masculine argument and maneuvering as the second Queen Elizabeth, who reigned but did not rule. In fact, their tasks and responsibilities were as opposite as Her Majesty and Madame President themselves.

Men spoke for the Crown in Britain's Parliament. In the Big Glass House, Vijaya Lakshmi Pandit was literally a watcher for the world. She must sit hour after hour, small in her throne-like presidential chair, overlooking the dais from which delegates spoke, never able to see the speaker's face, alert for change of emphasis or indicated shift in policies. Presiding over the Central or Steering Committee, composed of vice-presidents and chairmen of the seven Assembly committees representing all races on the earth, she must never depart from the proper path through an organizational maze that left many statesmen bewildered.

She could no longer think and act as a woman of India. Partiality must be erased from mind and heart. She had led, and won, the first debates on racism in South Africa. Now she must protect the parliamentary privilege of South African delegates who stormed that their country's treatment of Indians and other Coloureds was no concern of the United Nations. She had seen horror when Pakistan split off from India. Now she must be unmoved by Pakistan charges of Hindu outrage against Muslims in Kashmir. She had been deeply involved in implementing the Korean truce. Now she must divorce herself from personal opinion, while Soviet representatives claimed full *kudos,* praised the U. S. S. R. as the Great Peacemaker and at every opportunity obstructed cold war easement.

For the majority in the General Assembly, being guided however deftly by a woman was something experienced previously, if at all, only within their families. Many represented countries in which religion or tradition or both still kept womenfolk secluded in *purdah* or its equivalent. Each word she spoke, each gesture, must be confident; yet she must never give excuse for any delegate to say or think "Now she is 'acting like a woman.'"

On her first day as Madame President, delegates put forward seventy-two separate items for the provisional agenda. "She knew the matters to be discussed involved conflicting views and intense feelings, and quietly appealed to all concerned to conduct debate calmly and objectively." All very well; but those concerned were used to women asking them to shout less and listen more. From ingrained habit, or deliberately probing for feminine reaction, at first some delegates ignored her plea. "Usually, they ended by apologizing and saying they would try not to let it happen again." This was in certain instances a Pyrrhic victory. "Men get accustomed to saying 'Yes, my dear.' It doesn't necessarily mean they are convinced; they just feel noble, for letting us have the last word, which is supposed to be all we want."

What Vijaya Lakshmi Pandit did not want was deference accorded to the weaker sex. *What should I have done, to make them listen as they would to a man?* Delegates coming to the dais bowed, as they would not to any man. A gallant Latin American diplomat, presenting the report of the Commission on the Racial Situation in the Union of South Africa, placed a bouquet of roses on the document he handed up to her. A reporter, new in the Big Glass House, took no notes during tense dispute regarding Israel-Syria rights to River Jordan waters, but when the session recessed asked how she would describe the color of her *sari*. For a moment, the Nehru temper nagged. "Would you have asked my predecessor the color of his necktie?" Then her disarming smile returned.

At a dinner given in her honor by the United Nations Correspondents Association, she said "No press corps anywhere is as zealous in the pursuit of news." The correspondents applauded *pro forma* compliment, but sobered when she went on. "You of the press have the power to sway men's minds and influence their judgment. Will you not help us to reach our common goal through love and faith, rather than through fear?"

Fear, more than love and faith, was the order of the day. In Indochina, France moved toward Dienbienphu. Fifteen Afro-Asian nations demanded inquiry into French operations in North Africa. France told the United Nations "Keep out." For Russia, Malenkov proffered an olive-branch. "There is no disputed or unsolved problem which cannot be resolved by peaceful means on the basis of mutual understanding between the countries concerned . . . including the United States of America." Then the Soviet exploded a hydrogen bomb. *Peace, peace, and there is no peace!* But Vijaya Lakshmi Pandit had decided long ago that it was a sin to abandon hope.

To women who came to introduce themselves and tell her she was their guiding light, she said, "This hall has begun to take on an atmosphere that we associate with a place where friends come to think and work together." Some of them said, "Well, they don't seem to agree on very much." She said no miracles should be expected. What counted was that for the first time in history, concerted attempt was being made "to harmonize dissimilar interests, and reconcile forces, and channel energy and genius toward cooperative action." Their hope was renewed by her faith.

Thousands of women wrote to her, as a confidante to whom

they told their troubles, asking what she would do in their place. She answered as many as she could. Frequently, she gave small luncheons or dinners, often preparing a special Indian dish, inviting selected delegates and guiding informal conversation into exchange of ideas. Perceptibly, her status changed. "I think gradually the delegates forgot I was a woman."

This was unlikely. But the press said "Her dignity and control as Madame President owes nothing to exercise of 'femininity' in the general usage of that misused word." A London editorialist said it had been a wiser act than some at the United Nations might realize, "that in this critical period they chose as their president one who is not only the most distinguished woman but the ablest diplomat in Asia."

On United Nations Day, October 24, 1953, the American Association for the United Nations arranged an outdoor celebration. Addressing a throng, she said, "We are members of the first generation of men who dared to believe that the miseries which afflict two-thirds of mankind are not inevitable. We have set out to develop and share the resources of the earth and the resources of the mind for the good of all." Mrs. Eleanor Roosevelt presented her with a silver gavel, and said, "Madame President has lighted a lamp in our hearts, a lamp of understanding and good will."

During October, she conferred at the White House with President Eisenhower and John Foster Dulles. A note records: "Her personal charm is matched by her firmness against 'colonialism' and racial persecutions." At the time, Soviet domination of satellite countries was hardening, and the Kremlin was accused of reviving anti-Semitism. In the Big Glass House, she was as unreadable as the Soviet's delegates.

The seventh anniversary of UNICEF, the Children's Emergency Fund, fell on her brother's sixty-fourth birthday, November 14. Seven New York City schools sent seven children each, to present her with a seven-tiered cake. She gave each child a generous slice, then told them, "I'm feeling lonely today. It's my brother's birthday and I can't celebrate it with him." Then she smiled. "I don't really like cake very much, so you have had to eat it for me. What would make me happy would be if each one of you would give me a kiss." Sticky kisses marked her cheek. A hopeful youngster asked, "Now do you feel better?" She said, "I feel much better."

On December 8, with Dag Hammarskjöld, she escorted President Eisenhower to the podium in the Big Glass House. All the delegates felt they knew him, though many saw him closely for the first time. He told them "The United States pledges before you, and therefore before the world, its determination to help solve the fearful atomic dilemma, to devote its entire heart and mind to finding the way by which the miraculous inventiveness of man shall not be dedicated to his death, but consecrated to his life."

He offered to discuss, "with the Soviet and others," creation of an international atomic energy agency, "to pool for peaceful purposes atomic energy supplies from both the Western and Communist worlds." From her vantage, she studied the Soviet delegates. Their faces were wooden masks. Malenkov had boasted "We, too, have the H-bomb." President Eisenhower's pledge and proposal were answered with silence.

22.

On December 9, 1953, she called the Assembly to order for the year's last business. She rose and began, "It remains for me to thank you . . . ," then realized all the delegates were standing. Requests to be heard came from all sides. Lester Pearson of Canada, as a past president, was first to speak. He said he knew well the burdens borne by one presiding over an assemblage representing sixty nations, with always a hundred problems on the agenda. "You have carried this load and discharged your responsibility with queenly grace and unquestionable impartiality."

Belgium's spokesman said he would cherish memory of "the charming simplicity with which you have presided and the team spirit you have inspired." The French Ambassador said, "You have never deviated from the great impartiality which won our confidence from the very first." Mexico's leader called her "an example of the happy combination of the simplicity of greatness and the greatness of a profound and disciplined mind."

Then Iran's Muslim delegate spoke for Arab countries in which for a thousand years women had been in *purdah*. "When you sat in your chair for the first time, I looked to the rostrum and wondered how times have changed. Many of us could not have hoped in our wildest dreams, that an Asian woman would one day rise to this august position. It has come to pass because of you, and other women like you, who have broken the shackles of centuries."

Many voices have been raised in praise. Even that of

Krishna Menon. The last to speak, he said "We are extremely grateful to you, Madame President . . . and we are very proud of you." Even now, no man present could justly say "At last, she is 'acting like a woman.' " Quietly, the Woman of the Century thanked the men over whom she had presided, then asked for a closing moment of silence. Then her gavel sounded the session's end. She could go home again, and for a while be a mother and a grandmother.

"The telephone rang constantly after newspapers announced she was coming to stay with us in Bombay for a few days," Tara says. "A pile of letters awaiting her on the hall table grew to a mountain. I didn't know where to put all the flowers sent by friends, known and unknown." All this was less important to her mother than a homemaker's discovery. "In a few minutes she had inspected every corner of our apartment, including the kitchen shelves. Suddenly, she said, 'I see you have no *achar* in the house.' " *Achar* is a pickled conglomerate, fire to the palate of Americans, a tradition in India. Making *achar* with her own hands is a test of a housewife's domestic artistry. This, Tara says, explained its absence from her home.

"Mummie took charge. We sat crosslegged on the floor to slice cauliflower, turnips, potatoes and beans. We spent a blissful mother-and-daughter half-hour, preparing the vegetables, then pouring them into an earthen jar and sprinkling them with mustard. We then put the jar in the sun. In two days' time, the *achar* was ready, and we were enjoying it with our lunch."

The morning after her mother's arrival, Tara rose at seven. "I wandered into her bedroom. It was empty. I found her in the kitchen, adding finishing touches to several vases. A twisted twig I had intended to discard and a spray of golden-brown chrysanthemums displayed her handiwork, in a crystal vase. In another, a few stalks of tuberoses towered like sentinels over a cluster of pink roses. I admired her talent. 'The flowers aren't important,' she said. 'All that is required is a little imagination.' "

Tara guessed what her mother denied. She was weary to the edge of exhaustion. But like her brother, she refused to rest while there was work to do. When Tara's cook fell ill at the last moment, with sixteen guests invited for New Year's Eve, her mother took charge in the kitchen. "I knew she wasn't well, but no one else could have guessed it, seeing her sitting cool and decorative in white silk, presiding over the banquet she had cooked, as charmingly as she presided over the United Nations."

On New Year's Day in 1943, she wrote in her diary, "The world has shrunk into two groups: Those who suffer for an ideal, and those who inflict the suffering." On New Year's Day, 1954, she looked back over eleven years of continuing effort towards making the two groups one, and ahead at frowning threat to what she hoped for most.

The General Assembly stood suspended, subject to being reconvened at her request or that of one or more members, concurred in by a majority of all member nations, should Korean developments warrant this. Things went badly in the Korean prisoner-of-war exchange, umpired by India. On January 10, 1954, India asked to have the Assembly reconvened immediately. There was no majority concurrence.

Back in her place in the House of the People, Vijaya

Lakshmi Pandit heard the report that her brother's appeal in February, to the opposing power blocs, for a cease-fire in Indochina, had been rejected as "impracticable." Nineteen nations, including Soviet Russia, Communist China, the United States and the United Kingdom, agreed that a Geneva conference on Indochina was preferable to debate in the General Assembly.

Massive American military aid poured into Pakistan. India's protest was answered by President Eisenhower's assurance that arms given to Pakistan would be used only for defense against the spread of Communism, never against India. But that India and Communist China exchanged guarantees of "respect for each other's territorial integrity and sovereignty, nonaggression, noninterference with each other's internal affairs, equality, mutual benefit and peaceful coexistence" was received in Washington as defiance of the Dulles dogma—*He who is not with us is against us.*

For the time being, not bound to impartiality by her duties as Madame President, she viewed developments as a woman of India. Mr. Dulles declared a policy of "massive retaliation," and gave his blessing to a new word: *brinkmanship.* Pakistan joined Greece, Turkey, Iraq and Iran in a Middle East Defense Organization, and subsequently joined the United States, the United Kingdom, France, Australia, New Zealand, Thailand and the Philippine Republic, in SEATO, the Southeast Asia Treaty Organization. Her brother continued refusal to depart from India's policy of nonalignment.

In the House of the People, he silenced clamor for seizure by force of Goa-in-India, but for Macao, the last small remnant of Portugal's once vast Empire in Asia. In 1950,

Vallabhbhai Patel had snorted, "We can take Goa in two hours." Jawaharlal Nehru held to determination against any act of aggression by India. "The fact that a war is a little war does not make it any less of a war."

At about this time, he wrote and then locked away, his *Will and Testament*. No one would read it for ten years. It began "I have received so much love and affection from the Indian people that nothing I can do can repay even a small fraction of it, and indeed there can be no repayment of so precious a thing as affection. I can only express the hope that in the remaining years I may live, I shall not be unworthy of my people and their affection." He would soon be sixty-five. More than long life for himself, he wanted a better life for India.

Americans remembered that Hitler chose guns for Germany in preference to butter. Jawaharlal Nehru said guns could wait until his people had enough to eat. Each month of peace meant a little more food; each threat to peace, anywhere in Asia, endangered India's slow and arduous progress. A briskly confident negotiator from Washington explained at length why no nation could be an island entire of itself, and therefore why India must stand up and be counted, as a Free World ally. He was courteously attentive, until his lecturer completed a peroration that merited inclusion in the *Congressional Record*. Then finally he said, "It surprises me sometimes, to find that Americans are surprised I am an Indian."

This was taken badly. In Pakistan en route to India, John Foster Dulles made statements interpreted as American endorsement of Portugal's refusal to follow the example of Britain and France in withdrawing from the subcontinent; then was visibly affronted by coolness of his reception in New

Delhi. He saw no reason to deny he had prevented the two-thirds vote that would have made India a participant in the Geneva conference. Thus he insured return of Krishna Menon to world headlines.

At the moment when the United States spoke of "intervention" and "direct action," Vijaya Lakshmi Pandit's former deputy appeared at Geneva saying "I am only a tourist, a bystander." In fact, his instructions from her brother went no farther than permission to pause at Geneva en route to New York, long enough to post himself on conference attitudes. However he plunged immediately into conferences of his own, with Chou En-lai of Communist China, Molotov from the Soviet, and Pham van Dong, representing Ho Chi Minh in North Vietnam. *Guilt by association* became a byword in the United States, left over from Senator Joseph McCarthy's adventures in search for State Department subversives. It was given substance by Menon's actions at Geneva.

He had no official standing, but nonetheless proposed a formula for truce in Indochina. It had Chou En-lai's announced approval. "Hardly anyone knew then," says Krishna Menon's apologist, "that Chou En-lai would soon betray the principles of Nehru's *Panchshila,* and stab India and Asia in the back." Whatever Americans knew or suspected regarding Chou En-lai, they knew Krishna Menon of old.

Vijaya Lakshmi Pandit, as head of India's delegations, as Ambassador, as Madame President of the United Nations, had won friends for her country. Now many of these, especially in the United States, were again convinced that Krishna Menon, not she, spoke for her country.

23.

The French Empire in Southeast Asia died at Dienbienphu on May 7, 1954. On July 21, agreement was signed at Geneva that, according to Krishna Menon's biographer, "brought to a close the eight-year war in Indochina." Elections for the whole of Vietnam were to be held before June 20, 1956. Execution of armistice between South Vietnamese and Ho Chi Minh's guerrillas, soon to be called Viet Cong, was to be supervised by a commission representing Canada, Poland and India. "The key role of 'tourist' Menon," says his biographer, "was acknowledged by spokesmen of many governments." His role was not applauded in Washington or London.

In April, Anthony Eden for Britain and Dulles for the United States had agreed a Southeast Asia defense treaty would be drawn up after the Geneva conference. Then it was decided not to wait. On June 28 at Washington, it was announced that Winston Churchill, Eden, President Eisenhower and Dulles had adopted plans for collective defense to meet whatever situation might arise from agreement or failure to reach agreement at Geneva.

Repercussions from the conflicting Geneva and Washington pacts greeted Vijaya Lakshmi Pandit while at the invitation of heads of state, she traveled from India to Ceylon, Burma, Thailand, Indonesia, Malaya, Japan, Yugoslavia, Switzerland and the United Kingdom. The first United Nations president to go to talk with people in as many countries, she was introduced in a dozen languages as "First Citizen of the World."

She had long since learned how wide the abyss can be between conferred title and real power.

Women just entering public affairs in their homelands found her "as feminine as they were, a mother as they were, and, for all her fame, sincerely unassuming." Some at least must have guessed what could be seen from her eminence. Women were still a long way from equality with men in deciding for or against action from which they and their children must suffer equally with men.

On September 8, at Manila, the United States, the United Kingdom, France, Australia, New Zealand, Thailand, the Philippines and Pakistan signed the Southeast Asia Defense Treaty, binding all to act against aggression in a vast area from which only Hong Kong and Formosa were excluded. "The importance of this for the United Kingdom was that it committed the United States in those parts of the globe where hitherto the United Kingdom had had to maintain peace alone."

John Foster Dulles appended to the treaty an "understanding" by the United States that "its recognition of the effect of aggression and armed attack . . . apply only to Communist aggression." A protocol stated that the parties to the Manila accord unanimously applied its provisions to Cambodia, Laos and "the free territory under the jurisdiction of the state of Vietnam."

India, Burma and Indonesia declined to join in the accord. For India, Jawaharlal Nehru warned "It increases the sense of insecurity in people's minds." It was denounced by the Soviet as "directed against the freedom and national independence of Asian peoples," on the day on which Vijaya Lakshmi Pandit resumed her post as Madame President in the Big Glass House in New York.

"Her arrival at United Nations headquarters was a personal triumph. Delegates welcomed her warmly however they felt about her country's attitude in international affairs. There was a touch of sadness in the greetings, for all knew these must be followed by farewell."

On September 21, 1954, as her last act in world authority, she opened the ninth session of the General Assembly. She spoke briefly, not "acting like a woman," and after due formalities, handed the gavel to her successor as president, Dr. Eelco van Kleffens of The Netherlands. Her service in and to the United Nations was over. Now at last she was going home, she thought, to settle and stay. On the way, she could baby sit in Tokyo, grandmothering her new grandson.

24.

In San Francisco, then in Honolulu, bound west across the Pacific, she was Madame President, Her Excellency, the world's most honored and headlined woman. On Wake Island, briefly, she was her private self, walking barefooted in the surf, talking as she pleased. At Tokyo, after presenting her public image to officialdom and the press, she established diplomatic relations with Rita's baby, Gopal Dar. But now she knew she was not, after all, going home to settle and stay. On October 2, 1954, she had been chosen for the highest foreign appointment her country could confer. She would go to the Court of St. James's as High Commissioner for India, a post first held by Krishna Menon.

She did not propose to go alone. In New Delhi she announced to Lekha and Tara, "Don't imagine for a minute that I am going six thousand miles from home to sit in solitary splendor in an enormous house with chandeliers in every room, unless members of my family visit me while I am there." They sat thinking of all that must be done if they were to leave their customary routine. "I have the oddest children," she said. "Anyone else's would have jumped at the opportunities I have offered them from time to time. Mine need engraved invitations. It was bad enough being president of the United Nations with all the advantages of that position, a box at the Opera and other wonderful things, and no one to share them with; but New York was much farther away. London is just a night's journey."

It had become that, and no more. Ten years before, going to the United States in an American transport plane was a leap into trackless space. Since then she had traveled more than any other woman in her times. "Hurry," Tara says, "is a word that for me splinters serenity into sharp fragments. It is the keynote of my mother's existence. She lives, as a matter of course, a strenuous life whose demands would exhaust a less energetic human being. We have none of us inherited any of these capacities, a fact she categorically refuses to accept. 'Of course you can do anything you make up your mind to do,' she is always pointing out. And it has been true for her."

At fifty-four, reviewing her youth, she said "I was never properly educated." She learned to read and write, add and subtract and play the piano. "This had been considered adequate preparation for a future that envisaged no exertion greater than presiding over a tea tray in the drawing room of a (preferably) rich husband. It would have got me nowhere," she told her daughters, "if I hadn't made some solid use of my brain myself. But struggling to use it at my present age is hardly the same as having to use it as a matter of course at fourteen."

Observers in England thought she had no problem. The *Sunday Times* saluted her. "Mrs. Pandit has had more experience as a diplomat than any other woman in history including Mother Eve." A woman writer said there were three stars in the diplomatic firmament: Moscow, Washington and London. "Mrs. Pandit has pinned them to her personality as she would diamond stars in her silver-grey hair."

The High Commissioner's house at Number Nine, Kensington Palace Gardens, purchased and furnished, but occupied only *en passant* by Krishna Menon, was "full of mirrors, satin-quilted Marie Antoinette furniture, with a salon whose walls were imported from a French chateau, and an Adam fireplace in the dining room." She opened it, aired it, rearranged it and made it a friendly and never too formal home.

"Each Ambassador's ghost lingers a while after him and some ghosts are more persistent than others. In London, after Mr. Krishna Menon, there had been Mr. Kher, but Mr. Menon's was the more persistent ghost, still roaming the corridors." Very much alive, he claimed credit for Chou En-lai's visit to India, and Jawaharlal Nehru's return visit to Communist China. It is worthy of note that Vijaya Lakshmi Pandit heard, when her brother returned from Peking, a comment indicating prescience that does not appear to have been shared in Washington or in Moscow.

"They are supposed to be Marxists in China," he said, "but the way they are interpreting Marxism is very different from the way the Russians did. I don't say there is a conflict. That is for them to say." It was said openly at last, and Free World leaders hailed themselves as first discoverers of a new star of hope, ten years afterward.

In London in 1954, an ornate landau drawn by two caparisoned horses, with liveried driver and footman, arrived at India House. The Marshal of the Diplomatic Corps handed Her Excellency the High Commissioner for India into the carriage. She rode along streets where she and Ranjit Pandit walked in 1926, when they were young and gay together, and free to remain in the London they loved, and might have lived happy ever after, except that they loved India more.

Her *sari* was black, not in mourning but in lieu of formal garb prescribed for other Ambassadors. A crowd stared, traffic was halted, guards stood to attention, as the landau lumbered through the gates at Buckingham Palace, across the courtyard to the palace entrance. The Vice Marshal of the Diplomatic Corps and the Queen's Equerry-in-Waiting presented the Master of the Household.

Together, they conducted Her Excellency into the Bow Room, then into the 1844 Room and the Presence of the Queen. The Marshal and the Master of the Household took one step, bowed, took another step, bowed again. The Marshal proclaimed "The High Commissioner for India!" Then the men withdrew, and the two Great Ladies were alone.

Motilal Nehru's Little Daughter bowed to the daughter of the last King-Emperor of British India, and presented her letter of credence, written in Hindi, with an English translation, and signed by her brother. Credentials bearing the signature of Her Majesty's father, presented when she went to

Moscow as Ambassador before India was free, were elaborately
phrased. At the Court of St. James's, she presented the first
that read simply "We request that you will give credence to all
she will communicate in our name."

Queen Elizabeth II was twenty-eight. Her life had been
managed by others; she had experienced no harsh treatment;
her crown came to her by inheritance. Behind Vijaya Lakshmi
Pandit's poised elegance were more years, than the young
Queen had lived, of sacrifice and loss, prison, loneliness and
heartbreak. But there was no barrier of bitterness between
them. They talked as women, and before they parted were
friends.

Vijaya Lakshmi Pandit had begun another conquest, in
which her weapons included such oddments as her written
notice to the staff at Number Nine, Kensington Palace
Gardens, heavily underlined, thumbtacked to the serving-
pantry door: *Peanut butter sandwiches must on no account be
served for tea when guests are present.*

She added her own collection of jade to a golden dancing
Nataraj, Persian miniature paintings, an heirloom silver tea set
on a tray fit for a museum, other treasures that filled the house
Krishna Menon bought. She also added Buddhi, the cook.
They had known each other since she was a bride in Allahabad and he came from an Army Mess. He called her Bibiji,
and argued with her each morning about the menus for the
day.

"We are now on the edge of the continent of Europe, the
cradle of Western civilization and culture," she told Buddhi.
"You and every member of this mission are going to cooperate
with me and make it a success." Buddhi muttered in Hindi,

and demonstrated his independence when Sir Anthony Eden, then Prime Minister, came to dinner. "Intoxicated with ale and righteous indignation, Buddhi swept the chicken off the kitchen table, brandished the soup ladle, and declared he was not preparing dinner for any Prime Minister whose country had sent Bibiji to prison."

Leaving Sir Anthony, Countess Mountbatten and other guests of high degree, sipping sherry in the drawing room, Her Excellency Madame Ambassador quieted Buddhi in the kitchen, assembled the dinner while Buddhi sobered, and received Sir Anthony's compliments on the excellence of her chef. Next morning, she served warning on Buddhi and all others concerned. "This is not Moscow, where we had no formal entertaining to do. And it is not Washington, where cocktail parties solve a lot of problems. There are going to be no cocktail parties here. All my parties, and there will be plenty, are going to be sit-down dinners. People want to talk, sometimes to discuss matters of importance, while they eat. The food has to be perfect and the evening must pass without incident. We have special ties with this country, and we cannot afford to have them endangered."

Buddhi was unimpressed. As he saw it, Bibiji took her position much too seriously. She would be really important, by his standard, only if some day she became Chief Minister of the United Provinces, at home in India. She said, "I shall be nothing of the kind." He said, "You might even be President of India if you're lucky." She said, "Get all those grand ideas out of your head. I am going to live in a small house with a large orchard which you are going to manage." Buddhi said, "We shall see."

25.

Social success came easily. But concurrently, she kept long office hours at India House on Aldwych Street. All departments of the Government of India had representatives in London; all operations were channeled through the High Commissioner. In an inherited chair much too big for her, behind a desk the size of a billiard table, she checked contents of tin dispatch-boxes tagged green for *Urgent* and orange for *Immediate*. Files bound in red piled up before her.

On March 1, 1955, she became India's first Ambassador to Eire. Hurrying from London to Dublin, speaking in Hindi, she said Ireland's struggle for freedom had influenced her generation in India. "Even though we walked different roads, the courage and sacrifice of Irish leaders was an inspiration to us. A new bond we now share is the democratic way in our national lives, and our desire to create peace in the world." She timed her visit to coincide with the running of the Irish Derby; she had never lost her love for horses. She told the Irish she earned her first and only gold medal, in an All-India essay contest, by writing about Ireland; and added Irish books to her library. It was said, and was true, that no matter what her schedule might be, she read at least one book a day.

Invitations to speak took her to many places in England, Scotland and Ireland. Again, she realized that when Commonwealth Commissioners consulted with the Prime Minister at Ten Downing Street, "It seemed odd to have a woman present, though perfectly natural to her." Again, she surmounted the obstacle. "She was accepted as official representative of the largest country in the Commonwealth family."

There were a hundred thousand Indian nationals in England, and it seemed all of them came to India House on January 26, Republic Day, and on Gandhi's birthday, October 2. Celebrations began as Gandhi had begun them, with a prayer meeting. "She loved having children there and was delighted when they clustered around her, reminding her of her own grandchildren."

Queen Victoria had made it a custom of the Royal Family to invite certain high-ranking individuals "to dine and sleep" at Windsor Castle, usually during the Easter season. The invitation came to her from Queen Elizabeth II. Again, they talked alone together. On November 24, 1955, the Queen Mother, as Chancellor of London University, presented her with the honorary degree of doctor of laws, *honoris causa*.

Sir Ifor Evans, as Public Orator, said she had in her early youth responded to the call "for self-sacrifice, endurance and discipline in her country's struggle for independence," and added, "This world figure, this Great Lady of the Commonwealth, has never lost her feminine qualities. Through her family there shines a wealth of devotion. Her love of her daughters is matched and strengthened by the admiring affection they feel for her. The indulgences her grandchildren receive or entice from her is testimony to their cunningly correct appreciation of her warm heart. Her deep humanity, her understanding, her concern for others, are founded upon a simple dignity and courtesy, a composure of thought and bearing, and a delight in the graceful things of life."

Women crowded the members' dining room in the House of Commons, for a reception "in honor of Her Excellency,

Madame Vijaya Lakshmi Pandit." She told them her brother had gained passage in India of the Hindu Marriage Act and the Hindu Succession Act. For the first time in India's history, women, including widows, were granted equality with men in matters of inheritance and possession of personal property. It was another victory in achievements that began with Gandhi. "Thanks to him, India's women did not have to fight for equal status; they have earned it, by work, not by sex struggle."

None present knew that eleven years before, she was widowed and penniless, deprived, by Hindu law perpetuated by British India's government, of rights now at last conferred by Free India. Some asked why it had taken so long for her brother's government to do justice to women. Neither diplomacy nor her unfailing courtesy permitted her to point out that the reception was sponsored by the Fawcett Society, named for Dame Millicent Fawcett, who in 1868 launched England's women's suffrage movement, that won equality for Englishwomen only after sixty years of failure. It had taken eight years in the Republic of India.

The Austrian Government invited her to address a seminar for diplomats at Salzburg, on "Women in Diplomacy." An English school inaugurated a plan to name its various houses for world leaders, and asked her to preside at the opening of the first, the Lakshmi Pandit House. Over it flew the flag her daughters raised as children, when Englishmen arrested their mother and father for rebellion against the Raj. "Now we are friends, involved in the same effort for peace and goodwill."

Named from New Delhi to serve also as India's Ambassador to Spain, she went to Madrid, and rode in a royal coach built for Queen Isabella II, to present her credentials to Generalissimo Franco. Invited to deliver a series of lectures at McMaster University in Canada, she received another honorary degree. Her lectures were published as *The Evolution of India*. The University of Göttingen in Germany chose her as first recipient of the Dorothy Schlozer Medal "for distinguished women," because of "her outstanding public services not only in the public life of her country, but also for her unique achievements in the international world."

Göttingen's rector praised her as "one of the strongest symbols of the fundamental change in the position of women in modern society." She said, "In most parts of the world, men and women now walk together as equals, sharing privileges and opportunities as well as the obligations which equality imposes"; but concluded, "Now they need to take a new course of study and graduate in the art of living together."

26.

There was favorable reaction in her mission area, when her brother, after visiting Moscow, flew directly to Rome to discuss Goa-in-India with Pope Pius XII. A Vatican statement declared there was no religious issue in the Goan case, and praised India's scrupulous fairness to her Christian minority. But American distrust was renewed, when Soviet Russia's Khrushchev and Bulganin visited India, and the press reported "The welcome they received was massive and tumultuous."

To Vijaya Lakshmi Pandit, the report was a classic proof of her brother's belief that truth is round, not flat. What was left out was the fact that only a minuscule fragment of India's populace was affected by or even knew about Communist ideologies. "To the great mass of the Indian people a guest from Russia was a novelty, as exciting as an interplanetary visitor from Mars." This did not mean that the visitors gained converts, though perhaps they thought they had.

"They were exuberantly friendly, donning Gandhi caps, threatening to climb coconut trees, quipping gaily with all manner of people, backslapping farmers, workers, students and officials in a truly *tovarisch* trauma. To the masses, this was more fun than a circus. To more sophisticated Indians, the exhibitionism of the Soviet guests was crude, contemptuous and annoying."

Privately, her brother said, "The thing you've got to remember is that the Russians, throughout their history, have never known democracy as the West understands it. When the Bolsheviks came to power, the Russians jumped from one autocracy to another, from Czarism to Communism. Therefore, to talk to them of democracy and personal liberty is like trying to explain the color white to a blind man. Once you understand this you begin to understand the Russian mind. That doesn't mean you agree with it." Still, American editors called her brother pro-Communist.

Five years later, when President Eisenhower visited India, she had cause to wonder why the American press made no point of the visible truth: that the representative of a democracy was given a much warmer and numerically more impressive welcome. It is doubtful if Mr. Eisenhower himself ever heard one reason why this was so.

In a hamlet a hundred miles from Delhi, a camera crew recorded dialogue between two village elders who had just heard

All-India Radio announce Mr. Eisenhower's impending arrival. One told the other in Hindi, "Abraham Lincoln's son is coming to India." The other echoed, "Lincoln's son?" The first speaker was annoyed. "Of course. President, President's son. Like Kings." The doubter was convinced. Rising, picking up his staff, he said, "We must go and receive *darshan* by seeing Abraham Lincoln's son." They walked for five days, to reach Delhi, where they were lost in the throngs that hailed the eighteenth American President since the Great Emancipator.

When I told this story at a dinner party in California, my hostess and the other guests thought I thought it was amusing. My host asked, "What can you do about people as ignorant as that?" and continued his indictment of That Man Krishna Menon. Nor would I argue a case for the *Tremendous Representative* whose presence, Vijaya Lakshmi Pandit's daughters thought, haunted the mansion he bought in London's Kensington Palace Gardens.

At the United Nations, then at the Bandung Conference, his biographer says admiringly, "In the process of building up Afro-Asia, Krishna Menon built up himself." No longer hampered by "a leader who had her own ideas of what India's representatives should and should not do," he climbed so rapidly toward apogee that on February 3, 1956, he was made Minister-Without-Portfolio in her brother's Cabinet.

"But it was not yet time to put his teeth into New Delhi's politics. By and large Menon confined himself to foreign policy." The result of this brought him to London, and again put him in the foreground, displacing her in the English press and in public regard, as spokesman for their country.

Gamal Abdel Nasser of Egypt had nationalized that profitable monument to Benjamin Disraeli, Queen Victoria's empire-builder, the Suez Canal. The Soviet backed his action. So did Krishna Menon, injecting himself into Franco-British conclaves in London, then producing another Formula Menon that pleased none of the Free World powers. Whatever he achieved by this, for good or ill, his next appearance in world headlines placed a black mark against India that time has not entirely erased.

He was en route from India to resume his duties at the United Nations in New York, when on November 4 in Hungary, Soviet tanks and infantry rolled over freedom fighters, killing thousands. In the General Assembly on November 9, in India's name he voted "No" on a five-power motion proposing free elections in Hungary, and "No" again on a resolution condemning the Soviet for use of brute force in crushing the Hungarian revolt.

Furore burst out against India. "The West condemned India in general and Krishna Menon in particular for practicing double standards. India's attitude on Hungary proved to Western statesmen what they had always suspected: that India was 'neutral' in favor of Soviet Russia and Communism." Menon's answer took full responsibility on himself. "Having counseled the Arabs not to condemn Britain and France for invading Egypt, he could not possibly support any move to condemn the Soviet over Hungary."

In India, political leaders and newspapers demanded his recall or dismissal and "removal from the political scene," on the ground that he voted "No" contrary to instructions from

Jawaharlal Nehru. At the United Nations, resentment of his votes on Hungary stiffened resistance to India's case against Pakistan in the Kashmir controversy. But to many in India, his defiance of the West made him a hero. Elected for the first time, he took his place in the House of the People, and volunteered for and was given the Cabinet post of Minister of Defense.

It is perhaps the greatest tribute paid to her, that whatever was said against Krishna Menon, India or her brother, press and public set Vijaya Lakshmi Pandit apart. She sought no such separation. Nor did she utter a woman's "I told you so" when on March 21, 1959, Krishna Menon's valued friend, Chou En-lai of Communist China, cast off his peace-lover's mask.

All-India Radio reported fierce fighting at Lhasa, between Tibetans and Communist Chinese. The young Dalai Lama, the fourteenth Living Buddha, was summoned to Peking. He refused to go, and was ordered to surrender without his bodyguard. Monks defending him were machine-gunned. With his mother, sister, brother and a small entourage, he escaped across the mountains, and after fourteen days reached Towang, a village on India's side of the frontier, where he asked for and was given political asylum.

Now India was placed in a position as ambiguous as that of India's Ambassador to the Court of St. James's. She went on doing as much as she could, as well as she could, until in January, 1961, another duty assigned to no woman before her took her home at last. Again, she was briefly reunited with her grandchildren. There were eight of them now.

27.

Again her task was one for which there were no guiding
precedents. This was to plan in advance for royalty's first visit
to India since, when she was Little Daughter, aged eleven,
King George V and Queen Mary traveled nearly a month by
boat to see their empire in the East.

At the Prime Minister's House in New Delhi, she joined
Indira Gandhi. Widowed five months before, Indira, like her
aunt, had mourned, then put mourning aside to return to work
that must be done. She was First Lady now in her father's
house, his confidante and pupil, being schooled in the subtleties and sorrows of politics and policy. She welcomed her
aunt. They stood side by side when on January 21, 1961, the
British plane *Britannia,* flying the newly adopted personal flag
of Queen Elizabeth II, ended a twenty-hour flight to what was
no longer British India.

Cannon thundered a twenty-one gun salute. The Queen
and the Duke of Edinburgh came down the steps to be greeted
beneath a bright-colored *shamiana* by India's President, Dr.
Rajendra Prasad, and Vice-president, Dr. Sarvepalli Radhakrishnan, and by the three Nehrus. A great but quiet crowd
lined the route along which Her Majesty was taken to
Rashtrapati Bhavan, the President's House, once the Viceroy's
Palace. Vijaya Lakshmi Pandit escorted her royal friend to
Rajghat, where the Queen laid a wreath on the Gandhi
Memorial and planted a living tree, "to honor the man who
defied the government she represented but did so without
bitterness, hatred or warfare."

In the Durbar Hall, where in days of British India the Viceroy sat on an ornate throne above the crowd, the Queen talked with reporters, standing below the throne. It was occupied now by a statue of Gautama Buddha, with the inscription *Wisdom resteth in the heart of him that hath understanding*.

The two Great Ladies of the British Commonwealth were together, when on Republic Day, January 26, Free India's Armed Forces paraded. Famed regiments commanded for generations by British officers were officered now by Indians, Hindus, Muslims, Sikhs. Softly, massed bands played *Abide With Me*. The Queen was told "It was Mahatma Gandhi's favorite hymn." She said, "It was my grandfather's favorite, too."

Together, they toured India. "It was a pleasure for those with her to share Queen Elizabeth's delight in the tapestry of India's past, present and hope for the future that unrolled before her." It was renewal for Vijaya Lakshmi Pandit. Returning to England, she made arrangements for her brother's arrival to attend the annual Commonwealth Conference. The Queen and her consort came to dine in Kensington Palace Gardens. Buddhi the cook created no contretemps; he was at last converted to forgiveness of the British who put Bibiji in jail.

On July 8, she received an honorary degree from the University of Edinburgh. The *Scotsman* of Edinburgh said editorially, "There can be no doubt about it. Mrs. Pandit will go down in history as one of the greatest statesmen of our time. She has taken politics out of the marketplace into the hearts and consciences of men and women, and she has done it without abating a jot of her patience, serenity, humor, and tolerance for the modern world. With the years her great personal beauty has seemed to deepen, as though her experiences of the worst and best of human behavior have served only to strengthen the inner flame."

On August 14, 1961, she went to the Court of St. James for the last time, to pay her parting respects. Her service as High Commissioner had come to its end. For the first time in fifteen years, she need not hurry to some other place; no new assignment was given to her. She had done her best for India for half a century, since she was Little Daughter asking her father and her brother "Why?" and "Why not?"

Those who received cards she sent on New Year's Day, 1961, treasure them. They bear an ancient Indian saying: *The light of a small lamp may dispel great darkness; so does understanding dispel suspicion.* Four days before her sixty-first birthday, the lamp that had given light not only in India for so long was put away on a shelf in a shadowed corner.

Two months later, in her brother's house in New Delhi, she said, "My public life is over. There is no work left for which I am needed." An intruder from America had no right to say what many of her people said: that it was a time of all times when light to dispel suspicion was needed. Only she can say, and I doubt if she ever will, what she thought and felt while once again she could only watch, listen and wait, as she did when her father and her brother debated what was best for India and hardly realized Little Daughter's presence.

Seven years before, Tara wrote, "She is often asked what she will do when she retires from political life. She speaks wistfully of having a home of her own at the foot of the Himalayas where she can live in solitude, grow fruit, write books and be visited by her grandchildren. It is only natural that she should dream of peace and permanence, but I cannot believe that a person with her vitality and her capacity to serve can ever retire to any corner of the world, however inviting it may be."

Nor could I believe it, on the morning when she told her brother "Today is his birthday, and he is away from his family," and thus gave me opportunity to ask for what might have been refused, if request had been submitted according to prescribed protocol. We had heard in California that he planned to come to the United States. We hoped he would visit California, as his sister had, and speak to the Los Angeles World Affairs Council. Formal invitation would follow, if he indicated interest.

He said his sister had told him much about California. So had many Californians, including Harvey Slocum, the hard-fisted dam-builder from a place called Anaheim who bossed the job at the gigantic Bhakra-Nangal project in the East Punjab, and died with his hobnailed boots on, and is greatly revered in India. Before he stopped being *Chacha,* Uncle, to the children who came to talk with him that morning, and said, "Now I become a statesman," he promised he would come to the part of America in which his sister stirred up so much commotion as a purposeful uninvited guest, when the United Nations was being organized.

28.

He came in November 1961, just before his own seventy-second birthday. Indira Gandhi accompanied him. Vijaya

Lakshmi Pandit remained in India, where another election impended. She had no part in it. All attention centered on Krishna Menon, a candidate for reelection. The Swatantra Party proclaimed a crusade to put him out of office. His supporters alleged that in fact this was a campaign for revenge, inspired and secretly supported by Western nations, and especially by the United States.

It would be impossible to put off much longer a final confrontation regarding Portuguese Goa-in-India. Goans in exile, attempting to enter the enclave in unarmed *Satyagraha* march, were fired on by conscripts from Portugal-in-Africa; thirty died. Pakistan's bellicose pressures increased along the Kashmir cease-fire line. Communist China, still blandly professing brotherhood, completed a military highway across frontier areas claimed by India, and massed troops in view of India's Himalayan outposts. It was a bad time to be out of India; yet it seemed vital to Jawaharlal Nehru, to mend misunderstanding between India and the United States.

He said he had three objectives: to demonstrate India's friendship and gratitude for American support in her fight for independence; to learn more about American thinking; and to explain with a good neighbor's frankness why "What is good for the United States or Russia is not necessarily good for India." En route to Washington, he studied *The Affluent Society,* by John Kenneth Galbraith, then American Ambassador at New Delhi. He said, "Even when I was a university student, I could see the United States forging ahead of all other countries technically and scientifically."

Two dozen speeches, nine banquets, nine receptions and press conferences, two hours on three television networks under cross-examination by critical questioners, made him the first Prime Minister accorded a banner-headline in the theatrical newspaper, *Variety*. It read *Nehru: Take Me to Your Media!* His long private talks with President John F. Kennedy were headlined *Two Historians Meet*.

The President's daughter, Caroline, then four, stood beside her mother to welcome him. She had been told that once a little refugee girl gave him a rose, and ever since, each day, he wore a fresh rose pinned over his heart. She presented him with a rose, and curtsied. Her father said "You did that exceedingly well." Then her mother and Indira Gandhi made plans for Mrs. Kennedy's future visit to India, while President and Prime Minister talked about many things. On some, they thought alike; as to others, their philosophies differed. Both were idealists by preference, but political out of necessity; each was master and captive of a personal *mystique*. They got on well, but neither converted the other.

"Mr. Nehru agreed with the President that his chief United Nations delegate, V. K. Krishna Menon, exaggerated in equating small United States underground nuclear tests with large Soviet tests in the open air." They disagreed on escalation from American commitment to bolster the Ngo Dinh Diem regime in South Vietnam. They agreed that "Hunger and despair are the enemies of freedom; Asia and Africa will cling to democracy if these enemies can be defeated," and that "If democracy fails in India, the Communists will win another great victory." They told each other they hoped to meet again, and parted, to go on toward their appointments in Samarra.

In California, the tired and aging man India's children

called *Chacha*, Uncle, was welcomed by American children when he visited such a playground as no Indian child of this generation can hope to see in India. When his plane landed at Los Angeles on Sunday, November 12, a helicopter waited to take him and his daughter, where he had asked to go: to Disneyland. There he faced in surprise a hundred scrubbed and smiling youngsters who sang *Happy Birthday, Mr. Nehru!* two days prematurely. While he was with them, weariness left him, and years fell away.

That night, he spoke for the last time in the United States, to a thousand Californians at a dinner sponsored by the Los Angeles World Affairs Council. Afterward, my wife showed him pictures of Ojai, a green nest in the hills seventy miles from Los Angeles. She told him, "It's a lovely valley." He answered with the Nehru smile. "It has lovely people, too." She said we wished he could come there and rest for a while. He said, "Some day I'll rest. Some day."

There was no rest for him in India. He had no more than resumed his New Delhi regimen, when on December 19, 1961, Americans to whom *Goa* had been a three-letter place-name useful in completing crossword puzzles reacted indignantly to tall headlines: *India Troops Engulf Goa; U. S. Demands Withdrawal.* Vijaya Lakshmi Pandit, India's truth-teller in America in the past, was still without assignment. There was a case for India; but on evidence presented in the United States, it appeared that her brother's *Panchshila* doctrine was repudiated by an act of unprovoked aggression.

Washington dispatches reported that "Secretary of State Dean Rusk bluntly told India's Ambassador that the United

States 'deeply regrets' India's use of force in Goa." Portugal had excoriated the United States for voting with the United Nations majority in censuring Portuguese repression of human rights in Africa. Now Portugal's Ambassador, accusing India of "brutal premeditated attack," demanded United States support in the Security Council, "to help obtain a cease-fire and force withdrawal of Indian troops."

Unless India was compelled to give Goa back to Portugal, he declared, "the United Nations is sick and has suffered perhaps a mortal blow." Concurrently, and perhaps more impressively, Dr. Salazar, a dictator since 1936, hinted broadly that failing satisfactory American action, he would order NATO defense installations out of Portugal.

Vijaya Lakshmi Pandit had heard Communists in the House of the People charge Dean Rusk's predecessor, John Foster Dulles, with endorsing Portugal's continued possession of the last enclave of European colonialism in India, in return for secret agreement with Dr. Salazar, allowing the United States to build secret missile-launching sites and jet-bomber hide-aways. She had heard her brother dismiss these accusations as "sheer rabble-rousing nonsense."

It was as well-known in Pakistan and in Communist China as in India, that submarines prowled the Indian Ocean. They were not American. A foreign power based in Goa, which is walled by mountains on three sides, and has a sheltered deep-water harbor, could play havoc with India's industrial heart-land, with transport and communications, with oil fields just being developed near Bombay. But in fact, security against armed attack had little if anything to do with the decision, taken reluctantly and only after twelve years of fruitless negotiations, to do what Vallabhbhai Patel had said in 1950 could be finished in two hours. It took only a little longer.

29.

There were no casualties from what Portugal called "brutal attack." Portuguese troops, black conscripts from Angola in Africa, threw down their arms without firing a shot. Indian troops "engulfing" Goa were greeted with music and flower garlands. Less than one percent of the Goan population was Portuguese. The rest was Indian, half Catholic, half Hindu and Muslims. All were accustomed to praying together at the shrine of Francis Xavier, Apostle to the Indies, who reported in 1542 to Ignatius Loyola, founder of the Jesuit Order, that "Exploitation and enslavement of the native people here is a crime against the Almighty." Goans said conditions had changed very little since then.

Under Portugal in 1961, per capita taxation in Goa was twice that borne by citizens of India; per capita income was two-thirds less. Eight-tenths of all arable land was controlled by Portuguese landlords. Under Dr. Salazar's *Carta Organica* and *Acto Colonial,* Goans called themselves the Irish of India. "Like Ireland until she was free, we have nothing to export but our young people." Since India gained independence, a fifth of Goa's population had fled across the mountains to freedom. For those who remained, there was no freedom.

Birth, death and marriage announcements, even scores of sports events, had to be passed by Portuguese censors. Newspaper publishers had to deposit estimated cost of six months' publication, to be forfeited at pleasure of the censors. Even wedding invitations had to bear the censor's stamp. Permission had to be obtained three days in advance, for any gathering however small. No political party was permitted but Dr. Salazar's *Uniao Nacional.* Its only members in Goa were Portuguese officials, most of them military careerists drawing double pay, and forty rich civilians, the only persons in Goa who could vote.

There had been recurrent uprisings since Portugal's conquests in the East began with Albuquerque's capture of a beachhead at Goa. Several had been led by priests. The last, in 1912, led by the Goanese hero, Dada Rane, was crushed by conscripts brought from Portuguese Africa. In 1961 the *Free Goa* movement, financed by expatriates living in India, was at explosion point. Communist infiltrators promoted a Goan Liberation Front. Meanwhile narcotics, gold, whiskey and other contraband reached Goa from across the Arabian Sea, and flooded into India. Indian police called Goa the smuggling capital of Asia.

This, and the very present danger of managed revolt within striking distance of the Gateway to India, sums up a story Americans did not read or hear. Vijaya Lakshmi Pandit was in New Delhi, not in Washington. There, a high-ranking Indian Foreign Service Officer said, "We are too young, too poor and too inexperienced to carry on a proper public-relations program. We are only too well aware that our reasons for acting in Goa should have been made clear in the United States, and were not. Now we can only hope that some day the truth will be known."

Whatever was known by those who made policy for the

United States, and in the United Nations, Portuguese demands and threats were rejected, though only on the basis that "We cannot change *un fait accompli.*" The United States, the United Kingdom, West Germany, Canada, Japan, France and the International Bank for Reconstruction and Development joined in extending $2 billions in long-term, interest-bearing credits, for purchases abroad to progress India's Third Five-Year Plan. This hard-money showing of confidence did not, however, erase doubts from the minds of Americans. And however this troubled Jawaharlal Nehru or Vijaya Lakshmi Pandit, it did not disturb Krishna Menon.

Triumphantly elected to represent North Bombay in the House of the People, he was said by supporters to be "seen for the first time by some political experts as a possible successor to Nehru." He is not known to have objected to this trial balloon. "He had become convinced that the Western combination, under American leadership, was out to suppress India. The conviction in turn led to an anger which affected all his actions."

In fact, he was far from alone in finding cause for anger. At Karachi in March 1962, a public symposium on Pakistan foreign policy ended with a summing-up: "Pakistan aligned herself with the West, primarily with a view to improving her overall position against India. She assumed, naively it seems in retrospect, that if she supported the United States in disputes with the Communist bloc, the United States would reciprocate and back Pakistan against India. But such an assumption was completely unwarranted. The change in American foreign policy, consequent upon the death of John Foster Dulles, has reinforced Pakistan's disenchantment with the United States' unwillingness to support her against India."

Pakistan and Communist China, said speakers at Karachi, "have an unsettled dispute with India which creates a basic, albeit limited, harmony of interests between them." It was recalled that as early as 1955, Pakistan's then-Prime Minister Chaudhri Mohammed Ali announced that he would seek "to cement friendly relations with China." But American arms continued to flow into Pakistan.

30.

Vijaya Lakshmi Pandit read Pakistan newspapers, listened to All-Pakistan Radio. So did official Americans in India. But though they were polite when the matter was mentioned, they made it clear that they declined to alter their conviction that Pakistan was a loyal Free World watchdog.

On June 8, after forty-four months of martial law in Pakistan, Field Marshal Mohammed Ayub Khan was sworn in as "first President elected under the new Constitution of the Second Republic." Almost concurrently in Peking, a note was delivered at the Indian Embassy, declaring Communist China's support of Pakistan in the Kashmir dispute. The note warned India that "Anyone who persists in an attitude of Great Power chauvinism in international affairs will always knock his head against a stone wall."

Pakistan's Foreign Office protested officially that "India is constantly threatening Pakistan." The Pakistan Air Force announced that F-104 jet-fighters delivered by the United States "have no offensive capacity and are purely defensive weapons," and alleged that "India has an air force which is more than three times the total strength of all its neighbors except China." India was accused of "militarism, violence and colonialist expansion."

General K. S. Thimayya, India's chief-of-staff, a Nehru family friend, reported "Whereas in the case of Pakistan I have considered the possibility of a total war, I am afraid I cannot do so in regard to China. I cannot as a soldier envisage India taking on China in an open conflict on its own. It must be left to the politicians and diplomats to insure our security." Krishna Menon said security could and should be left to him. General Thimayya resigned, saying, "I have reached an impasse with Menon." He was persuaded to stay on, but the breach between them widened.

Vijaya Lakshmi Pandit saw one more burden placed upon her brother. He bore too many already. He rose at dawn, to work through letters, telegrams, reports, complaints. His time for meeting children in the gardens, for riding and swimming to keep himself fit, for visiting and personally feeding his favorite pets, two droll pandas, Bhimsa and Pashi, was cut and cut again. Occasionally, not often, he spent a few minutes spinning fine yarn, as he had done in prison. He limited himself now to twenty minutes for reading, before he fell asleep, never earlier than one in the morning. His sister and his daughter realized how he drove himself, as a runner does near the end of a long race.

His seventy-third birthday neared. He had talked with his sister about a young American medical Samaritan, Dr. Thomas Dooley, who built jungle hospitals in Laos, and continued his work even after he knew he was dying of cancer. Dr. Dooley took as his personal commitment lines from a poem by Robert Frost. Now she found her brother had written them in a notebook he kept beside his bed.

> The woods are lovely, dark and deep,
> But I have promises to keep,
> And miles to go before I sleep,
> And miles to go before I sleep.

On September 8, 1962, Communist Chinese troops and armor pouring out of captured Tibet invaded India's North-East Frontier Agency. Indian *javans,* armed with rifles long obsolete, died without being able to return the fire of modern weaponry. By October 20, invasion extended along the Himalayan Wall, as far as Ladakh, the Hidden Kingdom, in view of Pakistan border observation-posts.

On October 26, Dr. Sarvepalli Radhakrishnan, now India's President, proclaimed a state of national emergency. There was a mass rush of Indians, of all races, castes and creeds, volunteering to fight the neighbors who vowed eternal friendship only a few weeks before. Many signed enlistment papers with their blood. Dr. Radhakrishnan hailed "a great awakening such as India has never had in all her history." The brave new world of *Panchshila* lay in ruins. In the United States, a headline read *Never Again the Same.*

31.

His sister and his daughter were in the gallery when Jawaharlal Nehru rose to face the House of the People. Quietly, he announced he had removed Krishna Menon as

Minister of Defense, and assumed the post as his own responsibility. In the same toneless voice, he continued with the first report of decisive defeat of Indian Army units at Se Pas and Walong. A member from Assam leaped up, demanding, "What is the government going to do? Are we going to get men and materials from friendly countries to fight a total war, or is the government contemplating a cease-fire and negotiations with the Chinese?" The answer came slowly but firmly, and was echoed even by Indian Communist Party leaders: "India must not and will not surrender to the Chinese."

The United States and Great Britain offered military supplies, but seemed to set a bargaining price: India must move troops from stations facing Pakistan, to meet the Chinese attack. This India refused to do. The American press decried misguided stubbornness. American military hardware continued to flow into Pakistan.

"Americans have a wonderful special quality. Contrary to the habit of people in some other rich and powerful countries, they want to be liked, not feared." Vijaya Lakshmi Pandit could say this with sincere fondness, while she watched Americans trying to be liked in Pakistan, with well-founded premonition of what was soon to come as sad surprise for Pakistan's prodigal benefactors.

Official Washington policy had denigrated her brother's attempt to be neutral between Soviet Communists and American anti-Communism; but there seemed to be no concern about Pakistan's increasing involvement with Communist China, that went back to favored-nation trade-agreements initiated by Pakistan in 1950. Few countries had gained more from American aid than Pakistan, economically and militarily. American gifts and long-term loans totaled more than $2.5

billions, about $20 per capita for ninety million Pakistani. Aid
to India, with a population five times larger, was $3.9 billions.
In either case, assistance was enormous; but only Pakistan received arms, planes, tanks, munitions, that built a war-machine
far more formidable than the British ever had on the subcontinent. Delhi pointed out repeatedly that very little of this
defense potential was allotted to Pakistan's frontier facing
Communist China or Soviet-influenced Afghanistan. American observers took no stand against this strategy. The American press called India's fear of Pakistan attack "hysteria."

Seven hundred thousand Pakistani welcomed President
Eisenhower when he visited Karachi. Vice-President Johnson
"captured the peoples' hearts in Pakistan," American newspapers said, "by stopping to talk at length with a camel-cart
driver named Bashir Ahmed." President Ayub Khan, visiting
the United States, was feted at Mount Vernon and cheered
when he addressed a joint session of Congress. Mrs. Jacqueline
Kennedy received tumultuous welcome during a five day stay
in Pakistan. Against all this, scant space or notice was spared
for disquieting questions.

In the House of the People, it was learned that although he
now held no portfolio, Krishna Menon still had a foothold in
the Cabinet. The Congress Party majority threatened to walk
out en masse "unless Krishna Menon is completely removed."
On November 7, Menon finally stepped down, "because he
believed that war-time was no time for recriminations and that
recriminations would end if he sacrificed himself." The text of
his lengthy letter of resignation included no expression of
regret addressed to the man whose trust in him had raised him
so high.

Peking halted invasion thrusts, and pulled back to positions still on Indian soil. Shooting stopped; but there could be no more talk of peaceful coexistence. On March 2, 1963, Pakistan signed a pact with Communist China under which Peking endorsed Pakistan's claim to some eight hundred square miles of strategic territory in Kashmir, while Rawalpindi endorsed Communist Chinese ownership of much larger areas in Indian Kashmir. These encompassed what Peking wanted most: the barren section of southern Ladakh called Aksai Chin, the whitestone desert. Few Muslims live in the Aksai Chin. Pakistan had no use for it. But the Chinese had already completed a military highway across it, targeted on India. Now finally, Pakistan's Foreign Minister warned Washington that if India received massive military assistance "from the Western powers," without prior solution of the Kashmir dispute, "it will mark a turning point for Pakistan, abandoned by our friends and allies."

Washington announced that Pakistan's fear of India was "recognized," but that the United States would continue its India assistance. In that case, Rawalpindi said, "Pakistan's policies will be reshaped." As first step in this direction, Pakistan's government-owned international airline was extended to Peking, and Chinese trade officials began discussions at Rawalpindi. Somehow, from Vijaya Lakshmi Pandit's view, it seemed that Americans were still pro-Pakistan, contra-India.

In August, 1963, her brother's government faced its first motion for a vote of no confidence. The motion, alleging "weakness in dealing with Chinese aggression, failure to maintain economic stability, and widespread corruption," was overwhelmingly rejected. But that it had even been proposed was seen by a section of India's press as "symptomatic of the

diminishing popularity of the ruling Congress Party, and of
the man who has led us since the achievement of independence."

He was criticized in personal terms, for the first time, during debate on the Language Bill; accused of "interfering with
the judiciary," when he requested abolition of the office of
Attorney General, its functions to be merged with those of the
Law Ministry; castigated for accepting a *Voice of America*
transmitter in India and granting broadcast rights to its programs aimed at Southeast Asia. From one side, he was attacked for considering Ceylon's offer to arbitrate the Chinese-
Indian border controversy; from the other, for accepting military assistance from the United States and the United Kingdom. The din of complaint and accusation was louder day by
day.

His sister and daughter remembered him saying after a
quarrelsome Congress conference, when independence was
still not won, "I wish we would not break each other's hearts
so easily and so constantly." Now Congress latecomers forgot
they would be nobodies but for him, and there was a sound of
small dogs yelping where he passed. He suffered a slight
stroke, but would let no one speak of it, and rose determinedly.
"He said, 'I am irritated with myself for being ill.' He seemed
to feel his body had no right to interfere with the work his
mind saw before him to do."

A brownish bristle which devout Muslims believed was
from the beard of the Prophet Mohammed was reported stolen
from a mosque in Kashmir. The report spread anti-Hindu rioting from Kashmir to East Pakistan. Hindus struck back. In a
week, three hundred killed each other. Tribesmen in Bihar,

recent converts to Christianity, were convinced by agitators that Pakistan was persecuting Christians. Armed with bows and arrows, they wiped out two Muslim villages before Indian troops, predominantly Hindu, herded them back to their jungled hills. For once, Field Marshal-President Mohammed Ayub Khan of Pakistan agreed with Jawaharlal Nehru. Hindu-Muslim conflict, both said, "is fatal for all of us." A meeting was scheduled. It was never to be held.

There was work again for Vijaya Lakshmi Pandit. Now she was her brother's eyes and ears at Bombay, where Congress Party strength was concentrated. Officially, she went there as the appointed Governor of Maharashtra State. Normally, this is a ceremonial post, calling for laying cornerstones, certifying *pro forma* the enactments of elected office-holders, and receiving distinguished foreign visitors. Hardly anyone thought she would be a mere decorative figurehead; nor was she.

For the first time in history, there was to be an Asian Eucharistic Congress, bringing Catholics to Bombay from everywhere. Pope Paul VI would be the first Roman pontiff to visit India, where in Indian belief St. Thomas the Apostle preached and was martyred seventy-two years after the Crucifixion. Pope Paul would be received by India's first Cardinal, Valerian Gracias, whose Hindu forebears were converted by St. Francis Xavier in Goa in 1545. India has only twelve million Christians, but Jawaharlal Nehru declared "It is no longer possible to speak of Christianity as a foreign religion. It is part of our national heritage." His sister continued the preparations he had initiated.

On May 27, 1964, he died. His *Will and Testament*, written ten years before, opened and read at last, asked "that a handful of my ashes be thrown into the Ganges at Allahabad to be carried to the great ocean that washes India's shore," and that "the major portion of my ashes" be scattered from a plane, "high over the fields where the peasants of India toil, so that these might mingle with the dust and soil of India and become an indistinguishable part of India."

From the United States, President Lyndon B. Johnson wrote to Indira Gandhi that her father's death "left this country and all mankind, to whom he gave so much in word and deed, the poorer. I shall always treasure my all too brief association with Prime Minister Nehru. His comfort at the time of the assassination of President Kennedy was a great source of strength to me. That we should lose this man, so soon after our own loss, grieves us more deeply than we can express."

The New York *Herald Tribune*, which had not always treated him respectfully while he lived, said "Gandhi led a revolution; Nehru built a nation." *The New York Times*, often critical of much that he did or that was done in his name, said "He loved India and he died beloved by her." At the United Nations, Adlai Stevenson said "He was one of God's great creations in our time."

At his funeral rites, a Minister who had never failed his trust said, weeping, "Life is out; the light is out." He was wrong. The lamp in the corner shone against the night.

V❀

"The fight for freedom is never really finally won."

On May 29, 1964, the second earth tremor in two days shook New Delhi. At Rajghat, near the Gandhi Memorial, where thousands of men and women and children scattered flowers on the ashes of his funeral pyre, and in silent throngs along streets leading to Parliament House, it was said that like her people, Mother India trembled with fear because Nehruji was gone. Meanwhile behind closed doors, men who had placed him on a pedestal above themselves, and men who had tried but failed to pull him down, disputed rights of succession.

Who would take the place of the leader they loved and lost was not for the masses to say. Under constitutional provisions adapted from the British parliamentary system, choice rested wholly with the hierarchy of the ruling Congress Party. This created two kingmakers. To many, it seemed that in them, two Indias were synthesized.

Nominal precedence belonged to India's President, Dr. Sarvepalli Radhakrishnan. Brahmin by heritage, world-

traveled, world-known as an interpreter of Eastern mysticism
to the West, turned late in life from scholar-philosopher into
political tactician, at seventy-six he showed remarkable energy,
resilience, practicality in party give-and-take and, some believed, ambition to go up higher.

His opposite in all ways was Kumaraswami Kamaraj, the
Congress Party president. No Brahmin, Kamaraj liked to say
he wasted only three years in schools, had no desire to see any
country but his own, saw no reason for speaking English
where his native South Indian Tamil tongue was sufficient to
his purposes, and thought "India should look in, not out."
Unusually tall and heavily built, brusquely unabashed by
accusations of ruthlessness, he held the power to make or
break, and frankly gloried in it, offering no objection when
American correspondents called him "India's Jim Farley,"
grinning when they dubbed him "Big Daddy."

Sleep softly, eagle forgotten! Indira Gandhi said of her
father that "He had the unique advantage of having within
him all parts of India. He could be at ease with the old, with
the very young, with the peasant, with the thinker, with all
aspects of our people. That contributed greatly, I think, to the
unity of India. Today, you find a division between the politicians and the intelligentsia, between the old generation and
the new." Both she and Vijaya Lakshmi Pandit knew that star-
chamber debate, in which they took no part, was predicated on
determination that there should be no Nehru dynasty.

A Congress wheelhorse, Gulzarilal Nanda, was closest to
the throne by virtue of his *pro tem* position as caretaker Prime
Minister. T. T. Krishnamachari, who had been in and out of
the Nehru Cabinet as Finance Minister, had strong backing

from business and industry. But it was Morarji Desai who would not discuss a successor "while Jawaharlal Nehru lives," whose campaign deadlocked the voting, and who threatened "public airing of party quarrels" unless opposition to his candidacy was withdrawn.

Party solidarity, already flawed, would crack apart if decision was long delayed. Facing this prospect, still the kingmakers would not, or could not, surrender to Desai. Then someone recalled that only days before his death, "Nehruji told Lal Bahadur Shastri to get ready to go with him to the British Commonwealth conference in London." Someone else said "I once heard Nehruji say of Shastri, 'No man could wish for a better colleague.'" The kingmakers looked at each other, and then at the smallest and shyest of those who had formed the Nehru Cabinet, the least of them as factotum Minister-Without-Portfolio.

No one cried "Eureka!" or "Needs must when the devil drives!" There were, and still are, conflicting interpretations of the reasoning behind hierarchical decision to interpret "Get ready to go with me" as designation of a chosen heir. One thing is certain. Lal Bahadur Shastri was more surprised than Morarji Desai by the announcement that "Nehruji's place will be taken by Shastri."

Newspaper editors searched their files for past-performance clippings, and found few. New Delhi wits asked, "Can you imagine little Shastri at a summit conference? President Johnson will pick him up by the ears!" Broadcast by All-India Radio, booming from loudspeakers in the villages, the news gave no surcease from fear to millions who had never heard of

Shastri. But in the Governor's Palace in Bombay, Vijaya Lakshmi Pandit listened thoughtfully to reports of Shastri's first act after the crown was thrust upon him.

In a government plane he flew from Delhi to Nagpur in Central India. From Nagpur, he set off across monsoon-soaked countryside in a car that soon stalled in a quagmire. He went on in a jeep. It, too, soon bogged down. He walked muddy roads until he reached a thatched hut in an isolated village. There he waited patiently until the lone occupant invited him to enter. Then the new defender of India's destiny bent to touch the bare feet of Vinoba Bhave, Vinobaji the Self-Giver, whose "Land for the love of God!" inspired revival of Gandhian compassion thirteen years before.

For two hours, seated on the dirt floor, Shastri and Vinobaji talked quietly, not about politics. Before departing, Shastri told the villagers, "In olden days kings used to travel great distances to receive *darshan,* the gift to the soul that comes from seeing saints. I have made such a trip. I have drawn courage from this pilgrimage."

Back in Delhi, on the morning of his swearing-in he rose as usual at dawn. His rising from the rope-webbed cot he shared with his second son, then sixteen, waked two other sons, his wife and his aged mother. All, in the tradition of the Hindu poor, shared a single small sleeping-room. He drank a cup of tea, breakfasted on orange juice and a handful of almonds, and went on foot to take his oath as Prime Minister of the earth's second most populous nation.

His salary equaled $300 a month, ten times his previous income. He arranged to have this paid to the Servants of God, a charity initiated by Gandhi. In return he accepted a dole just sufficient to feed himself and his family. To cynics, this was of a piece with his pilgrimage to see Vinobaji. Vijaya Lakshmi Pandit had known Gandhi much too well to be impressed by imitators of his humility and asceticism, whose assumed cloaks were as transparent as the Emperor's new clothes. But increasingly, she sensed that there was no pretense in Shastri.

He lacked Gandhi's conquering *charisma*. He had none of her brother's ease and eloquence. Most of the time, he spoke in a whisper. He was barely tall enough to see over the top of the massive Cabinet conference table at which her brother presided for so long. But the American Ambassador, John Kenneth Galbraith, reported conclusions soon confirmed in her own thinking. "There is more iron in Shastri than appears on the surface. He listens to every point of view, he makes up his mind firmly and his decisions stick. He is the kind of man who is trusted."

He announced, "There will be no change from Nehruji's policies," and retained all members of the Nehru Cabinet, including Y. B. Chavan, Krishna Menon's successor as Defense Minister. Then he added to the Cabinet two Congress strong-men, S. K. Patil from Bombay, a veteran negotiator with Pakistan and with the United States, and N. Sanjiva Reddy, from South India. This was regarded by many as shrewd politics.

Then Delhi buzzed, and the press guessed contradictorily, when he announced, "I have offered the portfolio of Minister of Information and Broadcasting to Mrs. Indira Gandhi." If this was anticipated by the kingmakers, it had not been hinted to those outside their closed circle. The post carried control of

All-India Radio and of India's Films Division, which produces documentary films all theaters must screen, and third rank in the Cabinet. Yet Indira hesitated to accept.

Her father had been beset by cries of *Nehru nepotism*. Like her aunt, she was well aware that his death had loosed the tongues of many who feared to speak out while he lived. For herself, she had said, "I do not like politics. I do not like being in the public eye." But Shastri was insistent. Finally, she accepted; and Delhi weathervanes veered.

It became the fashion now to say her appointment was a move to mollify her father's die-hard disciples; wait a bit, and her resignation would be arranged. "And that will be the end of the Nehru Era." This went on being said while she used skills learned from her father, unraveling red-tape in the Ministry, setting new ideas in motion, impressing foreign correspondents with her administrative efficiency.

Her father had never yielded to Communist Party machinations. Split now in halves, pro-Soviet, pro-Peking, Communist Members of Parliament formed strange alliances. Protests rose, not only from Communists, when without warning Shastri ordered arrest of five hundred party card-carriers on charges of "having plotted revolutionary action." Communist China exploded its first nuclear device. He met radical shouts of "India, too, must have The Bomb!", by declaring that although India's physicists, headed by the world-known Dr. H. J. Babha, had the capability to produce atomic weapons, "India will not put nuclear energy to any but peaceful uses." This reiterated the Nehru position.

He held the meeting his predecessor had planned with Field Marshal Mohammed Ayub Khan. There were scattered cries of "Appeasement!" The Sandhurst-graduated, bemedaled, towering professional soldier whose bloodless military *coup d'etat* had made him President of Pakistan, and the diminutive, soft-spoken, Gandhian Prime Minister-by-compromise reached no agreement that lessened tensions. Now the saying was "Ayub growled and The Sparrow flew out the window!" According to her custom, Vijaya Lakshmi Pandit formed her own conclusions.

Hoarders and profiteers fattened on food shortages. S. K. Patil negotiated successfully in Washington for added shipments of American surplus grains. Shastri imposed partial rationing, and heavy penalties for black-market trading. Accused offenders claimed mutual-profit arrangements with Congress office holders. Newspapers exhumed the axiom that a party rots progressively, from the bottom upward, as it continues in power. Vijaya Lakshmi Pandit reached another decision not taken easily.

2.

If cameras and the awed stare of crowds and the company of the wise and notable had mattered most, she would have remained in Bombay, to head up official welcome as Her Excellency Madame Governor when the Eucharistic Congress and the arrival of Pope Paul VI brought such a gathering of delegates from Christian countries abroad as India had never seen, attended by the largest corps of correspondents and photographers ever sent to Asia except in time of war. She was not there.

While two million non-Christian Indians thronged into

Bombay to receive *darshan,* the gift to the soul that comes from seeing saints, no matter what their faith may be, she was back in Allahabad, beginning her campaign for election to India's Parliament from what had been her brother's constituency. While India's Brahmin President and Muslim Vice-President, and Bombay's Christian Mayor, and the heads of India's Hindu, Muslim, Sikh, Jain, Parsi, Jewish and Buddhist communities joined in welcoming the first head of a world church ever seen in India, Vijaya Lakshmi Pandit went forth from Anand Bhavan to find out if United Provinces villagers had forgotten her.

Political experts, including longtime friends, had warned her earnestly against relinquishing her secure and honored post and returning to politics. Conditions had changed, they argued, more than she realized. Defeat at the polls, which was almost certain, would end her distinguished career disastrously. "There has never been a Nehru defeat. Now of all times there should not be one." She said this was so, and sent in her resignation.

Confounding the experts, villagers flocked to greet the Great Lady who did good things for poor people, and elected her by a dramatic majority. Again one voice, one vote, among more than four hundred members of the House of the People, she soon made clear why she had decided it was her duty to be there.

When she rose to speak for the first time, Congress Party leaders told each other she reminded them of Motilal Nehru rising to address a jury. Then they blinked, in realization that she put them on trial. As surprised American Aid administrators said admiringly, when she was Madame Ambassador in

Washington, she had done her homework. Dispassionately, she catalogued instances of ineffectiveness and ineptitude, ill-considered planning, ill-managed spending, at levels low and high. A Congress housecleaning, she said, was too long over-due.

Her speech set off no immediately apparent change, nor can she have expected that it would. But with it, she made herself a presence not to be ignored. The next day's newspapers head-lined *Nehru's Sister Castigates Shastri*. Second thoughts re-vised this arguable interpretation. Editorials recalled her brother's own pleas, and in his last days, demands, for Con-gress reforms from within. As for Shastri, subsequent events gave credence to surmise that he welcomed restatement of Nehru principles by a Nehru.

Her brother had opposed the Hindi Act, that would make their birth-speech the official language of all India. She op-posed it now, arguing as he had that no more than half of India's many millions know Hindi, that it is only one of four-teen major languages recognized by India's Constitution, that in fact there are one hundred and fifteen altogether, and more than five hundred regional dialects. And although the British were gone, English remained as the only bridge between linguistic divisions. Still the measure was pushed through.

Tamil-speaking South Indians reacted violently. Her voice and vote backed Shastri, who suspended the Language Act, ruling that English would continue to be the language of his government, while each state might transact internal affairs in the language of its preference. The issue would rise again. "Religion and language are the two forces that dominate the life of India." Temporary truce, the most that could be hoped for, gave time to deal with another recurring and even more explosive problem.

Sheikh Abdullah, the Muslim agitator who liked to be called "the Lion of Kashmir," had been Gandhi's friend and had asked Jawaharlal Nehru for help in ridding Kashmir of its Hindu Maharajah; but since partition, he had made himself a hero in Pakistan, not in India. In 1953 Adlai Stevenson, defeated by General Eisenhower in the American presidential elections, visited him at Srinagar. Stevenson had hardly departed, when Sheikh Abdullah called on the United States for intervention to establish "an independent Vale of Kashmir."

Indian Kashmir's Muslim Chief Minister, Bakshi Ghulam Mohammed, ordered Sheikh Abdullah's arrest, "on suspicion of conspiring with foreign powers." In the United States, Edward R. Murrow, most respected of American commentators, told his listeners, "No doubt the Lion of Kashmir expressed his views to Mr. Stevenson. But it was ridiculous for Indian circles to hint that he and Mr. Stevenson conspired to take Kashmir out of the Indian Federation."

Murrow's voice was one of the many raised in praise of Vijaya Lakshmi Pandit when she was president of the United Nations General Assembly. Now he implanted opinion that alienated friends she had won for India by telling truths to Americans. "Mr. Nehru," he said, "must have assented to Sheikh Abdullah's arrest. The British are out of India, but Indians seem capable of oppressing each other. The moral may be that the fight for freedom is never really finally won." With this, she could agree. For the rest, what had happened since 1953 made Murrow's case a poor one.

In 1958 her brother ordered Sheikh Abdullah's release.

Immediately, the Lion of Kashmir was the center of Kashmiri Muslim demonstrations. He was again arrested, then again released, on agreement that he would cease activities which in India's view made him "a hazard to security," and leave the country. His travels took him to Algiers, where he met and conferred at length with Chou En-lai of Communist China. Soon he was back in Kashmir.

According to *The New York Times,* he was "scrupulous in refraining from any incitement to violence." New Delhi's information was to the contrary. Still, fainthearts in the House of the People cried that any action against Sheikh Abdullah might bring reprisal from Pakistan, Communist China or both. Shastri, however, ordered the Lion of Kashmir caged, at Ootacamund in South India, twelve hundred miles from his hunting-grounds. Again, Shastri had Vijaya Lakshmi Pandit's full support. He would need it increasingly.

Fighting broke out between American-armed Pakistan detachments and Indian border patrols, in the desolate West Coast wasteland of sand and swamps called the Rann of Cutch. The brushfire blaze spread rapidly. Sent to America, Vijaya Lakshmi Pandit might have been able to prevail on American policy-makers to see what India saw behind conflict deliberately provoked, in an area of no actual importance to Pakistan. There was no time for this.

Washington, warning "The United States has no intention of financing war on the subcontinent," curtailed wheat deliveries and economic assistance to India; but went on delivering military hardware to Pakistan. Shastri's proclamation that "Our country must be independent, able to fight and live on

what it can produce" was read as reckless defiance, not of
Pakistan but of the United States.

Under Shastri's orders, Indian troops were rushed to the
Rann of Cutch from watch-duty along the cease-fire line in
Kashmir. This time, there was no Indian Army debacle.
Shastri exhorted India's people: "Hold up your heads and be
proud!" Indian newspapers said, "Shastri the Sparrow has be-
come Shastri the Hawk."

Harold Wilson of the United Kingdom, senior Prime Minister in the British Commonwealth of Nations to which both
Pakistan and India belonged, hurried from England to plead
for a truce before escalation went further. Firing stopped.
Washington and London hailed Wilson as a peacemaker.
Then in early August 1965, just before her sixty-fifth birthday, Vijaya Lakshmi Pandit saw the beginning of the tragedy
her brother foresaw in 1947.

3.

Lieutenant General Robert Nimmo of Australia, chief
United Nations military observer in Kashmir, reported to the
Security Council that "Armed men, not in uniform but with
Army-issue weaponry, are crossing the cease-fire line from the
Pakistan side, for the purpose of aggressive action on the
Indian side." Pakistan disclaimed responsibility. "There is
simply a rising of oppressed Muslims in Kashmir to throw off
the yoke of India." Shastri denied this. "The alleged 'revolt'
does not exist, and has not been noticed by independent
observers." On August 13 Shastri warned Pakistan, "Force

will be met by force." On August 14 Pakistan Armed Forces, spearheaded by American Saber-jets and Patton tanks, smashed into Indian Kashmir. From Rawalpindi, Ayub Khan proclaimed, "We are at war."

All-Pakistan Radio boasted, "We will have the Hindus crawling on their bellies in a week." In India, Hindus, Muslims, Sikhs, Christians, Jews, Jains, Parsis and Buddhists begged recruiting officers to let them go and fight for Mother India. Gandhian nonviolence was dead. *Panchshila* lay in ruins. At the front, brothers killed brothers. Generals, once comrades as Majors in the Royal Indian Army, matched skills at deploying expendables.

Again, India's women marched beside their men. Ministers of Information are rarely seen where bullets write communiqués. India's *javans,* under fire in Kashmir, cheered Indira Gandhi appearing among them. There was no precedent for sending a mere Member of Parliament, least of all a woman, to Europe as a wartime envoy. By Shastri's choice, Vijaya Lakshmi Pandit spoke for India in West Germany, the Netherlands and France.

In Indian belief, Pakistan strategy was keyed to coincide with outbreaks of Kashmiri Muslims, armed and led by infiltrating guerrillas, behind the Indian lines. Pakistan's Armed Forces would "protect our Islamic brothers from Hindu brutality," while completing conquest until Delhi was in striking range. Then Pakistan would present the United Nations with *un fait accompli.* "We have Kashmir; now legalize our ownership." And the United Nations would settle for peace at any price.

However accurate this assessment may have been, in fact

there were no Kashmiri Muslim uprisings. Infiltrators were rounded up. "With inferior weapons but superior tactics and *esprit,* our *javans* destroyed two hundred of the four hundred tanks the United States gave Pakistan. Our little home-made 'Gnats' shot American planes and their Pakistani pilots right out of the sky." Figures and facts were exaggerated by both sides. One fact was clear. The Pakistan attack, expected to crush defense "as easily as breaking an egg," ground to a halt.

Again as in the past, information reaching Americans was confused and dubiously accurate. Indira Gandhi and Vijaya Lakshmi Pandit knew this; so did Kamaladevi Chatto-padhyay, Mahatma Gandhi's secretary at nineteen, in 1965 director of the cottage industries he founded. "I am afraid," she wrote from India, "that more damage has been done to our relations with the United States. There have been inhibitions and mental reservations in Washington, due to several factors. Unfortunately, these trends, like press reports, get high-lighted, and they come to personify a country. The millions of people who comprise the country simply get wiped off the scene. We really do not know, and have little chance to know, what the American people really feel or know."

In the midst of war, women as participants continued learn-ing what their country must still learn. "I agree with you that our propaganda system and technique is very poor," Kamala-devi wrote from Kashmir. "There have been mistakes in han-dling the foreign correspondents who rushed here. Sending press personnel to the forward areas was slow, hesitant and such as to give an impression that India Government did not want them to go. All this has come out in our public press. We only hope this will be a lesson for the future."

She asked, as Vijaya Lakshmi Pandit had asked in the United States, "Why do those in authority in Washington and at the United Nations take their cues from what is published, when they are in possession of the true facts through their own channels and documents? Why go on pressing for 'a Kashmir plebiscite' when it was clearly understood at the U. N. that there was a Pakistan aggression, and Pakistan had to vacate Kashmir before India could take the next step? Why not insist Pakistan must pull out of Kashmir, and then see what happens?"

The questions, asked by many in India, went unanswered from abroad. On September 4, the United Nations Security Council called on both India and Pakistan to end hostilities and withdraw their forces to former positions along the cease-fire line. Fighting intensified. On September 6, Shastri sent Indian troops and artillery into Pakistan, driving toward Lahore. U Thant, successor to Dag Hammarskjöld as United Nations Secretary-General, found neither Rawalpindi nor New Delhi receptive to his personal pleas for an armistice.

Vijaya Lakshmi Pandit, back from Europe, her mission there concluded, was in the foreground in debate in the House of the People, where each day's Kashmir fighting multiplied the difficulty of finding funds to meet emergencies. "We shot away my entire budget for social improvement yesterday," a department head reported. "Today our guns fired off two badly needed irrigation dams."

Shastri had charged, before invasion began, "There is a conspiracy between Pakistan and Communist China." The charge had been dismissed by Free World powers. But on September 17, Peking served an ultimatum on New Delhi, threatening renewed invasion through the Himalayas unless India yielded within seventy-two hours to terms that would ease the pressures on Pakistan's faltering offensive in Kashmir.

This was when an American correspondent described Lal Bahadur Shastri as "India's equivalent of Harry Truman, a small man with a big backbone made of iron." Shastri told the House of the People, "The might of China will not deter us from fighting for our territorial integrity. If we are attacked, we shall fight for our freedom with grim determination." There was silence for a long breath. Then Vijaya Lakshmi Pandit and every other member of the House, of whatever party or persuasion, gave Shastri the highest salute permitted by parliamentary rules, pounding their desks, then rising in unison.

The three-day time limit set by Peking's ultimatum passed. Communist Chinese troops made no menacing move. A little longer, All-Pakistan Radio blared *Kadam Bararhijao:* "One step, one more step, one step at a time, and we shall conquer all!" In a tirade before the Security Council, Zulfikar Khan Bhutto of Pakistan called all Indians "dogs," and swore Pakistan would fight on until India surrendered. Then Bhutto ceased to be heard. Ayub Khan himself spoke for his country.

He was ready to talk terms. The question of Kashmir was put over to some other time. Hostilities ceased, with nothing settled, nothing gained and much irreparably lost. There were no victory celebrations. Pakistan's former favored position had been as badly damaged as the American war *matériel* that littered Kashmir. For India, the cost of unwanted war left progress programs in wreckage. The long hard road had lengthened; and some who walked it were too weary to go on.

General J. N. Chaudhuri, India's chief-of-staff, expressed what millions had come to feel. "Nonalignment is a good policy provided that in a pinch you have strong allies." Princess Amrit Kaur of Kapurthala, who renounced her heritage to march with Gandhi, wrote to friends in America, "I never dreamed a day could come when I would pray for the American nuclear umbrella over India. It has come, and I weep for what is gone." Soon after, she was dead.

Writing from Delhi, for the American *Saturday Review,* William D. Patterson summed up: "It is keenly felt here that London, caught between two warring members of the Commonwealth, confused the issue by following Washington in the sterile policy of regarding the conflict in Kashmir as though it were merely a clash between two equally irresponsible belligerents. Such a Western policy, it is argued in highly placed quarters, is morally wrong and is, moreover, dangerous to our national security in the struggle in which we are engaged in Vietnam and other parts of Asia."

Vijaya Lakshmi Pandit had served India, and studied policies toward India, in Moscow, Washington and London. Now she watched the United States and the United Kingdom present Soviet Russia with the role of Asian peacemaker. From the Kremlin, Premier Kosygin arranged for Shastri and Ayub Khan to meet at Tashkent, capital of the Uzbek Soviet Republic. Before they met, she began another truth-telling mission in the United States. Her program was arranged to take her across the continent to California, where she was to be our guest, and to speak to the Los Angeles World Affairs Council, as her brother had five years before.

On January 11, 1966, headlines told that the Tashkent

Declaration, renouncing use of force between Pakistan and India, had been signed. *Peace In Kashmir!* We talked with her on long-distance, and planned a celebration in Los Angeles of the dawn of a new day for India. Columnists and reporters called, asking for interview appointments when she arrived. Among the callers was the Hearst papers' Cobina Wright, who said, "I believe Mrs. Pandit will remember me from meetings when she was president of the United Nations."

She said, "Please tell Cobina Wright I do indeed remember her, but that I am not one of the glamourous society women she writes about. As a woman still working hard for India, I shall be happy to speak with her about my country." She was about to board a plane for California, when she saw newspaper headlines. *Shastri Dead.*

He died among strangers, alone, not quite nineteen months after he was brought from shadows to do the best he could as successor to Nehruji whom he idolized. Again in India, people cried *The light has gone out, and there is darkness every where.* Again, a lamp was lighted.

Vijaya Lakshmi Pandit turned back toward home, and twenty hours later was in New Delhi. She did not go to place herself in prominence. She went, as she always had, to be useful where and how she could.

4.

Again, Gulzarilal Nanda was caretaker Prime Minister. Again, no one urged "Friend, go up higher." Again, Morarji Desai avowed himself as candidate for the throne, and stated confidently there could be no better choice. Again, there were other aspirants, and rumors of strange coalitions. But ten out of fifteen Chief Ministers, representing states of the Indian Federal Union, and twelve out of fifteen Cabinet members, told Congress Party kingmakers "Our choice is Mrs. Indira Gandhi."

Vijaya Lakshmi Pandit, questioned by the press, said "Indira has risen by sheer value of her worth, and the work she has done. Of course she has had the advantage of being her father's daughter, as I had the advantage of being his sister. But once that's accepted, you can't pin that on a person forever. She has worked hard all these years, and it's absolutely in the fitness of things that she has reached the position she has today."

Once she herself might have been chosen, *viva voce*. Now she aided toward the result that caused the Associated Press to report worldwide, "By her victory, Mrs. Indira Gandhi not only resumes the Nehru Era, but the leadership of India passes to a second generation of freedom fighters." What Americans had learned about the aunt was said now about the niece. "Although India has had a reputation for the subjugation of women, actually they were beaten and imprisoned and they shared all the tribulations of the bloody revolt against the British Raj. So Indian women in public office are not automatically to be suspected of being shrewish or flighty as so often happens of their sisters in more developed countries."

Correspondents agreed unwontedly. "Mrs. Gandhi was chosen by hard-nosed politicians, and is herself a seasoned, disciplined party politician." This was true, but those in her family knew it was incomplete. "My public speaking started," she said, "at the age of three. My favorite occupation as a child was to deliver thunderous orations to the servants while standing on a very high table." Her father had often reminded her of how as a young girl she dreamed of "being something like Joan of Arc." So her aunt had dreamed of being Jhansi-ki-Rani.

Still, though she had been in politics all her life, she shrank from concessions and compromise. In Congress conclaves, she made speeches only when she must. Her aunt and her cousins knew how sincere she was in saying "I always wanted to be like my mother. She was the gentlest creature in the world." Slight, small-framed like all the Nehrus, at times forbiddingly austere, there was sadness in her large brown eyes, shyness in her manner except when the Nehru temper flared.

Like Vijaya Lakshmi Pandit, she resisted "being treated 'like a woman.' " She said "I faced firing when we were fighting for independence. No one thought 'This is a woman. We can't fire on her.' I have been beaten up. I have been in jail." She, too, labored to learn "how to make men listen as they would to a man."

Presiding at Congress sessions, she had gaveled her father down when he spoke beyond his allotted time. In debate, she asked for no special privilege, and gave none. Called on to fill the post her father held for seventeen years, she said "I am not conceited enough to say others cannot handle it, but I am not modest enough to say I cannot do the job."

On January 24, 1966, two days before India's sixteenth Republic Day, Indira Priyadarshini Gandhi was sworn in as her country's third Prime Minister. An American radio interviewer hailed her as "the most powerful woman in the world." She was also the most heavily burdened. "She's been a lonely person all her life," a friend said sadly. "Now she'll be lonelier than ever. She is putting on a crown more of thorns than of roses." One of those closest to her wrote to America "Indi's election of course has made us very proud. She is very capable and I have great faith in her ability. But frankly I do not envy her position one little bit. You well know the problems facing our country. Now they are all hers."

For herself, she said "I make no promises. We are entering our most crucial period since independence nineteen years ago. I can't do anything more than try to establish some positive trends that may have long-term results." She would, she said, try to follow the path charted by Gandhi and her father and Lal Bahadur Shastri. "But if it becomes necessary to turn another way, I shall not hesitate to do so."

In a yellow convertible made in America, she rode through thronged streets to accept Dr. Sarvepalli Radhakrishnan's request to her to form and head a new government. For hours, she stood in the gardens of the Prime Minister's House, where her father had walked so often, with her children, her aunt, her cousins and their children close around, while men, women and children offered the *namasthe* gesture, which is in a way a prayer, and garlanded her with flowers.

A very old widow, come out of *purdah* into a new world, pressed a rupee-note into her hands. "I give what I have for India." When Morarji Desai approached, Indira said "I would like to have your blessing." He responded "Who am I to give you blessing? We need everybody's blessing!" and disappeared into the crowd. Next day, he sent her warning. "The task of being Prime Minister in this country is very difficult." She knew this without being told, perhaps better than he was born to learn.

She made no Cabinet changes that removed men who had earned her father's confidence. A fiction circulated, that she was under Krishna Menon's influence. Actually, they met only in passing. Measures she proposed had Vijaya Lakshmi Pandit's vote and support in the House of the People. They held briefing sessions before she went to the United States. She had been there last as only her father's daughter, content to be jostled or overlooked by dignitaries and the press surrounding him. Now she was received as a head of state, and conferred privately with President Johnson. Like her aunt before her, she won American friends, for India and for herself.

Back in Delhi, she lifted the ban on trade with Pakistan. Diehards protested. She told them, "I must pursue the policies which I consider are best for the country as a whole." Food riots took her to densely populated, Communist-troubled Kerala. Organized demonstrators shouted, "Give us rice or shoot us!" She cut through bureaucratic tangles to expedite delivery of rice, but refused to give ground when pro-Peking Communists staged strikes and riots in Bengal.

Maharashtra and Mysore wrangled over which should absorb former Portuguese Goa. Her Ministers took sides in the quarrel. Later, several of them said, "She made us quiet down. She did it without raising her voice." The Johnson Administration, impressed by needs she had summarized in Washington, proposed to expend $300 millions in blocked rupees (expendable only in India though credited to the United States as payment for shipments of American surplus grains), to finance a massive education program. Her approval of this was assailed by Outs, and by some Ins. "The C.I.A. will masquerade as teachers!" She silenced those who tested her strength by offering to quit office "if India is dissatisfied with my leadership." Meanwhile her aunt was traveling again, to Europe, then to Australia and Malaysia, on truth-telling missions.

In the House of the People, and in her constituency, that had been her brother's, Vijaya Lakshmi Pandit worked with more and more women taking the lead in public affairs. Dr. Sushila Nayar was Minister of Health. Dr. Soundaram Ramachandran was Deputy Minister of Education. Mrs. Maragatham Chandrasekhar was Deputy Minister of Social Welfare. Ninety-five women were Members of Parliament. One hundred and ninety-five served in state legislative assemblies. A Congress Party bylaw required that at least 15 percent of its candidates must be women; but she could testify from personal knowledge that "being able to do the job as well or even better than men, and not just 'equal rights for women' was the test that both men and women applied."

Shortly after her sixty-sixth birthday, by choice amidst the rank-and-file, she watched her niece face assembled Congress delegates at Ernakulam in Kerala, to present her platform for the coming national elections. Morarji Desai, now seventy but still vigorously set on climbing to the heights, was there. So was Kumaraswami Kamaraj. So were other kingmakers and aspirants.

Chosen initially by the Congress hierarchy, in January and February 1967, Indira Gandhi must go to the people for their votes, for the first time. She must carry Congress candidates with her. If she failed in this, her first year as Prime Minister would be her last. At such a time, practical politics dictated "Walk warily." Professional strategists wanted nothing done that could be put off to next year.

She shocked them frankly declaring she could promise, if her program was ratified by the people in India's fourth general election in February 1967, no more than three more ounces of food per head per day for India's hungry millions in 1976. It would take that long at best, she said, for India to become self-sustaining. And this was only the beginning of a show of independence that soon produced reports that Kumaraswami Kamaraj had withdrawn his support and might even decide she was expendable, if a change in Prime Ministers would serve Congress Party purposes.

Refusing to buy votes by avoiding issues, she took sudden drastic action, ordering devaluation of India's rupee currency by 36.5 percent, in an effort to slow inflation. There was shock, then clamor, in cities and industrial centers. In the United States, newspaper pundits complained that rupee de valuation reduced American holdings in counterpart funds by hundreds of millions of dollars, neglecting to mention that these blocked rupees were spendable only in India, and only for India development.

Congress campaigners wailed that they were victims of a decision on which they should have been consulted. But in the villages, the masses talked about another Delhi order, announced in Kashmir. This was that Indira Gandhi's government would provide marriage dowries for girls living in refugee camps, to consist of two *saris,* a shawl, two quilts, cooking utensils and a purse of rupees worth nearly $30 even at the new rate of exchange. This largess might seem small, in any other country. In India where average cash income is less than $100 American per annum, it was a fortune to those who, like their country, start into the future *not merely from Zero, but from Zero Minus One.*

But goodwill gained was offset by unrest that worsened until American correspondents reported, "1966 is the year of popular agitation in India." Vijaya Lakshmi Pandit saw her niece beset by more problems than any other leader of a nation bore. "The late Prime Minister Nehru," one summary read, "was to most Indians such a father-figure that they were glad to let him tell them what was best for them. Shastri's brief regime saw the country united against enemies outside. Mrs. Indira Gandhi, however, must contend with opposition from within, that capitalizes on one crisis after another."

The summing-up included "resentment and demonstrative violence leading to the burning of buses in New Delhi, Calcutta and Allahabad; derailing of trains in Central India, looting of grain-shops in several localities, student strikes that led to closing of schools and colleges." Police and troops used tear gas against demonstrators. Resistance led to gunfire. "The wide variety of reasons given for the violent manifestations makes any general explanation difficult if not impossible. But in each case those doing the demonstrating have had specific grievances."

Border dispute flared in South India, where Marathi-speaking villagers were absorbed against their will into Tamil-speaking Mysore. Language conflict in the Punjab forced imposition of martial law, lifted only after Indira Gandhi surrendered to demands that split the Punjab into two states: one

Sikh, one Hindu. Meanwhile no monsoon rains fell in Bihar, or in the eastern third of the United Provinces, the Nehru birthland. Inspecting a vast dust-bowl in Northeastern India, she traveled forty miles without seeing a foot of land on which any green thing grew.

Canals dried up and wells failed. Villagers abandoned their farms. Those who did not die along the way swarmed into already overcrowded cities, where cows roam unmolested in the teeming streets. Famine-plagued India has two hundred and fifty million cows. To orthodox Hindus, they are sacred symbols. The devout would rather starve than feed on beef. *Cow-slaughter* is, as it has been for centuries, a synonym for mortal sin. Unfounded rumor sent hundreds of *sadhus,* holymen in loincloths, bearing metal tridents, rallying demonstrators in New Delhi. Fanaticism sparked the worst rioting in nineteen years.

There was arson and looting. Police opened fire. Eight rioters were killed, and hundreds hurt. Mobs fought back with stakes and stones. Five hundred *sadhus* were arrested. A curfew was imposed, and schools and colleges closed. Gulzarilal Nanda, the Home Minister, twice Prime Minister *pro tem,* was held responsible for mishandling matters, and forced to resign. Members of her own party castigated Indira Gandhi for "a tendency to capitulate to pressure groups, allowing them to bully the government."

In Parliament, six separate no-confidence motions alleged failures in economic development, in preventing famine, in ending corruption and in "a self-righteous foreign policy." Minoo Masani, a spokesman for the rightist Swatantra Party, rising near Vijaya Lakshmi Pandit in the House of the People, shouted at her niece, "For God's sake, go, while there is still some administration and order left!" Indira Gandhi weathered an uglier storm than any her father had endured. The no-confidence motions were voted down. But the Indian press said, "Certain party leaders are only waiting for Mrs. Gandhi to stumble, so they themselves can make a bid for power."

Correspondents called her "A lady at a tea-party with a bunch of toughs." Older members of Parliament spoke of her as "Nehru's little daughter." Critics, both Indian and foreign, professed "alarm at her departures from her father's philosophy." Her aunt supported her with vote and personal influence. Some women, in government and out, said they sensed behind carping, accusation and outright revolt an age-old motivation. "Men simply can't bear being led by a woman." None were more aware than Indira Gandhi and Vijaya Lakshmi Pandit that the hard-won right of India's women to share equally in determining their country's destiny was in increasing jeopardy.

"As a proud and somewhat willful lady," *Time,* the American newsmagazine, reported, "Indira Gandhi smarts under the accusation that she was picked as Prime Minister largely because the Congress Party's political pros reckoned that she would be easy to control. Last week, as if to assert her independence, Mrs. Gandhi made some Cabinet changes." What she did was viewed quite differently in India.

Changes she made began with transfer of Y. B. Chavan, her father's choice to succeed Krishna Menon as Minister of Defense, to the post of Home Minister, succeeding Gulzarilal Nanda. "In so doing," said *Time,* "she created a powerful potential rival for the future." If this was the case, her friends declared, it was a showing of statesmanship, not of feminine pique; for she did what seemed best for India, no matter if it lessened her own chances of continuing as Prime Minister.

Seemingly, only neighboring Pakistan read significance in other changes she ordered. Succeeding Chavan in control of India's Armed Forces was turbaned, bearded Swaran Singh, a Sikh. Time was when Sikhs ruled what is now West Pakistan. With partition, they were expelled. During Kashmir fighting, their holiest temple, at Amritsar, was bombed by Pakistan pilots. Sikh officers and *javans* bore heavy losses yet held and counterattacked. Now a Sikh headed up preparations against possible breach of the Tashkent Pact.

His place as Foreign Minister was taken by Mahomedali Currim Chagla, a Muslim, Oxford-educated, formerly India's Ambassador in Washington and to the United Kingdom. He moved over from the Ministry of Education. Succeeding him there was another Muslim, Fakhruddin Ahmed. Muslims moved up in grade in other ministries, and there were informed observers who thought that the over-all result should be regarded as sound strategy. They saw courage, not indecision, in Indira Gandhi's appeal on All-India Radio.

"My heart is filled with great sadness," she told India's people. "There is hunger and distress in millions of our homes. Let us have a truce. This is no time for agitation." Listening to this, Vijaya Lakshmi Pandit looked backward over half a century. Truly, *The fight for freedom is never really finally won*. But still it was not lost.

Her daughter Tara quoted Somerset Maugham's bleak dictum: "Life's meaning is contained in the sentence, 'Man is born, he suffers, and he dies.'" She said reflectively "Well, yes, of course. But lots of interesting things happen in between." This might not be enough, for those who loved too little. She has always loved.

5.

In an old American DC-3 lumbering through the darkness over India, an American woman talked while the rest of us were silent. Helen Hokinson pictured her sisters, in their flowered hats and cloistering corsets, for many issues of *The New Yorker*. At first, I hardly listened to her.

India's shortage of foreign exchange makes it necessary to keep planes in service, on some runs, that would have been retired long since in countries where anything built ten years ago is an antique. Ours had been carrying cargo and passengers since the third year of the Second World War. But it was not the feeling that this might be its final flight that kept me looking out through the window at my elbow.

Almost anywhere else on earth, the night traveler by air can take reassurance from sprinkles of light in scattered constellations far below. There are cities and towns down there, and people, snug and safe in houses. He is not, after all, alone. But over India, night blacked out seven hundred thousand villages, and four hundred and eighty million human beings. I had mentioned this to Indian friends, after a previous flight from Calcutta, the City of Dreadful Night, to Bombay which is becoming another Chicago. They said "We are trying to turn the lights on. It takes time."

The lady from America said two weeks in India had convinced her there will be darkness there forever. She was glad to be going home. On the lecture tour she would begin as soon as she reached Kansas City and had a good hot bath and had her hair done, she would tell her countrymen and mine that *Mother India* is truer now than when she read it as a schoolgirl. "There is just no hope for India."

How much better things must have been, she said, when the British carried the White Man's Burden. How ungrateful India was, to make them go away. And it was too much to expect, that we Americans should go on pouring money into a country that refuses to help itself. She was sorry for India, but India's people had only themselves to blame. She would say this in her lectures in utter sincerity; and those who heard her would tell each other "She must know. She was there."

But because she was so well-meaning, she asked for another opinion. She spoke to the American nearest her only because shortsightedness kept her from realizing his condition. Washington would never choose him as a people-to-people ambassador. An engineer, or more accurately a water-witch, he works electronic wizardry locating catch-basins deep underground, tapping them, bringing cold, clean water gushing up through iron pipes in villages where there was no water at all until he came. He had squandered his last pay-check in Calcutta, the last of it for a bottle of *Made In India* gin.

The lady from America tested him with the question many Americans ask. "What's going to become of India?" A whiff of his gin-soured breath mixed with the scent of her talcum powder, while cogitation furrowed his forehead. Finally, he said "Well, ma'am, I haven't quite made up my mind. I've only been here since 1947." Then there was silence in the plane until, an hour late, we touched down at the Gateway of India.

There in Bombay, and in Lucknow and Patna and

Bangalore and Darjeeling and Panjim, and at Motibagh Palace in Patiala and at Udaipur where Mrs. Jacqueline Kennedy was a guest in the Lake Palace that is now a hotel, and in Cochin and Madhya Pradesh and Hyderabad and Bihar and Gujerat and Mysore, and at Allahabad where Vijaya Lakshmi Pandit was born, and in New Delhi where the House of the People sits, it was easy to find evidence that the lady from America was right: There is no hope for India. Unless, that is, you remembered the lamp in the corner.

"The next ten or twelve years," Indira Gandhi said as her first year in her father's place drew to a close, "will be only the first milestone. But within the time-span of the next decade or so, India, we believe and we pray, will emerge as a fully self-reliant nation." How long and how far a woman will lead, India's men and women had still to decide. But beside her stood another woman, another widow, another Nehru, who has proved that for a woman who cares with all her heart, no victory, no fortune is beyond accomplishment.

In Acknowledgment

Only Vijaya Lakshmi Pandit could tell all of the story that should be told. Thus far, she has been too busy being a part of it, to write about it. She is credited with only one bit of writing about herself, *So I Became a Minister,* which was published only in India, in 1939. The late Richard Walsh told me ten years ago, "I've waited ten years to publish Mrs. Pandit's *Autobiography*. She still hasn't found time to finish it." What has happened since is evidence that however long it may be, before she writes *The End,* the time will not have been wasted.

For myself, in what I have written I have tried to adhere to her brother's principle, that the truth is round, not flat. For twelve years, as a working traveler in India and in countries that are her next-door neighbors, I have listened, watched, guessed, been entrusted with confidences, carried on always-increasing correspondence, read many books and other publications recommended by persons with variant viewpoints. For what I am reasonably sure of, I owe thanks to friends who ask not to be named, as well as to many I have named or who will recognize themselves within quotation marks.

Above all, I am indebted to Irene, my wife, my research assistant, on occasion my staff photographer, and always, the one to whom I turn if the writing goes badly, or when it will not go at all. It is no accident, that *A Lamp For India* is published on our twenty-fifth wedding anniversary.

As for a bibliography, it is hard for a magpie to remember where each bright bit in his collection came from. However, I would be remiss if I failed to mention, among references I have consulted:

The Autobiography of Jawaharlal Nehru. John Lane, The Bodley Head, Ltd., London, 1936.

The Discovery of India, by Jawaharlal Nehru. John Day, New York, 1946.

Glimpses of World History, by Jawaharlal Nehru. John Day, New York, 1942.

Mahatma Gandhi, by Jawaharlal Nehru. Signet Press, Calcutta, India, 1949.

Jawaharlal Nehru: A Biography, by Frank Moraes. The Macmillan Company, New York, 1956.

Report on Mao's China, by Frank Moraes. The Macmillan Company, New York, 1953.

So I Became a Minister, by Vijaya Lakshmi Pandit. Kitabistan Press, India, 1939.

Prison and Chocolate Cake, by Nayantara Pandit Sahgal. Alfred A. Knopf, New York, 1954.

From Fear Set Free, by Nayantara Pandit Sahgal. W. W. Norton & Company, New York, 1963.

This Time of Morning, a novel by Nayantara Pandit Sahgal. W. W. Norton & Company, New York, 1965.

Talks With Nehru, by Norman Cousins. John Day, New York, 1951.

The Story of My Experiments With Truth: An Autobiography, by Mohandas Karamchand Gandhi. Navajivan Trust, India, 1929.

The Life of Mahatma Gandhi, by Louis Fischer. Harper & Brothers, New York, 1950.

Gandhi, His Life and Message for the World, by Louis Fischer. New American Library, New York, 1954.

With No Regrets, by Krishna Nehru Hutheesing. Padma Publications, Bombay, India, 1944.

Many Worlds: An Autobiography, by K. P. S. Menon. Oxford University Press, London, 1965.

Krishna Menon: A Biography, by T. J. S. George, Taplinger Publishing Company, New York, 1965.

Lead, Kindly Light, by Vincent Shecan. Random House, New York, 1949.

Jinnah: A Biography, by Hector Bolitho. John Murray, London, 1954.

Mission With Mountbatten, by Alan Campbell-Johnson. Robert Hale, Ltd., London, 1951.

Madame Ambassador: The Life of Vijaya Lakshmi Pandit, by Anne Guthrie. Harcourt, Brace & World, Inc., New York, 1962.

India and the Awakening East, by Mrs. Eleanor Roosevelt. Harper & Brothers, New York, 1952.

India: A Modern History, by Percival Spear. The University of Michigan Press, Ann Arbor, 1961.

India in the New Era, by T. Walter Wallbank. Scott, Foresman and Company, New York, 1951.

The Nature of the Non-Western World, by Vera Micheles Dean. Mentor Books New American Library, 1957.

Perspective of India: An Atlantic Monthly Supplement, edited by Harvey Breit. Intercultural Publications, Inc. (The Ford Foundation), 1952.

Imperial Commonwealth, by Lord Elton. Reynal & Hitchcock, New York, 1946.

Mother India, by Katherine Mayo. Jonathan Cape, London, 1929.

The History of India, by the Hon. Mountstuart Elphinstone. John Murray, London, 1916.

Indika, by Bishop John F. Hurst. Harper & Brothers, New York, 1891.

Sorrowing Lies My Land, by Lambert Mascarenhas. Hind Kitabs, Ltd., Bombay, India, 1955.

Pakistan: Birth and Growth of a Muslim Nation, by Richard V. Weekes. The Asia Library (D. Van Nostrand Company, Inc.), New York, 1963.

Foreign Policy of Pakistan. Department of International Relations, University of Karachi. Allies Book Corporation, Pakistan, 1964.

Red China: An Asian View, by Sripati Chandra-Sekhar. Frederick A. Praeger, Inc., New York, 1961.

A Passage Through Pakistan, by Orville F. Linck. Wayne State University Press, Detroit, 1959.

The Pathans: B.C. 550–A.D. 1957, by Sir Olaf Caroe. Macmillan & Company, Ltd., London, 1965.

The Narrow Smile, by Peter Mayne. John Murray, London, 1955.

Kashmir, by D. R. Goyal (Kanwar Lal, editor). R. & K. Publishing House, New Delhi, India, 1965.

Tibet and the Tibetans, by Tsung-lien Shen and Shen-chi Liu. Stanford University Press, California, 1953.

Royal India, by Maud Diver. D. Appleton-Century Company, New York, 1942.

Restless India, by Lawrence K. Rosinger. Foreign Policy Association Headline Series, New York, 1943.

Ambassador's Report, by Chester Bowles. Harper & Brothers, New York, 1954.

Halfway to Freedom, by Margaret Bourke-White. Simon & Schuster, New York, 1949.

Nehru: A Pictorial Biography, by Michael Edwardes. Thames and Hudson, London, 1964.

Inside Asia, by John Gunther. Harper & Brothers, New York, 1939.

After Partition. Government of India Publications Division, 1948.

The Wonder That Was India, by A. L. Basham. The Macmillan Company, New York, 1954.

Eastern Religion and Western Thought, by Dr. Sarvepalli Radhakrishnan. Oxford University Press, London, 1939.

2500 Years of Buddhism, edited by Prof. P. V. Bapat. Publications Division, Government of India, New Delhi, 1956.

The Life of Buddha as History and Legend, by Edward J. Thomas. Barnes & Noble, New York, 1952.

The Edicts of Asoka, edited and translated by N. A. Nikam and Richard McKeon. University of Chicago Press, Chicago/London, 1959.

The Making of the Indian Princes, by Edward J. Thompson. Oxford University Press, New York, 1943.

Prime Minister Nehru in China. Embassy of the People's Republic of China, New Delhi, India, 1955.

Nehru Your Neighbor. Edited by P. D. Tandon. Signet Press, Calcutta, India, 1946.

1857: A Pictorial Presentation. Publications Division, Government of India, New Delhi, 1957.

The United Nations: Blueprint for Peace, by Stephen S. Fenichell and Phillip Andrews. John C. Winston Company, Philadelphia, 1951.

About India. Publications Division, Government of India, New Delhi, 1950.

The Princes, by Manohar Malgonkar. The Viking Press, New York, 1963.

Land Reforms in India, by H. D. Malaviya. Indian National Congress, New Delhi, India, 1954.

Pioneering in Indian Business, by Sultan Chinoy. D. B. Taraporevalla Sons & Co. Pr. Ltd., Bombay, 1959.

The Cultural Heritage of Pakistan, by S. M. Ikram and Percival Spear. Oxford University Press, London, 1954.

Beyond the High Himalayas, by Justice William O. Douglas, Doubleday & Company, New York, 1953.

Philosophies of India, by Heinrich Zimmer. World Publishing Company, Cleveland, Ohio, 1956.

The Story of the Pakistan Army, by Maj. Gen. Fazal Muqeem Khan. Pakistan Branch, Oxford University Press, Karachi, 1963.

Afghanistan: 1919, by Lieut. Gen. G. N. Molesworth. Asia Publishing House, New York, 1962.

Millions on the Move: The Aftermath of Partition. Publications Division, Government of India, New Delhi, 1948.

World Opinion on Kashmir and Indian Reactions to It. Pakistan Mission to the United Nations, New York, 1951.

The Constitution of the Islamic Republic of Pakistan. Published at Karachi, 1957.

First Five-Year Plan. Publications Division, Government of India, New Delhi, 1952.

Second Five-Year Plan. Publications Division, Government of India, New Delhi, 1955.

An Indian Diary, by Edwin S. Montagu. Heinemann, Ltd., London, 1930.

Churchill in His Own Words: Years of Adventure, edited by F. W. Heath. Odhams Press Limited, London, 1962.

Other information sources have included the *Indian & Foreign Review,* published at New Delhi; *Pakistan Affairs,* published by the Embassy of Pakistan, Washington, D. C.; *Yojana,* from Publications

Division, Government of India; the *Pakistan Quarterly,* the *Times of India* and the *Indian Express,* the *Times* and *Dawn* in Pakistan, *The New York Times,* the New York *Herald Tribune,* the Chicago *Daily News, Saturday Review, Time, Life, Look, Newsweek, U.S. News & World Report, Catholic Digest,* the *Goan Tribune;* an interview by Arnold Michaelis in *McCall's Magazine;* the UNESCO Courier; speeches of Jawaharlal Nehru, Vijaya Lakshmi Pandit, Mrs. Indira Gandhi, Ambassador B. K. Nehru, et al.; and the Year-Books of the *Encyclopaedia Britannica,* 1945–1966 inclusive. Also the files of the Allahabad *Pioneer* and *Cure & Military Gazette;* and *Blitz, New Statesman, Hindustan Times* and other newspapers in India.

Glossary

For the Reader's Reference

Some words in this book may seem strange, though quite a few almost explain themselves. By and large, they pronounce as spelled. Their meanings in India are:

Abdar A servant to the rich. Literally, "wine-slave."

Achar A relish of mixed pickled vegetables. Making it properly is a traditional test of a housewife's qualifications.

Angrezi Anything English.

Ashram A retreat for those who withdraw from active life for study and meditation.

Bania Or *banya*. A sub-division of the *Vaisya* caste, third in the orthodox Hindu social order. Mahatma Gandhi was a *bania*.

Bapu Father. India called Gandhi *Bapu*.

Bhavan Also written *Bhawan*. House or home, in the sense of a manor, even a palace.

Brahmin The highest Hindu caste: the Twice-Born. By birth, custodians of the sacred texts, thus rewarded for good deeds in past lives. The Nehrus were a Kashmiri Brahmin family.

Burra Big, wide, strong. The Angrezi drink *burra pegs:* double Scotches.

395

Caste Borrowed by the British from the Portuguese *casta*. Correctly, the structure sanctified by the ancient Laws of Manu, outlawed by the Constitution of the Republic of India, is described as *varuna* —which originally meant "color." The lowest order is that of the Sudras. *Sudra* originally meant "black."

Chacha Uncle. India's children called India's first Prime Minister *Chacha* Nehru.

Community In India, applied to an organized religious or linguistic majority or minority, not as in the West, to describe the body of people in a place.

Congress The Indian National Congress, founded in 1885, spearheaded and eventually won India's independence crusade; and since 1947, as a political party, has held ruling powers under India's adaptation of the British parliamentary system.

Daridranarayan "God that resides in the poor."

Darshan The act of going "to receive the gift to the soul that is conferred by seeing a superior being."

Dhoti The strip of cloth which India's poor twist around themselves to form their sole garment.

Durbar A ceremonial occasion of state.

Fakir From the Arabic *faqir,* poor. A religious mendicant or ascetic. In the West, confused with Germanic-derived *faker*—not always unintentionally.

Farangi Foreigner. Anyone not India-born.

Gram Seeds of plants such as the chick-pea; a staple food for millions in India.

Gurudwara A Sikh temple. (See *Sikhs* below.)

Harijans "Children of God." Gandhi conferred this new name on those who had been called Untouchables.

Hartal Organized work-stoppage, picketing, demonstrations, protest marches.

Howdah The box in which dignitaries ride atop an elephant.

Jai Hail! As in *Nehruji ki jai!* Hail to our beloved Nehru!

Jawaharlal Motilal Nehru, who gave his son this name, translated it to mean "A ruby jewel." Gandhi said "Jawaharlal Nehru is the jewel of India."

Ji Appended to a name, *ji* signifies respectfully possessive affection: thus Gandhiji, or Vinobaji for Vinoba Bhave. It can also mean simply "Yes."

Jihad Holy war. A rally-cry for militant Muslims.

Khadi Rough homespun cloth. Wearing *khadi* instead of imported goods was a facet of Gandhi's strategy of nonviolent noncooperation.

Ksatriyas Second in the scale of caste divisions; traditionally soldiers, administrators, kings. Prince Siddhartha who became Gautama Buddha was a *Ksatriya* of the Sakya tribe.

Lakshmi In the Hindu pantheon, the Goddess of Fortune.

Lathis Flexible, often steel-shod crowd-dispersers, wielded like whips by police and constabulary.

Maha Great or supreme.

Mahatma Great souled. When used by India's masses, *Mahatma* saluted Gandhi as one almost deified.

Mata Mother. *Bharat Mata:* Mother India.

Muslims They resent being called *Mohammedans.* Mohammed was their Prophet, but they worship only Allah. They also object to *Moslems.* Properly written in Arabic, the spelling is M S L M. They read this as *Muslim.*

Namasthe There are several spellings. A salutation, whether spoken in farewell or expressed silently by raising the hands, palms pressed together, in prayer-like gesture.

Pakistan A coined name for a created country. Pakistani interpret it as "The pure land."

Panchshila Jawaharlal Nehru's Five Tenets (*panch* means "five"): Non-aggression, non-interference, recognition of the equal rights of other nations, mutual help, peaceful coexistence.

Pandit Englished from the Sanskrit, to *pundit.* Courtesy title accorded to a learned person; hence Pandit Nehru. However many Sanskrit and Hindi words have also become family names: *vide* that of Ranjit Pandit, Vijaya Lakshmi Pandit's husband.

Parsis   From "Persians." Disciples of Zoroaster, who call God "Ahura-Mazda" or Being of Light, they came to India as fugitives from religious persecution in A. D. 706. There are only 100,000 Parsis, but their reputation for business acumen, probity, and charitable works made them, albeit the smallest of India's religious communities, influential both before and after independence. Mrs. Indira Gandhi's husband, Pheroze, was Parsi.

Pradesh   Province or state: as in Uttar Pradesh, the United Provinces.

Pukka   The very best. Before 1947, customarily applied to British things.

Purdah   Cloistered seclusion of women. Muslim tradition and the word for it were borrowed over the centuries by many Hindus. *Purdanashin:* a gathering of women, with men excluded.

Quaid-i-Azam   Peerless Leader. The title his countrymen legally conferred on Mohammed Ali Jinnah, Father of Pakistan.

Raj   Related to *Rajah,* ruler; derived, as was *Rajah,* from the Sanskrit *rajan,* "He who pleases the people." The Raj was British India's government. Headed by the Viceroy, it ruled over princes and peasants alike, with absolute authority.

Ramayana   India's *Iliad,* whose hero, Prince Rama, is believed by many Hindus to have been an avatar or incarnation of the paramount deity, Vishnu.

Rani   Queen. Jhansi-ki-Rani: Queen of Jhansi.

Sabha   Assemblage of the people. India's Lok Sabha or House of the People equates with the British Parliament's House of Commons; the Raja Sabha is an appointive body with limited legislative powers, somewhat comparable to Britain's House of Lords although inherited titles are not the qualification for membership.

Sahib   One meaning of *sahib* is "holy." The word probably derives from the Arabic *cahib,* "master" or "friend." However Europeans in India, of whatever breed or quality, enforced its use in addressing them (and some still do), with the meaning only of "master." The feminine equivalent, *Memsahib,* merely added the Indian pronunciation of "Ma'am," *Burra sahib* was not—and is not—a compliment.

Samyavada Vinoba Bhave's word for Communism. Its opposite, *Samyayoga,* means equal freedom for all, and individual responsibility.

Sanyasi A man who has renounced the world. He wears a saffron-hued robe in token of his sacrifice. *Sanyasi* is sometimes, but not necessarily with accuracy, used interchangeably with *sadhu:* a self-elected holy man.

Sardar Leader, chieftain; with a connotation of militant if not military methods.

Sari The single long piece of cloth which India's women drape into what is certainly the most practical and possibly the most attractive dress worn by women anywhere.

Sati A virtuous woman; especially, a widow who immolated herself on her husband's funeral pyre. The practice, which the British mistakenly spelled *suttee,* was stopped more than a century ago.

Satyagraha "Holding onto truth"; total self-giving. Integral to Mahatma Gandhi's whole concept of victory achieved through nonviolent resistance to evil.

Shamiana A canopy or marquee rigged for outdoor parties.

Sherwani Long straight tunic-coat with high collar, row of buttons down the front; usually black, but Jawaharlal Nehru often wore white.

Sikhs From *Sikha,* "disciples." A religious community centered in the Punjab, founded in dissent from both Hinduism and Islam by Guru (the Teacher) Nanak, a contemporary of Martin Luther. Persecuted, the Sikhs became a nation of soldiers although farming is their natural occupation.

Srimati Great Lady. The honorific cannot be conferred; it must be earned, and granted spontaneously. Madame Pandit, entering Parliament in the House of the People, was greeted as *Srimati* Pandit.

Swadeshi Made by hand, or home-produced. Has the meaning of "do it yourself."

Swaraj Home Rule, as opposed to rule by *farangi*. When Gandhi called for *Purna Swaraj,* complete independence, the end of Empire began.

Zamindars Originally, tax-farmers; by virtue of growing power, a privileged class of landowners and capitalists; in effect, feudal barons.

Zindabad Long live!—as in *Inquilab zindabad!* Long live the revolution!

INDEX

47